Excel

Get the Results you W[ant]

YEAR 11
CHEMISTRY

Geoffrey Thickett

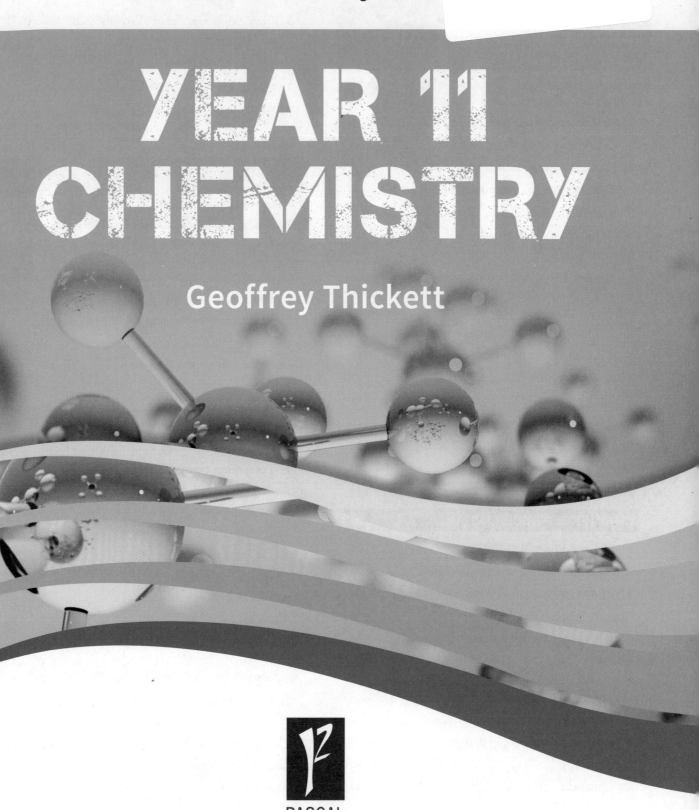

PASCAL PRESS

CONTENTS

CHAPTER 1
PROPERTIES OF MATTER

How do the properties of substances help us to classify and separate them?

Mixtures are substances that usually vary in their composition. Citrus juices vary in the amount of sugar, acid and vitamin C present. Air in a polluted industrial area has a different composition to air in an unpolluted rural area. The physical properties of the components of a mixture can be used to separate the components. Gravimetric analysis can be used to determine the percentage composition of mixtures as well as pure substances. Pure substances are elements and compounds.

1 Separation of mixtures

» Students explore homogeneous mixtures and heterogeneous mixtures through practical investigations using separation techniques based on physical properties.

Types of mixtures

→ Mixtures can be homogeneous or heterogeneous.
- Examples of **homogeneous mixtures**: sugar solution, filtered air, petrol, brass
- Examples of **heterogeneous mixtures**: suspension of clay and mud in water, concrete, orange juice containing orange pulp
→ Mixtures of different substances can be separated by a variety of physical separation techniques. These techniques rely on differences in the properties of the components of the mixture.

homogeneous mixture: all components are uniformly mixed and the composition is uniform
heterogeneous mixture: the components are not uniformly mixed

Separation of mixtures based on particle size

→ Sieving can be used to separate mixtures of solid particles of different particle size. For any one sieve, some particles in the mixture will be small enough to pass through the wire mesh while other particles are too large and are retained in the sieve.
→ **Centrifugation** is used to separate solids of different particle size in an aqueous suspension. The sedimentation process is accelerated using a centrifuge. If the suspension is spun rapidly in a centrifuge then the heavier particles are more rapidly separated from the lighter particles and are deposited at the end of the centrifuge tube. Red blood cells can be separated from whole blood by centrifugation.

Separation of insoluble solids from liquids

→ Filtration can be used to separate solids that are suspended in liquids or solutions. As long as the size of the particles of the insoluble solid is greater than the **porosity** of the filter, then the insoluble solid will be retained in the filter and separation has been achieved. Sand and salt, for example, can be separated by adding water to dissolve the salt and then filtering the mixture. Figure 1.1 shows how a salt solution passes through the filter but the sand is retained in the filter paper.

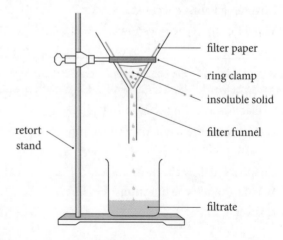

Figure 1.1 Filtration of a suspension of an insoluble solid/water mixture

Separation of dissolved solids from solution

→ Evaporation is the common procedure used to separate the components of a solution. The boiling point of the components in the mixture is a good indicator of the success of the evaporation method. Water has a boiling point of 100 °C whereas salt (sodium chloride) has a boiling point of 1465 °C. As the water evaporates into the air, the salt is left behind in the evaporating basin when a saltwater solution is evaporated (Figure 1.2).

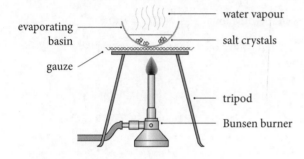

Figure 1.2 Evaporation of salt water

Separation of mixtures of miscible liquids

→ Distillation is a common method of separating a mixture of **miscible** liquids. The technique depends on the liquid components having significantly different boiling points. If the mixture is heated then the lower boiling point component is separated from the higher boiling point component due to a change in state. The vapour of the more volatile component is condensed back to a liquid using a condenser cooled by tap water. The condensed liquid is called the distillate (Figure 1.3).

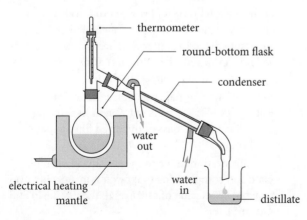

Figure 1.3 Distillation

→ If the boiling points of the components are too close then fractional distillation is used. In a school lab a fractionating column is inserted between the flask and the condenser. The vapours condense and vapourise on the glass beads in the column and over time the lowest boiling components reach the top of the column and liquefy in the condenser. The distillate (or fraction) is richer in the lowest boiling point component.

Separation of mixtures of immiscible liquids

→ Separating funnels can be used to separate immiscible liquids. These liquid mixtures separate into layers due to density differences.

→ Consider the following example of the separation of immiscible liquids. A mixture of mercury, water and kerosene is separated using a separating funnel. The mercury has the greatest density and sinks to the bottom of the funnel. The water floats on top of the mercury and the kerosene floats on top of the water as shown in Figure 1.4. The tap at the base of the funnel is opened and the mercury is allowed to flow out into a beaker. The tap is closed once all the mercury has been removed. The water layer is now allowed to flow out into a new beaker. The kerosene is released into a third beaker.

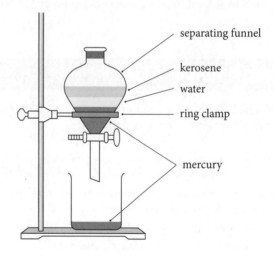

Figure 1.4 Separating funnel

Separation of magnetic materials

→ Some substances, such as iron and steel, are strongly magnetic. Cobalt and nickel have weaker magnetic properties than iron. Other metals and non-metals are non-magnetic. This difference can be used to separate a mixture of iron and copper particles. Figure 1.5 shows a simple experiment using a bar magnet to remove iron grains from a mixture of iron and copper.

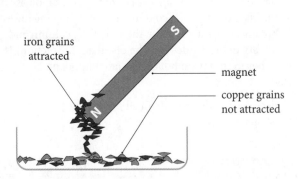

iron grains attracted

magnet

copper grains not attracted

Figure 1.5 Magnetic separation

→ KEY QUESTIONS

1 Identify which of the following mixtures are homogeneous and which are heterogeneous:

urban air   granite rock

muddy water   methylated spirits

glucose solution kerosene

2 Identify a physical separation technique that can be used to obtain fresh water from ocean water.

3 Identify a simple laboratory apparatus that can be used to separate a mixture of cooking oil and water.

Answers ⊃ p. 13

2 Gravimetric analysis

» Students calculate percentage composition by weight of component elements and/or compounds.

Percentage composition of mixtures

→ The proportion of each component in a mixture can be expressed as a weight percentage.

→ The analytical techniques used to measure these proportions are called gravimetric analysis.

→ This technique is important as it allows analytical chemists to test products for composition and purity. This is particularly important in the food industry where the percentage by weight of the food's components must be listed (by law) on the packaging.

→ The composition of a mineral obtained by mining an ore body or the composition of a mixture of different compounds or alloys can be determined using gravimetric analysis.

EXAMPLE 1

A sample of a copper alloy to be used for coins and medals was analysed to determine whether its copper content was in the acceptable range of 90–92%. A 5.00 g sample of the alloy was dissolved in concentrated nitric acid and the solution that formed was diluted and the copper extracted as pure copper metal by electroplating it onto a pre-weighed platinum electrode. Use the collected data to determine whether the alloy contained an acceptable amount of copper.

Calculate the mass of electroplated copper

Data:

Mass of platinum electrode = 12.365 g

Mass of electrode + electroplated copper = 16.915 g

Answer:

mass of copper = 16.915 − 12.365 = 4.550 g

% copper in alloy = $\dfrac{4.55}{5.00} \times 100 = 91.0\%$

This percentage of copper is in the acceptable range for the alloy.

⚛ FIRSTHAND INVESTIGATION

Gravimetric analysis of a mixture

» Students explore homogeneous mixtures and heterogeneous mixtures through practical investigations using separation techniques based on physical properties.

Aim

to determine the composition of a sand, water and salt mixture by gravimetric analysis

Method

1 The supplied sample tube contains a mixture of sand, salt and a little water to form a damp mass. Weigh the tube and contents and record the mass (m1).

2 Using a wash bottle and stirring rod, transfer the contents of the tube to a pre-weighed filter paper (m3) supported in a filter ring over a large pre-weighed evaporating basin (m2). Rinse the tube and wash the sand that collects in the filter.

3 Remove the filter paper and place on a clean watch glass. Dry to constant weight in a drying oven. Record the mass of the dried filter paper + sand (m4).

4 Partially evaporate the salt water slowly on a hot plate and complete the evaporation in a drying oven to avoid splattering of salt. Weigh the dry basin and salt (m5).

5 Weigh the clean, dry sample tube (m6).

Sample results

Some sample data is provided.

mass of sample tube + contents (m1) (g)	25.543
mass of evaporating basin (m2) (g)	125.332
mass of filter paper (m3) (g)	0.845
mass of filter paper + sand (m4) (g)	2.312
mass of evaporating basin + salt (m5) (g)	128.556
mass of sample tube (m6) (g)	18.457

Sample calculations

The data collected can be used to determine the masses of each component.

mass of mixture (m7 = m1 – m6) (g)	7.086
mass of sand (m8 = m4 – m3) (g)	1.467
mass of salt (m9 = m5 – m2) (g)	3.224
mass of water (m10 = m7 – m8 – m9) (g)	2.395

The percentage by weight of each component is then calculated:

$$\% \text{ sand} = \frac{1.467}{7.086} \times 100 = 20.7\%$$

$$\% \text{ salt} = \frac{3.224}{7.086} \times 100 = 45.5\%$$

$$\% \text{ water} = \frac{2.395}{7.086} \times 100 = 33.8\%$$

Experimental accuracy

The accuracy of the experiment could be improved by ensuring that all materials are quantitatively transferred from the sample tube to the filter paper and evaporating basin. The sand on the filter must be thoroughly washed to remove any salt. Splattering of salt during evaporation must not occur and a weighed clock glass to cover the basin may be needed to prevent loss of mass. Drying samples to constant weight is important. A pre-weighed filtering crucible will be more accurate than a filter paper as filter papers are absorbent. An electronic balance for weighing also improves accuracy.

Percentage composition of compounds

» Students calculate percentage composition by weight of component elements and/or compounds.

➔ Pure samples of compounds contain fixed percentages by weight of each element.

➔ Gravimetric analysis can be used to determine the % by weight of elements in a compound.

EXAMPLE 2

4.50 g of mercury (II) oxide was decomposed by heating and the mercury formed was weighed. The mass of mercury formed was 4.17 g. Determine the percentage by weight of mercury and oxygen in mercury oxide.

Answer:

mass Hg = 4.17 g

mass O = 4.50 – 4.17 = 0.33 g

Mass is conserved in a chemical reaction

$$\%\text{Hg} = \frac{4.17}{4.50} \times \frac{100}{1} = 92.7\%$$

$$\%\text{O} = \frac{0.33}{4.50} \times \frac{100}{1} = 7.3\%$$

➔ KEY QUESTIONS

4 5.00 g of an iron oxide was analysed. The sample contained 3.50 g of iron. Determine the percentage by weight of iron and oxygen in the compound.

5 A hydrocarbon compound was gravimetrically analysed and the percentage by weight of each element determined. The results of the analysis are:

92.26% carbon, 7.74% hydrogen

Calculate the mass of carbon and hydrogen present in 20.0 g of this hydrocarbon.

6 A student used a crucible to burn a piece of magnesium in air to form magnesium oxide. The following results were obtained.

mass of magnesium (g)	0.684
mass of crucible/lid (g)	28.540
mass crucible/lid + magnesium oxide (g)	29.674

Calculate the percentage by weight of magnesium and oxygen in the magnesium oxide.

Answers ⊃ p. 13

3 Nomenclature of inorganic compounds

» Students investigate the nomenclature of inorganic substances using International Union of Pure and Applied Chemistry (IUPAC) naming conventions.

➔ A pure substance is defined as a material that has a constant composition and fixed properties. Pure substances cannot be separated using physical separation techniques.

→ Pure substances can be classified into two groups called elements and compounds. Elements are the simplest pure substances.

→ Compounds can be separated into component elements by chemical means.

→ Compounds are composed of elements in fixed atomic ratios. Calcium chloride is composed of one calcium ion and two chloride ions. Its formula is $CaCl_2$.

→ Compounds can be classified as inorganic or organic. Organic compounds are based on the element carbon and are produced by living organisms. Sugars, fats and proteins are organic compounds. Inorganic compounds form most of the non-living world.

→ Many inorganic compounds are composed of metals bonded to non-metals.

→ The following naming rules apply to inorganic compounds:
  - The metal is named first.
  - The non-metal is named second.
  - The *ide* suffix is used for the non-metal in simple binary compounds. Binary compounds contain only two elements.

  Examples:

  1 CaH_2 metal = calcium; non-metal = hydrogen
  name = calcium hydride

  2 ZnS metal = zinc; non-metal = sulfur
  name = zinc sulfide

  - Inorganic compounds can be composed of more than two elements. Non-metals can join together to form stable groups. Examples of these are listed below:

  OH = hydroxide CO_3 = carbonate
  NO_3 = nitrate SO_4 = sulfate
  PO_4 = phosphate NH_4 = ammonium

  Examples:

  $Ba(OH)_2$ = barium hydroxide
  Na_2CO_3 = sodium carbonate
  KNO_3 = potassium nitrate
  $CoSO_4$ = cobalt (II) sulfate
  $(NH_4)_3PO_4$ = ammonium phosphate

→ **KEY QUESTIONS**

7 **Explain the distinction between inorganic and organic compounds.**

8 **Explain why elements are examples of pure substances.**

9 **Name the following compounds:**
  a Na_2O b $CaCO_3$ c $FeSO_4$ d $AlPO_4$

  Answers ⊃ p. 13

4 Elements and the periodic table

» Students classify the elements based on their properties and position in the periodic table through their physical properties and chemical properties.

A complete copy of the periodic table of elements is located on the inside front cover of this book.

→ The majority of elements are metals. Metals have the following physical properties:
  - lustrous (shiny) when polished
  - good electrical conductors due to the presence of mobile (delocalised) electrons in the metal crystal
  - good heat conductors
  - malleable (able to be beaten or rolled into thin sheets)
  - ductile (able to be drawn out into thin wires by application of tensional forces).

mobile (delocalised) electrons: electrons that are not bound to a particular atom but are free to move in a metal

→ All metals are solids except mercury, which is a liquid at 25 °C.

→ The non-metallic elements are located on the right-hand side of the periodic table. Non-metals can be solids, liquids or gases at room temperature. Non-metals have the following physical properties:
  - solid non-metals are dull in appearance
  - very poor electrical conductors (exception: carbon graphite)
  - poor heat conductors
  - brittle: solid non-metals shatter into small crystals when hammered.

→ Many non-metals exist as molecules rather than single atoms. The noble gases are all monatomic (i.e. composed of single atoms). Other non-metals exist as diatomic molecules. Chemical bonds called covalent bonds join the atoms together. Covalent bonding will be discussed in a later section. The diatomic molecular non-metals are H_2, N_2, O_2, F_2, Cl_2, Br_2 and I_2. The first five of these are gases at room temperature whereas bromine is a liquid and iodine is a solid.

→ Six elements are classified as semi-metals. These elements have properties which are intermediate between metals and non-metals.

→ The six semi-metals are boron (B), silicon (Si), germanium (Ge), arsenic (As), antimony (Sb) and tellurium (Te).

The periodic table

→ The modern periodic table arranges the elements in order of their increasing atomic number (Z).

Hydrogen has an atomic number of 1. Helium has an atomic number of 2.

> atomic number (Z): the number of protons in the nucleus of an atom; each element has a unique atomic number

➜ The following diagram shows an outline of the structure of the periodic table. The periodic table contains:
  - 7 horizontal rows called periods
  - 18 vertical columns called groups
  - Groups 1, 2, 13, 14, 15, 16, 17 and 18 that are called the main block
  - the transition metals that belong to Groups 3, 4, 5, 6, 7, 8, 9, 10, 11 and 12
  - a subsection of the transition metals called the lanthanoid series and the actinoid series; the lanthanoids are rare-earth elements
  - elements (Z = 84 – 118) that are radioactive.

➜ The colour coding in Figure 1.6 shows that most elements are metals. Six elements are semi-metals and the remaining elements are non-metals. Semi-metals have properties intermediate between metals and non-metals.

➜ The vertical groups are numbered from Group 1 to Group 18. (An older method uses Roman numerals but they are less commonly used in modern chemistry. Group 15, for example, is also known as Group (V).)

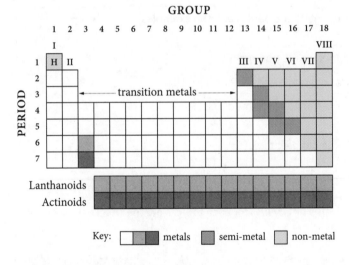

Figure 1.6 The periodic table outline

Chemical properties of periodic groups

➜ Group 1 is known as the alkali metals. These metals are very soft and highly reactive. When these metals react with water they produce solutions that are strongly alkaline. Alkaline solutions have a high pH due to the presence of hydroxide ions (OH^-). The reactivity of Group 1 metals increases down the group.

➜ Group 2 is known as the alkaline earth metals. These metals also produce alkaline solutions when they react with water. Group 2 oxides, hydroxides and carbonates are not as strongly alkaline as the equivalent Group 1 compounds. The reactivity of Group 2 metals increases down the group.

➜ Group 17 elements are called the halogens. This name arises because these elements can combine with metals to form ionic compounds called salts. Fluorine is the most reactive of these halogens.

➜ Group 18 contains gaseous elements known as the noble gases. They were originally called inert gases until chemists were able to make oxide and fluoride compounds with xenon. Noble gases are very unreactive elements under normal conditions.

➜ Transition metals (Group 3 to Group 12) are less reactive than the metals in Groups 1 and 2. The reactivity of transition metals decreases down each transition metal group. For example, in Group 8 (Fe, Ru, Os) iron is reactive whereas osmium is an unreactive metal.

➜ **KEY QUESTIONS**

10 Use the complete periodic table in this book to identify the groups of the periodic table to which strontium, nickel, tin and selenium belong.

11 Use the complete periodic table in this book to identify the periods of the periodic table where the following elements are located: rubidium, mercury and gallium.

12 Explain the distinction between elements classified as lanthanoids and those classified as actinoids.

13 Compare the chemical properties of Group 1 and Group 18 elements.

Answers ⊃ p. 13

Are you able to answer these questions from the syllabus for this chapter? Tick each question as you go through the checklist if you are able to answer it. If you cannot answer a question, turn to the relevant page in the study guide to find the answer. For NESA key word meanings, go to www.educationstandards.nsw.edu.au and search 'key words'.

	FOR A COMPLETE UNDERSTANDING OF THIS TOPIC:	PAGE NO.	✓
1	Can I distinguish between homogeneous and heterogeneous mixtures and describe examples of each?	4	
2	Can I identify a physical separation technique used to separate mixtures based on particle size?	4	
3	Can I identify a physical separation technique used to separate solids from liquids?	4–5	
4	Can I identify a physical separation technique used to separate dissolved solids from solutions?	5	
5	Can I identify a physical separation technique used to separate mixtures of liquids?	5	
6	Can I identify a physical separation technique used to separate immiscible liquids?	5	
7	Can I identify a physical separation technique used to separate magnetic materials from non-magnetic materials?	5–6	
8	Can I explain how gravimetric analysis is a useful technique in analytical chemistry?	6–7	
9	Can I calculate the percentage composition of a mixture based on gravimetric analysis data?	7	
10	Can I define the term *pure substance* and provide examples of pure substances?	7–8	
11	Can I calculate the percentage composition of a compound based on gravimetric analysis data?	7	
12	Can I use nomenclature rules to name simple inorganic compounds?	8	
13	Can I classify elements as metals, semi-metals and non-metals and name common examples of each classification?	8–9	
14	Can I describe the physical properties of metals, semi-metals and non-metals?	8	
15	Can I explain the structure of the periodic table in terms of groups and periods?	8–9	
16	Can I explain how the elements of the periodic table are arranged in terms of the atomic number of each element?	9	
17	Can I recall the chemical reactivity trends of groups in the periodic table?	9	

A QUICK NOTE! All the **dark green panels** with information (like the one below) have the **syllabus inquiry questions** and all the **light green panels** (like the one below) have the **syllabus dot points** for each topic. Note the checklist questions in the table above are based on these.

INQUIRY QUESTION:

How do the properties of substances help us to classify and separate them?

Mixtures are substances that usually vary in their composition. Citrus juices vary in the amount of sugar, acid and vitamin C present. Air in a polluted industrial area has a different

1 Separation of mixtures

» Students explore homogeneous mixtures and heterogeneous mixtures through practical investigations using separation techniques based on physical properties.

Chemistry Stage 6 Syllabus

Properties of Matter

• **Inquiry question:** How do the properties of substances help us to classify and separate them?

Students:

• explore homogeneous mixtures and heterogeneous mixtures through practical investigations:
  – using separation techniques based on physical properties (ACSCH026)
  – calculating percentage composition by weight of component elements and/or compounds (ACSCH007)
• investigate the nomenclature of inorganic substances using International Union of Pure and Applied Chemistry (IUPAC) naming conventions
• classify the elements based on their properties and position in the periodic table through their:
  – physical properties
  – chemical properties 🖥

Now for the real thing! The following questions are modelled on the types of questions you will face in the yearly examination in Year 11. Think about it: if you get extensive practice at answering these sorts of questions, you will be more confident in answering them in the yearly examination. It makes sense, doesn't it?

Another advantage for your exam preparation is the format of the answers: they are deliberately structured to give you strategies on how to answer examination questions. This will help you aim for full marks!

→ For each objective-response question you will have the correct answer and an explanation, and reasons why all the other answers are incorrect.

→ For each extended-response question you will have a detailed answer marked with ticks to indicate what part of the question gains which marks and also, when needed, an examiner's plan (Examiner Maximiser / **EM**) to help you get full marks.

When you mark your work, highlight any questions you found difficult and earmark these areas for extra study.

Objective-response questions

(1 mark each)

1   Select the set that contains only homogeneous mixtures.

A	brass	polluted air	salt water
B	methylated spirits	petrol	sand
C	muddy water	steel	limestone
D	filtered salt water	white wine	methylated spirits

2   Identify the appropriate method to separate a homogeneous mixture of liquid hexane (C_6H_{14}) and liquid decane ($C_{10}H_{22}$).

   A   filtration

   B   magnetism

   C   separation funnel

   D   distillation

3   Use the periodic table of the elements to select the true statement about cobalt and iodine.

   A   Cobalt is malleable whereas iodine is brittle.

   B   Cobalt and iodine are both good conductors of heat.

   C   Both elements are semiconductors.

   D   Cobalt is highly unreactive whereas iodine is very reactive.

4   Consider the properties of the elements P, Q, R and S.

   • Element P is lustrous and silvery in appearance and has a high electrical conductivity.

   • Element Q can be drawn into long thin wires.

   • Element R has a low melting point and shatters into tiny crystals when hammered.

   • Element S is a yellow-green gas at 25 °C.

   Select the correct classification of these elements:

	P	Q	R	S
A	metal	metal	non-metal	non-metal
B	non-metal	metal	metal	non-metal
C	metal	non-metal	non-metal	non-metal
D	non-metal	metal	non-metal	non-metal

5   The following data concerns the gravimetric analysis of a sample of copper alloy. The alloy was dissolved in acid and the solution was electrolysed and copper was deposited on the platinum electrode.

mass of alloy (g)	5.00
mass of platinum electrode (g)	15.00
mass of electrode and electroplated copper (g)	17.35

The mass of copper in the alloy and the percentage by mass of copper in the alloy are:

   A   2.65 g   53%

   B   12.35 g   86%

   C   2.35 g   47%

   D   12.65 g   16%

Extended-response questions

6   Bromine is slightly soluble in water (density = 1.0 g/mL) forming a yellow solution. Bromine is very soluble in an organic liquid called cyclohexane (density = 0.78 g/mL), forming an orange-coloured solution. Water and cyclohexane are immiscible in one another. Cyclohexane is less dense than water. A yellow solution of bromine in water is placed in a separating funnel. An equal volume of cyclohexane is now added. The stopper is replaced and the mixture shaken for several minutes and the separating funnel then placed back on its ring clamp. Draw a labelled diagram of the appearance of the final contents of the separating funnel.   (3 marks)

7   Three hydrocarbon liquids were mixed together and the mixture distilled. These liquids were:

   decane ($C_{10}H_{22}$):   m.p = −30 °C   b.p = 124 °C
   dodecane ($C_{12}H_{26}$):   m.p = −10 °C   b.p = 216 °C
   tetradecane ($C_{14}H_{30}$):   m.p = 5 °C   b.p = 255 °C

   Identify the hydrocarbon which will form the major component of the first distillate and explain whether separation is likely to be complete.   (2 marks)

8 Drawings A and B (Figure 1.7) show two properties of metals. Name these properties. (2 marks)

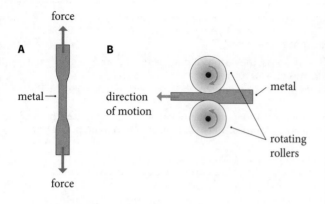

Figure 1.7 Properties of metals

9 A student filtered a 60.00 g mixture of green powdered chalk and water. The student removed the filter paper and residue and dried them to constant weight. A clean, unused filter paper was also weighed.

Results: mass of dry filter paper = 0.550 g
          mass of dry filter paper + residue = 14.630 g

a Identify the material that is present in the residue. (1 mark)

b Calculate the mass of dry residue. (1 mark)

c Calculate the percentage by weight of chalk and water in the original mixture. (2 marks)

10 50 g of copper (II) sulfate crystals were dissolved in 100 g of hot water at 80 °C. The solution was then slowly evaporated to remove half of the water and then cooled to 20 °C. At 20 °C, the solubility of copper (II) sulfate is 20 g per 100 g of water. Calculate the mass of copper (II) sulfate that will crystallise at 20 °C. (3 marks)

ANSWERS

KEY QUESTIONS

Key questions ⊃ p. 6

1. homogeneous: glucose solution, methylated spirits, kerosene
heterogeneous: urban air, muddy water, granite rock

2. distillation (Water's boiling point is much less than the boiling points of salts in the ocean water.)

3. separating funnel (Cooking oil and water are immiscible.)

Key questions ⊃ p. 7

4. $\%Fe = \dfrac{3.50}{5.00} \times \dfrac{100}{1} = 70.0\%$ $\qquad \%O = 100 - 70.0 = 30.0\%$

5. $m(C) = \dfrac{92.26}{100} \times 20.0 = 18.45\ g$ $\qquad m(H) = \dfrac{7.74}{100} \times 20.0 = 1.55\ g$

6. $m(\text{magnesium oxide}) = 29.674 - 28.540 = 1.134\ g$

   $\%Mg = \dfrac{0.684}{1.134} \times \dfrac{100}{1} = 60.32\%$ $\qquad \%O = 100 - 60.32 = 39.68\%$

Key questions ⊃ p. 8

7. Organic compounds are carbon based and produced by living things. Inorganic compounds form the non-living components of the world.

8. Elements are pure substances that cannot be separated into anything simpler using chemical separation techniques.

9. a sodium oxide   b calcium carbonate   c iron (II) sulfate
   d aluminium phosphate

Key questions ⊃ p. 9

10. strontium: Group 2   nickel: Group 10
    tin: Group 14   selenium: Group 16

11. rubidium: Period 5   mercury: Period 6   gallium: Period 4

12. Lanthanoid series: a subsection of the transition metals in Period 6 containing natural rare-earth metals

    Actinoid series: a subsection of the transition metals in Period 7 containing natural and synthetic radioactive metals

13. Group 1 are metals that are very soft solids and highly reactive. Group 18 are gaseous non-metallic elements that are highly unreactive.

YEAR 11 EXAM-TYPE QUESTIONS

Objective-response questions

1. **D.** The components of these mixtures exist in only one phase. **A** is incorrect as polluted air contains solid particles. **B** is incorrect as sand is a heterogeneous mixture of silica, crushed shells, organic matter and water. **C** is incorrect as muddy water is a suspension and limestone is a heterogeneous mixture of calcium carbonate and other solid impurities.

2. **D.** These liquids are miscible and have different boiling points. **A** is incorrect as the mixture will pass through a filter since there are no solids present. **B** is incorrect as these substances are non-magnetic. **C** is incorrect as the liquids are not immiscible.

3. **A.** Cobalt is a transition metal and malleable whereas iodine is a solid non-metal and therefore brittle. **B** is incorrect as iodine is a poor heat conductor since it is a non-metal. **C** is incorrect as cobalt is a metal and iodine is a non-metal. **D** is incorrect as cobalt and iodine are moderately reactive.

4. **A.** Metals are lustrous and ductile; non-metals have low melting points and many are gaseous. **B** is incorrect as P is a lustrous metal. **C** is incorrect as Q is ductile and therefore a metal. **D** is incorrect as P is a lustrous metal.

5. **C.** Mass Cu = 17.35 − 15.00 = 2.35 g. $\%Cu = \dfrac{2.35}{5.00} \times \dfrac{100}{1} = 47\%$.

   A, **B** and **D** are incorrect as the mass of Cu is 2.35 g.

Extended-response questions

6. **EM** Diagrams should be drawn with a pencil and ruler with labels for the main components. Students should use the density data to show that the cyclohexane floats on the water.

   ✓ correct apparatus drawn;
   ✓ correct labelling;
   ✓ cyclohexane layer floats on top of water

   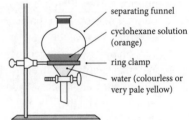

   Figure A1.1 Separating funnel experiment

7. **EM** In the distillation of a homogeneous liquid mixture, the separation depends on the boiling points and not the melting points. Fractional distillation would lead to greater separation of the components.

   Decane will distil first as it has the lowest boiling point. ✓ The boiling points are quite far apart so the separation process will be fairly complete. ✓

8. **EM** Diagram A shows forces pulling the metal into a thinner wire whereas diagram B shows the metal being rolled into a thin sheet.
   A = ductility ✓ B = malleability ✓

9. **EM** Students should remember that chalk is insoluble in water and will form the residue when filtered. The mass of dried chalk can be found by subtracting the mass of the filter paper from the total mass. The percentage of chalk is determined as a percentage by determining the ratio of the chalk mass to the total mass and then expressing that fraction as a percentage. All calculation steps should be shown.
   a chalk ✓
   b mass of dry chalk residue = 14.630 − 0.550 = 14.08 g ✓

   c $\%\text{ chalk} = \dfrac{14.08}{60.00} \times 100 = 23.47\%$ ✓
   $\%\text{ water} = 100 - 23.5 = 76.53\%$ ✓

10. **EM** Students should realise that a greater mass of crystals will form at 20 °C as only half the mass of water remains. Only 10 g of the copper (II) sulfate will dissolve in 50 g of water. Ensure all calculation steps are shown.

    50 g of water remains after evaporation. ✓

    10 g of copper sulfate will dissolve in 50 g of water at 20 °C. ✓

    Therefore 50 − 10 = 40 g of copper sulfate will crystallise. ✓

Why are atoms of elements different from one another?

Experiments performed in the late 19th and early 20th centuries revealed that atoms were composed of subatomic particles called electrons, protons and neutrons. The difference between elements is the number of protons in the nucleus of the atom. Further experiments revealed that some atoms of an element contain different numbers of neutrons. These are called isotopes. Elements can also exist in different structural forms called allotropes. When elements are heated they can emit light of characteristic wavelengths. These different wavelengths are related to the electron shell structure of the atom.

1 Atomic structure

» Students investigate the basic structure of stable and unstable isotopes by examining:
  • their position in the periodic table
  • the distribution of electrons, protons and neutrons in the atom
  • representation of the symbol, atomic number and mass number (nucleon number).

Subatomic particles

➜ All atoms have a similar basic structure. Atoms are composed of three fundamental subatomic particles called protons, neutrons and electrons.

➜ Protons are positively charged particles found in the central nucleus of the atom.

➜ Neutrons are neutral particles, which are also found in the nucleus. Neutrons are slightly heavier than protons.

➜ Electrons are negatively charged particles that are found outside the nucleus. They exist in energy levels or shells that surround the nucleus. The mass of an electron is much less than that of a proton.

Table 2.1 shows information about each subatomic particle.

Table 2.1 Subatomic particles

Particle	Symbol	Charge	Mass (u)
proton	p	+1	1.00759
neutron	n	0	1.00898
electron	e	−1	0.00055

(u = atomic mass unit; $1\ u = 1.661 \times 10^{-27}$ kg)

➜ Figure 2.1 shows the shell model of the atom for the element sodium which has 11 electrons in its shells around the nucleus. This model was developed by Niels Bohr in 1913. Bohr proposed that electrons could only occupy allowed energy levels or shells at fixed distances from the nucleus.

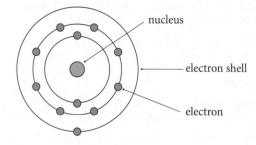

Figure 2.1 Shell model of the atom

protons: subatomic particles with a positive charge
neutrons: subatomic particle with no charge
electrons: subatomic particles with a negative charge

Isotopes

➜ Each element can be represented by a unique symbol. Thus hydrogen has the symbol H. Helium has the symbol He. The nuclear (nuclide) symbol for any element (X) shows its atomic number (Z) and its nucleon number (also called its mass number) (A).
  • Z = number of protons in the nucleus
  • A = number of nucleons (protons + neutrons) in the nucleus.

➜ The atomic number is written as a subscript and the nucleon number as a superscript before the symbol.

$$^A_Z X$$

Example

1 $^1_1 H$ The atomic number (Z) = 1; thus there is 1 proton in the nucleus

   The nucleon number (A) = 1; thus there are no neutrons in the nucleus

2 $^7_3 Li$ The atomic number (Z) = 3; thus there are 3 protons in the nucleus

   The nucleon number (A) = 7; thus there are 7 – 3 = 4 neutrons in the nucleus

➜ Most elements exist in nature as a mixture of isotopes. Isotopes of an element have the same atomic number but different nucleon (mass) numbers. Natural chlorine, for example, consists of a mixture of 2 isotopes: chlorine-35 ($^{35}_{17} Cl$) and chlorine-37 ($^{35}_{17} Cl$). These 2 isotopes have the same chemical properties but different relative atomic masses.

➜ Isotopes can be stable or unstable. Most elements exist as stable isotopes. Unstable isotopes are radioactive as they break down to more stable isotopes by the release of nuclear radiation.

➜ Elements with atomic numbers between 84 and 92 are natural radioactive metals. Elements with atomic numbers between 93 and 118 are synthetic radioactive elements. Technetium (Tc) (Z = 43) and promethium (Pm) (Z = 61) are very rare radioactive elements that have no stable isotopes.

➜ KEY QUESTIONS

1 Identify the subatomic components of the nucleus of an atom.

2 Compare the mass and charge of a proton and an electron.

3 Distinguish between the terms atomic number and nucleon number.

4 Determine the nuclear composition of chlorine-37.

Answers ➙ p. 24

2 Electron energy levels and orbitals

» Students model the atom's discrete energy levels, including electronic configuration and spdf notation.

➜ In the electron **shell** model of the atom, the electron shells represent the allowed energy levels for electrons.
  • Between each energy level were zones of forbidden energies. Electrons can move from a lower shell to a higher, unfilled shell by absorbing a small packet or quantum of energy that is equal to the energy difference between the two shells.
  • In the following diagram (Figure 2.2) of a lithium atom (Z = 3), the single electron in the L shell can absorb a quantum of energy and move into the vacant M shell. In this state, called an **excited state,** the electron is not very stable and will fall back down into the L shell with the emission of a quantum of energy. This quantum of energy will be usually observed as a light photon of a fixed frequency.

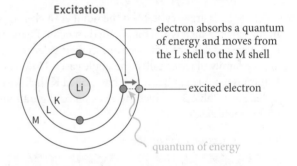

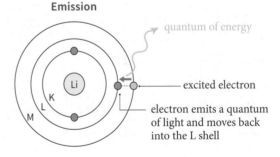

Figure 2.2 Excitation and emission

shell: alternative name for an electron energy level
excited state: electrons occupying a higher and unstable energy level above their normal, stable ground state

➜ The **electron configuration** of an element refers to the arrangement of electrons in each shell. There is a maximum number of electrons in each shell.

The K shell, which is closest to the nucleus, can hold 2 electrons, whereas the L shell can contain up to 8 electrons. The next shell is the M shell that can hold 18 electrons and the N shell can have a maximum of 32 electrons. For any element in its most stable state (called the ground state), the electrons occupy the lowest shells.

→ The electron configuration of an atom is the number of electrons in each shell, starting with the K shell. For example:
  • lithium (Z = 3): electron configuration = 2,1
  • fluorine (Z = 9): electron configuration = 2,7
  • magnesium (Z = 12): electron configuration = 2,8,2

→ The outermost shell that contains electrons is called the valence shell. Thus, in the above examples, lithium has 1 valence electron, fluorine has 7 valence electrons and magnesium has 2 valence electrons.

electron configuration: the number of electrons in each electron shell of the atom

valence shell: the outer electron shell of an atom which contains the valence electrons

→ Valence shells are very stable if the number of electrons in the valence shell is 8. This is called an octet. Elements that have a stable octet of electrons in their valence shell are the family of gases called the noble gases. However, helium is a noble gas because it has a filled K shell with 2 electrons. Table 2.2 shows the electron configurations of the noble gases.

Table 2.2 Electron configurations

Noble gas	Z	Electron configuration
helium	2	2
neon	10	2,8
argon	18	2,8,8
krypton	36	2,8,18,8
xenon	54	2,8,18,18,8
radon	86	2,8,18,32,18,8

→ Metals tend to form positively charged ions (cations) by the loss of electrons from their valence shell. Magnesium (Z = 12) has 2 valence electrons in the M shell. The loss of the 2 valence electrons produces a stable Mg^{2+} ion, which has a stable noble gas electron configuration (2,8).

→ Aluminium (Z = 13) has 3 valence electrons in the M shell. The loss of the 3 valence electrons produces a stable Al^{3+} ion, which also has a stable noble gas electron configuration (2,8).

$$Al \rightarrow Al^{3+} + 3e^-$$
$$2,8,3 \quad\quad 2,8$$

→ Non-metals tend to form negatively charged ions (anions) by the gain of electrons into their valence shell. Oxygen (Z = 8) has 6 valence electrons in the L shell. The gain of the 2 electrons produces a stable O^{2-} ion, which has a stable noble gas electron configuration (2,8).

→ Chlorine (Z = 17) has 7 valence electrons in the M shell. The gain of 1 electron produces a stable Cl^- ion, which also has a stable noble gas electron configuration (2,8,8).

$$Cl + e^- \rightarrow Cl^-$$
$$2,8,7 \quad\quad\quad 2,8,8$$

Subshells and orbitals

→ The modern atomic theory describes electrons in each electron shell (energy level) as occupying specific subshells and orbitals. Orbitals have specific shapes and orientations and are designated by the letters s, p, d and f. Figure 2.3 shows the shapes and orientations of these orbitals.

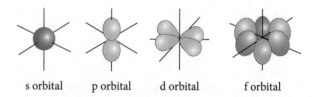

s orbital   p orbital   d orbital   f orbital

Figure 2.3 s, p, d and f orbitals

→ Table 2.3 lists the number of subshells, and symbols for the subshells. Thus 2s and 2p subshells are located in the L shell (n = 2). The letters s and p refer to the shapes of the orbitals found in that subshell.

Table 2.3 Shells, subshells and orbitals

Shell	Number of subshells	Symbols for subshells
K (n = 1)	1	1s
L (n = 2)	2	2s, 2p
M (n = 3)	3	3s, 3p, 3d
N (n = 4)	4	4s, 4p, 4d, 4f

→ The number of orbitals in a shell is equal to n^2. Thus in the L shell (n = 2) there are 2^2 or 4 orbitals. They are the 2s orbital, and the three 2p orbitals (called $2p_x$, $2p_y$ and $2p_z$). Orbitals can contain a maximum of 2 electrons.

→ Figure 2.4 shows the number and types of orbitals in each subshell for the first three shells of an atom. Each atomic orbital can contain a maximum of 2 electrons.

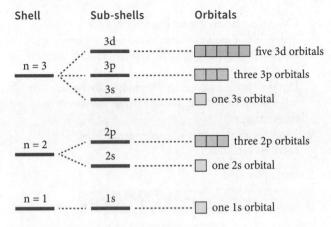

Shell	Sub-shells	Orbitals

Figure 2.4 Subshells and orbitals

→ Electron configurations of elements can also be expressed in spdf notation, as shown in the following examples:

Element	Electron configuration	spdf notation
hydrogen (Z = 1)	1	$1s^1$
helium (Z = 2)	2	$1s^2$
lithium (Z = 3)	2,1	$1s^2\,2s^1$
fluorine (Z = 9)	2,7	$1s^2\,2s^2\,2p^5$
neon (Z = 10)	2,8	$1s^2\,2s^2\,2p^6$
sodium (Z = 11)	2,8,1	$1s^2\,2s^2\,2p^6\,3s^1$

→ KEY QUESTIONS

5 Consider the following nuclear symbol: $^{56}_{26}Fe$

Determine the number of protons, neutrons and electrons in this atom.

6 Distinguish between the terms ground state and excited state in relation to electrons.

7 Write the electron configuration of silicon (Z = 14).

8 Write the spdf notation of sulfur (Z = 16)

Answers ⊃ p. 24

3 Relative atomic mass

» Students calculate the relative atomic mass from isotopic composition.

→ Due to the existence of different isotopes of each element, a standard isotope is used as the standard of mass. This standard is the carbon-12 isotope. Its mass is set at 12 atomic mass units (or 12 u) exactly. One atomic mass unit (or 1 u) is equal to one-twelfth (1/12) of the mass of a carbon-12 atom. The mass of single carbon-12 atoms has been measured using a mass spectrometer and found to be equal to 1.9927×10^{-23} g.

Thus, $1\ u = \dfrac{1.9927 \times 10^{-23}}{12} = 1.661 \times 10^{-24}$ g

→ Carbon exists in nature as a mixture of two stable isotopes and one radioactive isotope:

C-12 (98.9%); C-13 (1.1%): C-14 (trace; radioactive)

→ The relative atomic mass or atomic weight of natural carbon can now be calculated. C-13 has an isotopic mass of 13.00 u:

Relative atomic mass (C) = $\dfrac{98.9}{100} \times 12 + \dfrac{1.1}{100} \times 13.00$

= 12.01 u

→ The relative atomic mass of carbon is commonly called its atomic weight.

→ The atomic weights of other elements can then be calculated from their known isotopic masses and the proportion of each isotope in the natural mixture.

EXAMPLE 1

Natural boron consists of 2 isotopes. Calculate the atomic weight of natural boron from the following data:

B-10: isotopic mass = 10.013 u
percentage = 19.9%

B-11: isotopic mass = 11.009 u
percentage = 80.1%

Calculate the weighted average of each isotope

Answer:
Atomic weight of boron = $\dfrac{19.9}{100} \times 10.013 + \dfrac{80.1}{100} \times 11.009$

= 10.81 u

→ KEY QUESTIONS

9 Use electronic configurations to explain why xenon and krypton are examples of noble gases.

10 Explain why the atomic weight of hydrogen is 1.008 u and not 1 u exactly.

11 Natural bromine consists of 2 isotopes: Br-79 and Br-81. The atomic weight of natural bromine is 79.90 u. Identify which isotope is present in the greater amount.

12 Europium-151 has an isotopic mass of 150.920 u. Europium-153 has an isotopic mass of 152.921 u. The atomic weight of natural europium is 151.96 u. Determine the percentage of each isotope.

Answers ⊃ p. 24

4 Electron transfer between energy levels

» Students investigate energy levels in atoms and ions through:
- collecting primary data from a flame test using different ionic solutions of metals
- examining spectral evidence for the Bohr model and an introduction to the Schrödinger model.

FIRSTHAND INVESTIGATION

Flame testing

» Students investigate energy levels in atoms and ions through:
- collecting primary data from a flame test using different ionic solutions of metals.

Background
When aqueous solutions of various metal ions are atomised in a blue (non-luminous) Bunsen burner flame, they produce a characteristic colour in the flame.

Aim
to determine the flame colours when various salt solutions are injected into a blue Bunsen burner flame

Chemicals
- 1 mol/L solutions of: barium chloride; calcium chloride; copper (II) chloride; sodium chloride; strontium chloride
- concentrated hydrochloric acid.

Method
1 There are two common methods used to inject salt solutions into a blue Bunsen flame:
- Use a spray (atomiser) bottle to spray the solution into the flame.
- Use a platinum wire loop to place a drop of solution into the flame.

Figure 2.5 shows the use of a loop of platinum wire.

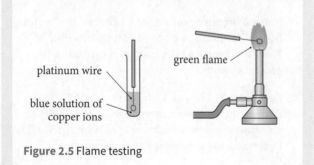

Figure 2.5 Flame testing

2 Clean the platinum wire in concentrated hydrochloric acid and then place it in the blue Bunsen flame. Repeat until no further flame colour results.
3 Dip the cleaned platinum wire loop into the selected salt solution and hold it in the flame to observe the flame colour.
4 Repeat with the other salt solutions. Clean the wire between each test.

Sample results

Metal ion	Flame colour
barium	pale yellow-green
calcium	orange-red
copper	green
sodium	yellow (yellow-orange)
strontium	crimson

Light emission

→ The colour of the flame is only a qualitative measure of the presence of the metal in the sample. The Bohr model of the atom can explain the observed frequencies of emitted light. The colour arises from the emission of light of specific frequencies due to excited electrons falling back to lower electron shells in the atom.

→ Figure 2.6 shows the stages of this process.
- When the metal ion sample is introduced into the hot flame, electrons in the valence shell absorb energy and move to higher shells. This is the excitation process.
- The excited electrons are unstable and fall back down to more stable shells or subshells. This is accompanied by the emission of light.
- If the frequency of this emitted light is in the visible region of the electromagnetic spectrum, then a coloured flame is observed. If the light frequency is in the non-visible region (e.g. ultraviolet), then the flame does not change colour.

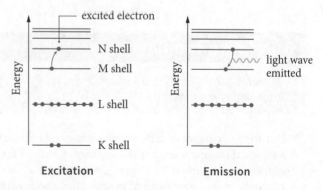

Figure 2.6 Excitation and emission

Atomic emission spectra

→ This light emission process can occur in a series of stages. The excited electron can drop back to a series of lower energy subshells. Different energy light photons are seen as coloured spectral lines in the visible emission spectrum. The greater the energy change in the electron transition, the higher the frequency (and the shorter the wavelength) of the emitted light photons.

→ Emission spectra are recordings of the intensity of each emitted photon versus wavelength. Bright lines in the spectrum indicated greater numbers of photons of a given wavelength. Pale lines indicated lower numbers of photons of a given wavelength.

→ The atomic emission spectra of sodium and mercury are shown in Figure 2.7. The yellow light emitted from the sodium flame is due to light of wavelength 589 nm. The light is produced when a valence electrons make a transition from the 3p orbital back to the 3s orbital (ground state).

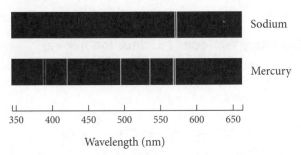

Figure 2.7 Atomic emission spectra for sodium and mercury

Schrödinger model of atomic structure

→ In 1926 Erwin Schrödinger improved the Bohr model of the atom using quantum mathematical equations in which electrons are described in terms of their wave nature. The solutions to these equations described the probability of finding electrons around the nucleus.

→ In this atomic model, the nucleus is surrounded by an electron 'cloud'. The Bohr electron shells were now envisioned as regions when the electron cloud was most dense (i.e. where the electron probability was greatest), and the inter-shell region was a region of low cloud density (Figure 2.8). This model is consistent with the electrons having both a particle nature and wave properties.

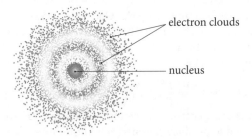

Figure 2.8 Electron cloud model of the atom

→ Schrödinger's model led to the concept of electron subshells and orbitals that were discussed previously.

 SECONDARY-SOURCED INVESTIGATION

Atomic emission spectra

» Students investigate energy levels in atoms and ions through:
  • examining spectral evidence for the Bohr model and an introduction to the Schrödinger model.

Aim

to identify the elements present in two alloys (X and Y) using their atomic emission spectra

Method

Figure 2.9 contains atomic emission spectra of two alloys, X and Y. Each alloy contains two elements.

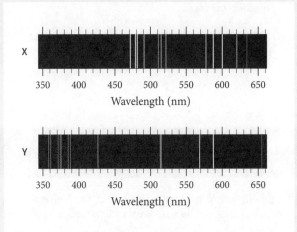

Figure 2.9 Atomic emission spectra

Use the wavelength data in Table 2.4 to identify the elements in alloys X and Y.

Table 2.4 Atomic emission wavelengths

Element	Line wavelengths in emission spectrum (nm)
carbon	392; 427; 515; 570; 589; 658
chromium	357; 361; 425; 429; 520; 521
copper	511; 515; 522; 578
iron	358; 361; 372; 374; 375; 386; 389; 517
lead	364; 367; 368; 374; 402; 406; 417
nickel	352; 362; 378; 381; 386
tin	381; 563; 607; 615
zinc	472; 478; 481; 491; 589; 602; 621; 636

→ KEY QUESTIONS

13 An unknown white salt was dissolved in water and a flame test was performed. The flame was orange-red. Identify the cation present in the salt.

14 Explain why all elements have unique atomic emission spectra.

15 Distinguish between the Bohr and Schrödinger models of the atom.

Answers ⊃ p. 24

5 Radioactivity and unstable isotopes

» Students investigate the properties of unstable isotopes using natural and human-made radioisotopes as examples, including but not limited to:
  • types of radiation
  • types of balanced nuclear reactions.

Radioisotopes

→ Some isotopes are stable and others are unstable. Unstable isotopes emit radiation (e.g. alpha, beta or gamma rays) and are called radioisotopes. The emission of radiation continues until the nucleus becomes stable.

→ Common nuclear radiations are:
  • Alpha particles—composed of helium nuclei ($^4_2$He)
  • Beta particles—composed of rapidly moving electrons ($^0_{-1}$e)
  • Gamma rays—high energy electromagnetic radiation (γ)

→ The stability of an isotope depends on the ratio of neutrons to protons (n/p), as well as the total number of nuclear particles (nucleons). Nuclear equations can be written for each decay. The A and Z values are conserved in nuclear equations.

n/p ratio is too high (excess neutrons)

When there are too many neutrons compared with protons then a neutron decays to form a proton and a beta particle (fast electron), which is emitted from the nucleus.

Example:

$$\text{iodine-131} \rightarrow \text{xenon-131} + \text{beta}$$
$$^{131}_{53}\text{I} \rightarrow ^{131}_{54}\text{Xe} + ^{0}_{-1}\text{e}$$
$$(53\text{p}/78\text{n}) \qquad (54\text{p}/77\text{n})$$

In this equation: $131 = 131 + 0$ and $53 = 54 + (-1)$

n/p ratio is too low (excess protons)

When there are too many protons compared with neutrons, then a proton decays to form a neutron and a positron (same mass as an electron with a positive charge).

Example:

$$\text{sodium-22} \rightarrow \text{neon-22} + \text{positron}$$
$$^{22}_{11}\text{Na} \rightarrow ^{22}_{10}\text{Ne} + ^{0}_{1}\text{e}$$
$$(11\text{p}/11\text{n}) \qquad (10\text{p}/12\text{n})$$

In this equation: $22 = 22 + 0$ and $11 = 10 + 1$

Too many nucleons (nucleus too heavy)

When there are too many nucleons, then alpha decay occurs. The loss of an alpha particle reduces the nucleus by 2 protons and 2 neutrons.

Example:

$$\text{thorium-230} \rightarrow \text{radium-226} + \text{alpha}$$
$$^{230}_{90}\text{Th} \rightarrow ^{226}_{88}\text{Ra} + ^{4}_{2}\text{He}$$
$$(90\text{p}/140\text{n}) \qquad (88\text{p}/138\text{n}) \qquad (2\text{p}/2\text{n})$$

In this equation: $230 = 226 + 4$ and $90 = 88 + 2$

Production of synthetic radioisotopes

→ Elements beyond uranium (Z = 92) in the periodic table are called **transuranic elements**. The first transuranic element to be synthesised was neptunium-239 (Z = 93). It was produced by bombarding uranium-238 with neutrons produced in **nuclear fission reactors**. Initially an unstable uranium isotope (U-239) formed, which quickly decayed by beta emission to form neptunium-239.

$$^{238}_{92}\text{U} + ^{1}_{0}\text{n} \rightarrow ^{239}_{92}\text{U} \rightarrow ^{239}_{93}\text{Np} + ^{0}_{-1}\text{e}$$

→ **Linear accelerators** and **cyclotrons** have been used to produce transuranic elements. Oganesson (Og) (Z = 118) was synthesised by firing a beam of calcium-48 ions at a californium-249 target. Three neutrons were emitted in the nuclear synthesis.

$$^{48}_{20}\text{Ca} + ^{249}_{98}\text{Cf} \rightarrow ^{294}_{118}\text{Og} + 3^{1}_{0}\text{n}$$

→ High energy particle accelerators and nuclear reactors are also used to produce commercial radioisotopes.

Example:

Iodine-123 is produced in a cyclotron by bombarding xenon-124 atoms with protons.

$$^{124}_{54}\text{Xe} + ^{1}_{1}\text{p} \rightarrow ^{123}_{53}\text{I} + 2^{1}_{0}\text{n} + 2^{0}_{1}\text{e}$$

→ Iodine-123 is a diagnostic radioisotope. I-123 is a beta and gamma emitter. It is used to detect thyroid gland abnormalities. The I-123 concentrates in the thyroid gland. The gamma rays emitted are detected by a gamma camera, and an image of the thyroid gland is produced. Its half-life is short (13.1 hours) and does not create waste problems or excessive radiation exposure to the body.

$$^{123}_{53}\text{I} \rightarrow ^{123}_{54}\text{Xe} + ^{0}_{-1}\text{e} + \gamma$$

transuranic elements: elements with atomic numbers greater than 92

nuclear fission reactors: reactors in which nuclear fission reactions occur with the production of energy

linear accelerator: a particle accelerator that increases the kinetic energy of charged particles using oscillating electric fields

cyclotron: a circular particle accelerator that increases the kinetic energy of charged particles using a static magnetic field and rapidly varying electric fields

half-life: the time for a radioisotope to decrease in mass by 50%

→ KEY QUESTIONS

16 Identify the nature of the common types of radiation emitted by radioisotopes.

17 Identify the factors that make radioisotopes unstable.

18 Identify two common methods that are used to produce synthetic radioisotopes.

19 Iodine-131 is a beta emitter used to treat thyroid abnormalities. Write a nuclear decay equation for this radioisotope.

Answers ⊃ p. 24

CHAPTER SYLLABUS CHECKLIST

Are you able to answer these questions from the syllabus for this chapter? Tick each question as you go through the checklist if you are able to answer it. If you cannot answer a question, turn to the relevant page in the study guide to find the answer. For NESA key word meanings, go to www.educationstandards.nsw.edu.au and search 'key words'.

	FOR A COMPLETE UNDERSTANDING OF THIS TOPIC:	PAGE NO.	✓
1	Can I name the sub-particles of the atom and classify them according to charge?	14	
2	Can I explain the electron shell structure of the atom?	14	
3	Can I explain the difference between the atomic number and the nucleon number?	14–15	
4	Can I explain the difference between the ground and excited states of an electron?	15	
5	Can I write the electron configuration of an element based on its atomic number?	16	
6	Can I explain how metals form positive ions and how non-metals form negative ions?	16	
7	Can I relate the stability of an ion to the stable electron configuration of noble gases?	16	
8	Can I explain the relationship between shells, subshells and orbitals?	16–17	
9	Can I state the standard of relative atomic mass?	17	
10	Can I calculate the atomic weights of elements based on their isotopic compositions and isotopic masses?	17	
11	Can I use the spdf notation to write electron configurations for elements given their atomic numbers?	17	
12	Can I explain the experimental method to observe flame colours?	18	
13	Can I explain why some metals produce flame colours?	18	
14	Can I recall the flame colours of some common metal ions?	18	
15	Can I explain how elements can produce emission spectra when samples are atomised in a flame?	18–19	
16	Can I explain the electron cloud model of the atom?	19	
17	Can I identify the types of radiation emitted during nuclear decay?	20	
18	Can I write nuclear equations for different types of nuclear decays?	20	
19	Can I explain how different radioisotopes can be synthesised?	21	

Objective-response questions (1 mark each)

1 Select the correct response concerning elements and the periodic table.

   A Iron-56 contains 56 electrons.

   B Hydrogen-2 has an atomic number of 2.

   C Bohrium is a synthetic radioactive metal.

   D Gold has fewer protons in its nucleus than platinum.

2 Select the correct statement concerning the atom.

   A Protons have a greater mass than neutrons.

   B The nucleus occupies most of the volume of the atom.

   C The nucleon number of an element is the number of protons and neutrons in the nucleus.

   D The nucleus is neutral as it contains equal numbers of protons and electrons.

3 The chloride ion has the same electron configuration as the:

   A potassium ion

   B neon atom

   C sodium atom

   D fluoride ion

4 The flame colour for the barium ion is:

   A orange-red

   B yellow

   C crimson

   D pale yellow-green

5 Natural carbon consists of 3 isotopes: C-12, C-13, C-14. Select the correct response.

   A These isotopes have different numbers of protons.

   B These isotopes have different structural crystalline forms.

   C C-12 is radioactive.

   D C-14 has 2 more neutrons in its nucleus than C-12.

Extended-response questions

6 Complete the following table by identifying S, P, Q and R. (4 marks)

Element	Symbol	Number of protons	Number of neutrons	Number of electrons
sodium	$^{23}_{11}Na$	11	S	11
chlorine	$^{35}_{17}Cl$	P	18	17
uranium	Q	92	146	92
R	$^{19}_{9}F$	9	10	9

7 Determine the electron configuration for the following ions and comment on their stability.

   a $^{24}_{12}Mg^{2+}$

   b $^{14}_{7}N^{3-}$

   c $^{27}_{13}Al^{+}$ (6 marks)

8 The following diagram (Figure 2.11) shows the visible emission spectrum of hydrogen. Four coloured lines are observed. Each line represents the transition of the excited electron back from a higher energy state to the first excited state.

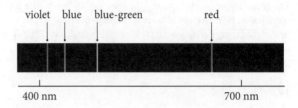

Figure 2.11 Hydrogen emission spectrum

   a Identify the first excited state shell for the hydrogen electron. (1 mark)

   b Identify the excited state shell for each coloured line in the emission spectrum. (4 marks)

9 Plutonium-241 decays by beta emission to form americium-241. Americium-241 is an alpha emitter and is used in smoke detectors.

   a Write a nuclear equation for the beta decay of plutonium-241. (1 mark)

   b If Pu-241 is a beta emitter, what can be said about the n/p ratio in its nucleus? (1 mark)

   c Write a nuclear equation for the alpha decay of Am-241 (1 mark)

10 Natural chlorine consists of 2 stable isotopes. Calculate the atomic weight of natural chlorine from the following data:

   Cl-35: isotopic mass = 34.969 u
              percentage = 75.78%

   Cl-37: isotopic mass = 36.966 u
              percentage = 24.22% (2 marks)

ANSWERS

Key questions ⇒ p. 15

1   Protons and neutrons

2   Protons have a much greater mass than an electron; protons have a positive charge and electrons have a negative charge.

3   The atomic number (Z) is the number of protons in the nucleus. The nucleon number (A) is the total number of protons and neutrons.

4   Chlorine (Z = 17): 17 protons; 37 − 17 = 20 neutrons

Key questions ⇒ p. 17

5   26 protons; 56 − 26 = 30 neutrons; 26 electrons

6   The ground state of an electron is the shell/orbital in which it is most stable. If an electron absorbs a quantum of energy it can move to a higher energy state, which is called the excited state. This is an unstable state.

7   2,8,4

8   $1s^2\, 2s^2\, 2p^6\, 3s^2\, 3p^4$

9   Both xenon and krypton have 8 electrons in their valence shell and therefore belong to group 18 (noble gases); krypton: 2,8,18,8; xenon: 2,8,18,18,8

10 Hydrogen-1 has an atomic weight of 1.008 u as it is not the standard against which atomic weights are compared. Carbon-12 is the standard atom, with a mass of 12 u exactly. 99.98% of natural hydrogen is H-1. Hydrogen-2 is also a stable isotope, with an abundance of 0.02%.

11 The Br-79 is present in a slightly greater amount as 79.9 is closer to 79 than 81.

12 Let $x\%$ represent the percentage of Eu-151, and $(100 − x)\%$ is the percentage of Eu-153.

$$\frac{x}{100} \times 150.920 + \frac{100 - x}{100} \times 152.921 = 151.96 \text{ u}$$

Solve for x: $x = 48.026\%$
Eu-151: 48.026%; Eu-153: 51.974%

Key questions ⇒ p. 20

13 Calcium

14 Each element has a different number of electrons in orbitals of varying energies. When energised these electrons become excited into higher energy levels before they de-excite and emit different radiation wavelengths. The atomic emission spectrum is therefore unique for each element.

15 The Bohr model of the atom states that electrons are confined to fixed energy levels (or shells) at various fixed distances from the nucleus. The Schrödinger model of the atom takes into account the wave nature of the electron. In this model the probability of finding electrons around the nucleus leads to the concept of an electron cloud of variable density. The zones of highest electron cloud density correspond to the radial distances of the Bohr energy levels.

Key questions ⇒ p. 21

16 Alpha particles: composed of helium nuclei; beta particles: composed of rapidly moving electrons; gamma rays: high energy electromagnetic radiation (γ)

17 An excess of neutrons (when n/p ratio is too high); an excess of protons (when the n/p ratio is too low); too many nucleons

18 Linear accelerators; cyclotrons; nuclear reactors (any 2)

19 $^{131}_{53}\text{I} \rightarrow\, ^{131}_{54}\text{Xe} +\, ^{0}_{-1}\text{e}$

YEAR 11 EXAM-TYPE QUESTIONS

Objective-response questions

1   **C.** Bohrium (Z = 107) is a radioactive element manufactured in a particle collider. **A** is incorrect as 56 refers to the nucleon number. **B** is incorrect as the atomic number of hydrogen is 1. **D** is incorrect as Pt has 78 protons and Au has 79 protons.

2   **C.** The term mass number is an alternative name for nucleon number; nucleons are particles inside the nucleus. **A** is incorrect as neutrons are slightly more massive. **B** is incorrect as the nucleus occupies only a very tiny volume of the atom. **D** is incorrect as there are no electrons in the nucleus.

3   **A.** Cl^- ion: (Z = 17) e = 17 + 1 = 18; K^+ ion: (Z = 19) e = 19 − 1 = 18. **B** is incorrect as the neon atom has 10 electrons. **C** is incorrect as a sodium atom has 11 electrons. **D** is incorrect as a fluoride ion (F^-) has 9 + 1 = 10 electrons.

4   **D.** Barium's flame is a paler green than copper's flame, which is much brighter. **A** is incorrect as calcium ions produce an orange flame. **B** is incorrect as sodium ions produce a yellow flame. **C** is incorrect as strontium ions produce a crimson flame.

5   **D.** Z = 6; C-12: A = 12 n = 12 − 6 = 6; C-14: Z = 6; A = 14 n = 14 − 6 = 8. **A** is incorrect as all the isotopes of carbon have 6 protons. **B** is incorrect as isotopes of elements have no effect on their macroscopic crystalline structure. **C** is incorrect as C-12 is a stable isotope.

Extended-response questions

6   **EM** In this question you are required to demonstrate an understanding of the relationship between Z and A values and the neutrality of atoms. The proton and electron number are equal in a neutral atom. The number of neutrons is found by subtracting the atomic number from the nucleon number.

S = A − Z = 23 − 11 = 12 ✓; P = Z = 17 ✓
Q = $^{238}_{92}\text{U}$, as Z = number of protons = 92;
A = number of neutrons + protons = 146 + 92 = 238 ✓
R = fluorine (symbol F, atomic number = 9) ✓

7   **EM** This question requires you to demonstrate how the number of electrons in an ion can be determined. Positive ions have fewer electrons than the neutral atom. Negative ions have more electrons than the neutral atom. Atoms or ions are stable if they can achieve a noble gas electron configuration.

   a Z = 12. Thus the uncharged atom would have 12 electrons. ✓
   This ion has a 2+ charge and so the atom has lost two electrons.

Therefore the ion has 10 electrons and its electron configuration will be 2,8. This is a stable ion as it has an octet in the outer electron shell. ✓

b Z = 7. Thus the uncharged atom would have 7 electrons. ✓ This ion has a 3– charge and so the atom has gained 3 electrons. Therefore the ion has 10 electrons and its electron configuration will be 2,8 (i.e. the same as example **a**). This is also a stable ion. ✓

c Z = 13. The uncharged atom would have 13 electrons. ✓ This ion has a charge of +1 and thus the atom has lost 1 electron. Therefore it has 12 electrons and an electron configuration of 2,8,2. This ion is not stable as it does not have a stable octet of electrons in the outer shell. ✓

8 **EM** In this question you are required to relate each spectral line to the energy levels in the atom. Hydrogen atoms have 1 electron, which is normally located in the K shell. Excited electrons temporarily occupy higher shells before they emit light and fall back to lower energy shells. Red light has the longest wavelength and is produced when the excited electron moves through the lowest energy difference. Violet light has the shortest wavelength and corresponds to the greatest energy change for the excited electron.

a L shell (The ground state would be the K shell.) ✓

b red: M shell (transition = M to L) ✓

blue-green: N shell (transition = N to L) ✓

blue: O shell (transition = O to L) ✓

violet: P shell (transition = P to L) ✓

9 **EM** In this question you need to demonstrate that in nuclear equations there is a conservation of nucleon numbers and atomic numbers. Electrons (beta particles) have a 0 nucleon number and an atomic number of –1. When there is an excess of neutrons in the nucleus, the decay process involves a neutron converting into a proton and an electron. This electron escapes from the nucleus as a beta particle.

a $^{241}_{94}Pu \rightarrow\ ^{241}_{95}Am +\ ^{0}_{-1}e$ ✓

b The n/p ratio is too high due to an excess of neutrons. ✓

c $^{241}_{95}Am \rightarrow\ ^{237}_{93}Np +\ ^{4}_{2}He$ ✓

10 **EM** In this question you need to demonstrate that the atomic weight of a natural sample of an element is the weighted average of its isotopic masses. The calculation should show all the arithmetic steps. The answer should be expressed to the correct number of significant figures. In this case, four significant figures are used because the percentage data has four significant figures.

$$\text{Atomic weight of chlorine} = \frac{75.78}{100} \times 34.969 + \frac{24.22}{100} \times 36.966 \checkmark$$
$$= 35.45\ u \checkmark$$

CHAPTER 3 PERIODICITY

Are there patterns in the properties of elements?

The natural and synthetic elements are shown in the periodic table. The periodic table we use today has developed over several hundred years as chemists began to classify elements according to their properties. In 1871, a Russian chemist Dmitri Mendeleev (1834–1907) constructed a table of the known elements based on atomic weight. He left spaces for undiscovered elements so that the vertical columns would contain only elements that had similar chemical properties. Using the known properties of surrounding elements, Mendeleev predicted the properties of the undiscovered elements, and these predictions assisted other chemists to search for these elements in various minerals.

1 The periodic table

» Students demonstrate, explain and predict the relationships in the observable trends in the physical and chemical properties of elements in periods and groups in the periodic table, including but not limited to:
  • state of matter at room temperature
  • electronic configurations and atomic radii.

Periodic table structure

➡ The discovery in 1914 by the English physicist Henry Moseley (1887–1915) that each element had a unique number of protons led to the development of the modern periodic table in which the elements were arranged in order of increasing atomic number (Z).

➡ The periodic table demonstrates the periodic law.

Periodic law:

> **The properties of elements vary periodically with their atomic numbers.**

➡ The periodic table consists of 7 horizontal periods and 18 vertical groups (Figure 3.1). Each group represents a family of related elements with gradations in physical and chemical properties.

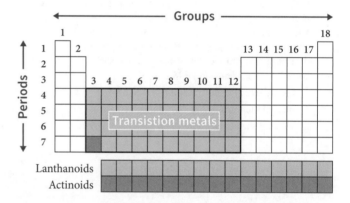

Figure 3.1 Organisation of the periodic table

➡ Figure 3.2 shows that the periodic table is divided into zones or blocks based on the filling of atomic orbitals.

➡ The s block (groups 1 and 2) are elements that have 1 or 2 valence electrons in an s orbital. Magnesium (Z = 12) is an example of an s-block element.

➡ The p block (groups 13 to 18) are elements that have valence electrons in p orbitals. Boron (Z = 5) is an example of a p-block element.

➡ The s block and p block are collectively called the 'main block'.

➡ The d block (groups 3 to 12) are called transition metals. This block contains metals that have some of their valence electrons in d orbitals. Titanium (Z = 22) is an example of a d-block metal.

➡ The f block contains two subseries of the d block. These series are called the lanthanoids and actinoids. These elements contain electrons in the f and d orbitals. Lutetium (Z = 72) is an f-block element. Actinoids are radioactive elements.

➡ Elements with atomic numbers of 93 to 118 are synthetic, radioactive elements.

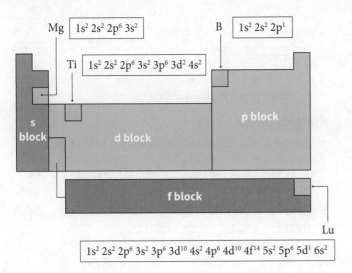

Figure 3.2 Blocks of the periodic table

→ **KEY QUESTIONS**

1 Identify which element is a member of group 6 of the periodic table:

   barium; tungsten; polonium; antimony

2 Identify which element is a member of period 4 of the periodic table:

   hafnium; tantalum; titanium; silicon

3 Identify which element is a transition metal:

   strontium; thallium; lead; palladium

4 Identify which element is a member of the lanthanoid series:

   manganese; neptunium; cerium; copernicium

Answers ⊃ p. 35

Groups in the periodic table

→ The group number is related to the electron configuration of the elements in a group. Within each group the elements have the same number of valence (outer shell) electrons (except He). Consider the following examples for groups 1, 2, 15 and 17.

Group 1

These elements have 1 electron in their valence shell and readily lose 1 electron to form a stable cation with a 1+ charge.

Examples:

  Na: 2,8,1
  K: 2,8,8,1
  Rb: 2,8,18,8,1

Group 2

These elements have 2 electrons in their valence shell and readily lose 2 electrons to form a stable cation with a 2+ charge.

Examples:

  Mg: 2,8,2
  Ca: 2,8,8,2
  Sr: 2,8,18,8,2

Group 15

These elements have 5 electrons in their valency shell. Non-metals in this group gain 3 electrons to form a stable anion with a 3− charge.

Examples:

  N: 2,5
  P: 2,8,5
  As: 2,8,18,5

Group 17

These elements have 7 electrons in their valence shell. These non-metals gain 1 electron to form stable anions with a 1− charge.

Examples:

  F: 2,7
  Cl: 2,8,7
  Br: 2,8,18,7

→ The noble gases (Group 18) have a stable octet of electrons in their valence shells. Helium, however, has a stable K shell. Consequently there is little or no tendency for these elements to react with other elements.

→ The transition metals have incompletely filled inner electron shells. They often form ions with variable charges. Consider the following examples:

Element	Electron configuration	Stable ion(s)
silver (Ag)	2,8,18,18,1	Ag^+
manganese (Mn)	2,8,13,2	Mn^{2+}
titanium (Ti)	2,8,10,2	Ti^{2+} and Ti^{4+}

→ In the case of titanium, if 2 electrons are lost from an N subshell, the Ti^{2+} ion is formed. More commonly titanium loses 4 electrons (to form the Ti^{4+} ion). This leads to a stable octet of electrons in the M shell.

→ **KEY QUESTIONS**

5 Identify which element is a synthetic, radioactive element:

   astatine; meitnerium; erbium; thorium

6 Identify which element is a member of the p block of the periodic table:

   holmium; bismuth; tungsten; caesium

7 Classify antimony (Z = 51) as a metal, semi-metal or non-metal.

8 The spdf notation of element A is $1s^2\,2s^2\,2p^3$. To which period and group does element A belong?

Answers ⊃ p. 35

Trends in physical properties in main block groups

States of matter at room temperature

➔ Most elements are solid at 25 °C. Two elements (Hg, Br) are liquids, and 12 elements are gases (see Figure 3.3).

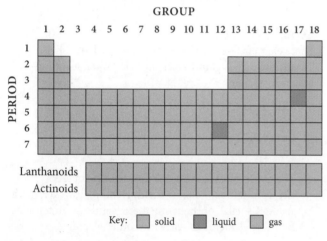

Figure 3.3 States of matter

➔ The state of an element at room temperature depends on its melting point (m.p) and boiling point (b.p):
  • If the boiling point is less than 25 °C, then the element is a gas.
  • If the melting point is less than 25 °C, but the boiling point is above 25 °C, then the element is a liquid.
  • If the melting point is above 25 °C, then the element is a solid.

  Example:
    mercury (Hg): m.p = −39 °C; b.p = 357 °C
  Mercury is a liquid at 25 °C.

Atomic radius

➔ Table 3.1 (see below) shows the atomic radii of the elements of the main block of the periodic table. The main block excludes the transition metals (d and f blocks).

➔ Analysis of the data in Table 3.1 reveals some generalised trends:
  • Atomic radius increases down a group.
  • Atomic radius decreases across a period.

➔ The radius of an atom depends on the number of electron shells and the size of the nuclear charge. Electron shells are attracted inwards as the charge on the nucleus increases down a group and across a period. Down a group the major cause of the radius increase is the increasing shell number whereas across a period the major cause of the radius decrease is the increasing nuclear charge.

➔ KEY QUESTIONS

9 Identify which of the following elements are gases at room temperature:

   fluorine; silicon; bromine; krypton; hydrogen; boron

10 Explain the trend in atomic radii for the elements in period 3.

11 Explain the trend in atomic radii for the elements in group 14.

Answers ⊃ p. 35

Table 3.1 Atomic radius (picometres, pm)

	1	2	13	14	15	16	17	18
1	H = 37							–
2	Li = 152	Be = 112	B = 73	C = 60	N = 54	O = 53	F = 53	–
3	Na = 186	Mg = 160	Al = 143	Si = 102	P = 94	S = 102	Cl = 93	Ar = 96
4	K = 227	Ca = 197	Ga = 122	Ge = 114	As = 106	Se = 107	Br = 110	Kr = 108
5	Rb = 248	Sr = 215	In = 136	Sn = 151	Sb = 127	Te = 121	I = 125	Xe = 122
6	Cs = 265	Ba = 217	Tl = 170	Pb = 175	Bi = 155	Po = 129	At = 138	Rn = 133

Note: A – symbol means no data is available.

Key: metals   semi-metals   non-metals

2 Ionisation energy and electronegativity

» Students demonstrate, explain and predict the relationships in the observable trends in the physical and chemical properties of elements in periods and groups in the periodic table, including but not limited to:
  • first ionisation energy and electronegativity.

First ionisation energy

➜ Figure 3.4 shows the ionisation of a gaseous lithium atom to form a lithium ion (Li⁺). The electron is lost from the outer L shell. The energy required to remove this electron is called the **first ionisation energy**.

> **first ionisation energy:** the first ionisation energy refers to the energy required to remove the most loosely bound electron from the valence shell of an atom in the gaseous state

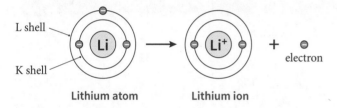

Figure 3.4 Ionisation of a lithium atom to form a lithium ion

➜ Table 3.2 shows the first ionisation energies of the elements of the main block of the periodic table. Figure 3.4 shows the ionisation of a lithium atom by the removal of the electron from the L shell.

➜ Analysis of the data in Table 3.2 reveals some generalised trends:
  • First ionisation energy decreases down each group.
  • First ionisation energy increases across each period.

➜ Down a group the valence electrons become further from the nucleus due to the increase in the number of shells. Valence shell electrons are more readily removed if they are further from the nucleus or if the nucleus has a smaller positive charge. The presence of shielding inner electron shells also reduces the energy required to ionise an atom.

➜ The first ionisation energy increases across a period because the atomic radius decreases across a period due to the increasing nuclear charge. Therefore it requires more energy to remove a valence electron.

Electronegativity

➜ Table 3.3 shows the trends in electronegativity in the periodic table.

➜ Analysis of the data in Table 3.3 reveals some generalised trends:
  • Electronegativity decreases down each group.
  • Electronegativity increases across each period.

> **electronegativity: a** measure of the electron-attracting ability of an element when bonded to another element in a compound

➜ Electronegativities for noble gases are not shown as they generally do not form compounds.

➜ Apart from the noble gases, non-metals have high electronegativity as they attract electrons to complete their valence shell. Fluorine (group 17) has the highest electronegativity. Metals are the opposite. They tend to lose electrons from their valence shell and so have very low electronegativity. Francium (group 1) has the lowest electronegativity.

➜ Therefore electronegativity decreases down a group as elements become more metallic, and increases across a period as elements become more non-metallic.

Table 3.2 First ionisation energy (kJ/mol)

	1	2	13	14	15	16	17	18
1	H = 1318							He = 2379
2	Li = 526	Be = 906	B = 807	C = 1093	N = 1407	O = 1320	F = 1687	Ne = 2087
3	Na = 502	Mg = 744	Al = 584	Si = 793	P = 1018	S = 1006	Cl = 1257	Ar = 1527
4	K = 425	Ca = 596	Ga = 585	Ge = 768	As = 953	Se = 947	Br = 1146	Kr = 1357
5	Rb = 409	Sr = 556	In = 565	Sn = 715	Sb = 840	Te = 876	I = 1015	Xe = 1177
6	Cs = 382	Ba = 509	Tl = 596	Pb = 722	Bi = 710	Po = 818	At = 888	Rn = 1043

Key: metals   semi-metals   non-metals

Table 3.3 Electronegativity

	1	2	13	14	15	16	17
1	H = 2.20						
2	Li = 0.98	Be = 1.57	B = 2.04	C = 2.55	N = 3.04	O = 3.44	F = 3.98
3	Na = 0.93	Mg = 1.31	Al = 1.61	Si = 1.61	P = 2.19	S = 2.58	Cl = 3.16
4	K = 0.82	Ca = 1.00	Ga = 1.81	Ge = 2.01	As = 2.18	Se = 2.55	Br = 2.96
5	Rb = 0.82	Sr = 0.95	In = 1.78	Sn = 1.96	Sb = 2.05	Te = 2.1	I = 2.66
6	Cs = 0.79	Ba = 0.89	Tl = 2.04	Pb = 2.33	Bi = 2.02	Po = 2.0	At = 2.2

Key: metals   semi-metals   non-metals

EXAMPLE 1

Arrange the following sets of elements in decreasing order of the indicated property:

1 Property = First ionisation energy;
Element set = N, Ba, He, Mg

2 Property = Electronegativity;
Element set = K, Si, O, Li

Review the trends across a period and down a group

Answer:

1 First ionisation energy decreases down a group and increases across a period. Thus the elements with the highest first ionisation energies are in the top right corner, and the lowest are in the bottom left corner of the periodic table.
The decreasing order is: He; N; Mg; Ba

2 Electronegativity decreases down a group and increases across a period. Thus the most electronegative elements in the main block are at the top of group 17 and the least electronegative elements are in the bottom left corner of the table.
The decreasing order is: O; Si; Li; K

📖 SECONDARY-SOURCED INVESTIGATION 1

Density trends in periodic table groups

» Students demonstrate, explain and predict the observable trends of elements in periods and groups in the periodic table.

Aim

to plot density graphs for elements in three periodic table groups and to determine the trend in density down each group

Method

1 Use Table 3.4 to plot column graphs of the density data for the elements in groups 2, 13 and 14.

2 Discuss the trends in density down each group.

Table 3.4 Density of elements in groups 2, 13 and 14

Group 2	Density (g/cm³)	Group 13	Density (g/cm³)	Group 14	Density (g/cm³)
Be	1.85	B	2.34	C	2.26
Mg	1.74	Al	2.70	Si	2.33
Ca	1.55	Ga	5.32	Ge	5.32
Sr	2.60	In	7.31	Sn	7.30
Ba	3.50	Tl	11.85	Pb	11.30

Sample answers

1 Figure A3.1 is a column graph of the density trends in the requested periodic table groups.

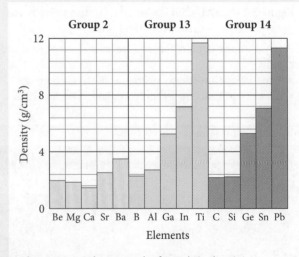

Figure A3.1 Column graph of trends in density

2 Density tends to increase down each of the groups examined. In group 2, the density initially decreases slightly, and then increases for heavier elements.

Atomic volume trends in the periodic table

» Students demonstrate, explain and predict the observable trends of elements in periods and groups in the periodic table through representing data in a variety of forms.

Aim

to determine the trend in atomic volume across periods and down groups from graphical data

Method

1 Examine the graph of atomic volume versus atomic number in Figure 3.5.

2 Answer the questions about this graph.

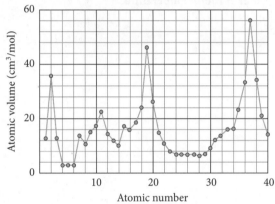

Figure 3.5 Atomic volume versus atomic numbers

Questions

a Using Figure 3.5, what are the trends in atomic volume:
  i across a period?
  ii down a group?

b Which elements form the maxima on the graph?

Sample answers

a i Apart from period 1, atomic volume initially decreases and then increases across each period in the main block elements (Z = 3–10; Z = 1–18; Z = 19–20, 31–36). The transition metals (Z = 21–30) show a decrease in atomic volume.

  ii Atomic volume generally increases down a group (e.g. group 1 (Z = 3,11,19,37), and group 2 (Z = 4,12,20,38).

b The maxima are helium (Z = 2), sodium (Z = 11), potassium (Z = 19), rubidium (Z = 37).

12 Describe the trend in the following properties across a period and down a group:
  a first ionisation energy
  b electronegativity.

13 An element in the p block has the following successive ionisation energies to remove the first 8 electrons: 0.79; 1.58; 3.24; 4.36; 16.10; 19.8; 23.79; 29.26 (MJ/mol). To which periodic group does it belong?

14 Explain why rubidium has a much lower electronegativity than iodine, even though they are members of the same period.

Answers ⊃ p. 35

3 Reactivity of elements with water

» Students demonstrate, explain and predict the relationships in the observable trends in the physical and chemical properties of elements in periods and groups in the periodic table, including:
  • reactivity with water.

Reaction of main group elements with water

→ Group 1 metals react very rapidly with water to produce solutions of metal hydroxides and hydrogen gas. The reaction becomes increasingly violent down group 1 as the heat released causes the hydrogen to explode in the air.

$$2K(s) + 2H_2O(l) \rightarrow 2KOH(aq) + H_2(g)$$

→ Group 2 metals (other than beryllium) react moderately with water to produce solutions of metal hydroxides and hydrogen gas. The reaction rate increases down the group.

$$Ba(s) + 2H_2O(l) \rightarrow Ba(OH)_2 (aq) + H_2(g)$$

→ Group 13–16 elements generally do not react with water. Aluminium in group 13 reacts very slowly with water to form aluminium oxide on the surface This oxide prevents further reaction.

→ Group 17 elements react with water, but the reaction rate decreases down the group. Fluorine reacts violently with water to release oxygen gas. Some ozone gas (O_3) also forms.

$$2F_2(g) + 2H_2O(l) \rightarrow O_2(g) + 4HF(aq)$$

Chlorine reacts to a very limited extent with water producing low concentration of hydrochloric acid (HCl) and hypochlorous acid (HOCl). Bromine and iodine react to a more limited extent than chlorine.

→ Group 18 (noble gases) have no reaction with water.

→ Transition metals generally do not react with water. Some of the transition metals in period 3 (e.g. Fe) react very slowly to release hydrogen gas, and metal oxide layers form on the surface.

Comparing the reactions of common metals with water

→ Table 3.5 compares the reaction of common metals with cold water, hot water and steam at red heat.

Table 3.5 Reaction of common metals with water

K Na Ca	Mg	Al Zn Fe	Sn Pb Cu Ag Au
React rapidly with cold water, releasing hydrogen gas; hydroxides form	Reacts with hot water, releasing hydrogen gas; hydroxides form	React with steam at red heat to release hydrogen gas; oxides form	No reaction with water

→ The rate of reaction decreases from left to right in Table 3.5. Tin, lead, copper, silver and gold will not react with water even at red heat. When a strip of magnesium is placed in a test tube of water at room temperature, bubbles of hydrogen gas very slowly form on the surface. The reaction is faster in hot water.

$$Mg(s) + 2H_2O(l) \rightarrow Mg(OH)_2(aq) + H_2(g)$$

→ KEY QUESTIONS

15 Compare the reaction of the following metals in water at room temperature:

magnesium; sodium; silver

16 Caesium and lithium are both members of group 1. Compare the reactivity of these two metals with water at room temperature.

17 Potassium and calcium are both members of period 4. Compare the reactivity of these two metals with water at room temperature.

Answers ⊃ p. 35

CHAPTER SYLLABUS CHECKLIST

Are you able to answer these questions from the syllabus for this chapter? Tick each question as you go through the checklist if you are able to answer it. If you cannot answer a question, turn to the relevant page in the study guide to find the answer. For NESA key word meanings, go to www.educationstandards.nsw.edu.au and search 'key words'.

	FOR A COMPLETE UNDERSTANDING OF THIS TOPIC:	PAGE NO.	✓
1	Can I recall and explain the periodic law?	26	
2	Can I recall the number of periods and groups of the periodic table?	26	
3	Can I recall the groups that form the transition metals?	26	
4	Can I identify which groups form the main block of the periodic table?	26	
5	Can I distinguish between the lanthanoid and actinoid series?	26	
6	Can I explain why the periodic table can be divided into four blocks based on atomic orbitals?	27	
7	Can I relate the groups of the periodic table to the number of electrons in their valence shells?	27	
8	Can I recall that transition metals have incompletely filled inner electron shells?	27	
9	Can I write the electronic configuration for an element given its atomic number?	27	
10	Can I describe the trends in atomic radius and states of matter of elements down groups and across periods?	28	
11	Can I define the terms *first ionisation energy* and *electronegativity*, and describe the trends in these properties across periods and down groups?	29	
12	Can I recall the differences in the reactions of elements of the periodic table with water?	31–32	

Objective-response questions (1 mark each)

Refer to the periodic table to answer these questions.

1 In 1829 the German chemist Johann Dobereiner discovered that groups of three elements such as sulfur, selenium and tellurium had similar physical and chemical properties. To which group in the modern periodic table do these elements belong?

   A 13   B 14   C 15   D 16

2 The number of periods in the modern periodic table is:

   A 5   B 6   C 7   D 9

3 Identify the most chemically unreactive element.

   A helium
   B gold
   C platinum
   D carbon

4 Identify the transition metal.

   A gallium (Ga)
   B zinc (Zn)
   C lead (Pb)
   D strontium (Sr)

5 Identify the set that contains only actinoid elements.

   A cerium; actinium; americium
   B uranium; neptunium; plutonium
   C samarium; europium; lutetium
   D osmium; iridium; ruthenium

Extended-response questions

6 Predict the periodic group in the main block of elements in which elements X and Y form the following stable ions:

   a X^{2-}
   b Y^{3+} (2 marks)

7 The electron configuration of titanium (Z = 22) is 2,8,10,2.

   a Classify titanium as a metal or non-metal.   (1 mark)
   b Write the orbital notation for titanium.   (1 mark)
   c Explain why titanium forms stable Ti^{2+} and Ti^{4+} ions.   (2 marks)

8 Copy and complete the table.

Element	Symbol	Metal, semi-metal or non-metal	Solid, liquid or gas at 25 °C
chromium			
krypton			
arsenic			
rubidium			

(4 marks)

9 In his 1871 periodic table, Mendeleev made predictions about the element immediately below silicon and above tin, which had yet to be discovered. He gave this unknown element the temporary name of 'ekasilicon'. In 1886 this element was discovered, and its properties measured. Some of these predictions and observed properties are tabulated below:

Property	Mendeleev's prediction for 'ekasilicon' (1871)	Observed properties of the discovered element (1886)
atomic weight	72	72.3
density (g/cm^3)	5.5	5.47
atomic volume (cm^3/mol)	13	13

   a Identify this element predicted by Mendeleev. (1 mark)
   b Explain why Mendeleev's predictions were so accurate.   (2 marks)

10 Consider the following elements and their atomic weights at the end of period 5 of the periodic table:

   antimony (121.8); tellurium (127.6); iodine (126.9); xenon (131.3)

   a Explain why the atomic weight of iodine is less than tellurium.   (2 marks)
   b Explain why the elements in the modern periodic table are arranged according to atomic number and not atomic weight, as used by Mendeleev.   (1 mark)

ANSWERS

KEY QUESTIONS

Key questions ➲ p. 27

1	Tungsten	3	Palladium
2	Titanium	4	Cerium

Key questions ➲ pp. 27–28

5	Meitnerium	6	Bismuth

7 Semi-metal

8 Element A: Z = 2 + 2 + 3 = 7; thus A = nitrogen. Nitrogen belongs to period 2 and group 15.

Key questions ➲ p. 28

9 Fluorine; krypton; hydrogen

10 Atomic radius decreases from left to right in period 3. The increasing nuclear charge causes the electron shells to be attracted closer to the nucleus, and this results in a decrease in atomic radius.

11 Atomic radius increases down group 14. The increasing number of electron shells results in an increase in atomic radius.

Key questions ➲ p. 31

12 a First Ionisation energy increases across a period and decreases down a group.
b Electronegativity increases across a period and decreases down a group.

13 Group 14, as the first 4 electrons are more readily removed than other electrons. Thus 4 electrons are present in the valence shell.

14 Rubidium is an active metal that gains stability by the loss of its 1 valence electron, resulting in an ion with a noble gas configuration. Thus its tendency to attract electrons is quite low. Iodine is a non-metal in group 17 and gains stability by gaining 1 electron to achieve a noble gas configuration. Thus iodine has a much higher electronegativity.

Key questions ➲ p. 32

15 Sodium reacts violently with water to release hydrogen gas, and a solution of sodium hydroxide forms. Magnesium reacts very slowly and some hydrogen gas forms. Magnesium hydroxide forms, which dissolves in the water. Silver has no reaction with water.

16 Caesium is much more reactive than lithium with water. The reaction with caesium is quite explosive, whereas lithium's reaction is quite moderate as hydrogen gas bubbles are evolved.

17 Potassium is much more reactive than calcium with water, as reactivity decreases across the period. Both react with water to produce hydrogen but the reaction is much faster with greater heat evolution for potassium.

YEAR 11 EXAM-TYPE QUESTIONS

Objective-response questions

1 **D.** Group 16 is the group that starts with oxygen. **A** is incorrect as group 13 contains Al, Ga and In. **B** is incorrect as group 14 contains Si, Ge and Sn. **C** is incorrect as group 15 contains P, As and Sb.

2 **C.** There are seven horizontal rows. **A**, **B** and **D** are therefore incorrect.

3 **A.** Helium is a noble gas; noble gases are very unreactive. **B** is incorrect as gold can react with other elements or compounds even though it is a noble metal. **C** is incorrect as platinum has low reactivity but it does react to form compounds. **D** is incorrect as carbon reacts with oxygen to form carbon dioxide.

4 **B.** Transition metals belong to groups 3–12 and zinc belongs to group 12. **A** is incorrect as gallium is a p-block element. **C** is incorrect as it is a p-block element. **D** is incorrect as strontium is an s-block element.

5 **B.** Actinoids are a subseries of period 7 (Z = 89–103). **A** is incorrect as cerium is a lanthanoid. **C** is incorrect as these elements are lanthanoids. **D** is incorrect as these are d-block elements.

Extended-response questions

6 **EM** Non-metals tend to form negative ions, and metals tend to form positive ions. The charge on the ion indicates the number of electrons gained or lost, and this is related to the group in which the element is located.
a X^{2-}: X belongs to group 16 as it has gained 2 electrons to form a stable ion. ✓
b Y^{3+}: Y belongs to group 13 as it has lost 3 electrons to form a stable ion. ✓

7 **EM** Students need to show that they are familiar with common transition metals. In transition metals, the d orbitals are filling. The stability of ions is related to the attainment of a noble gas configuration.
a Metal ✓
b $1s^2\,2s^2\,2p^6\,3s^2\,3p^6\,3d^2\,4s^2$ ✓

c Ti^{2+} is stable as the 2 valence electrons in the N shell are removed. ✓ Ti^{4+} is stable as the two 3d electrons are removed, leaving a stable octet in the M shell. ✓

8 **EM** Students are required to use the supplied periodic table to find the symbol of a named element. Students should remember that all metallic elements (except Hg) are solids at room temperature. All semi-metals are solids. All group 18 elements are gases.

Element	Symbol	Metal, semi-metal or non-metal	Solid, liquid or gas at 25 °C
chromium	Cr	metal	solid ✓
krypton	Kr	non-metal	gas ✓
arsenic	As	semi-metal	solid ✓
rubidium	Rb	metal	solid ✓

9 **EM** Students are required to locate silicon and tin in order to determine the identity of this element. The predictive nature of the periodic table is illustrated by the trends in physical properties down groups and across periods.
a Germanium ✓
b Mendeleev believed that elements in the same group had gradations in physical properties. Using his knowledge of the trends in physical properties of elements in this group (silicon and tin), he estimated the physical properties of ekasilicon. ✓ These predictions turned out to be quite accurate and this confirmed the importance of the periodic table as a predictive tool. ✓

10 **EM** In this question students need to understand that the percentage of different isotopes for each element is quite variable, and so the average atomic weight is variable. This leads to elements being placed in the incorrect group if atomic weight is used to arrange the elements in the periodic table. The use of atomic numbers overcomes this problem.
a The atomic weight is a weighted average of the isotopic masses, ✓ and iodine has a higher proportion of the lighter isotopes than tellurium. ✓
b The atomic number is used to classify elements as it ensures that elements are placed in the correct family group where they exhibit similar chemical properties and valencies. Using atomic weights only can lead to elements placed in the incorrect family group. ✓

What binds atoms together in elements and compounds?

Attractive forces bind particles of matter together. In compounds composed of oppositely charged ions, this attractive force is electrostatic in nature. Molecules attract each other through a variety of intermolecular forces that depend on the relative electronegativity of the elements in the compound.

1 Electronegativity and bonding

» Students investigate the role of electronegativity in determining the ionic or covalent nature of bonds between atoms.

Ionic and covalent bonds

→ Chemical bonds form due to interactions between the electrons of neighbouring atoms.

→ This interaction may involve the sharing of electrons between the atoms or the complete transfer of electrons in the outer electron shell from one atom to the other.

→ The electronegativity of interacting atoms determines whether electrons are shared or transferred. The higher the electronegativity, the greater the electron-attracting ability.

→ Metals have very low electronegativities. Non-metals have high electronegativities. This is shown in Table 4.1.

→ When the interacting atoms are identical non-metals, there is no difference between their electronegativities, and pairs of electrons are shared equally. This bond is called a **covalent bond**. This bond is also an example of a **non-polar bond** as the electron pairs are equally shared and electric charges are balanced due to bond symmetry. Figure 4.1 shows examples of three different covalent bonds.

H:H   O::O   N:::N
single   double   triple

Figure 4.1 Covalent bonds

> **covalent bond:** a bond formed by sharing electron pairs
> **non-polar bond:** a covalent bond in which electrons are symmetrically arranged

→ In Figure 4.1, the bond between hydrogen atoms has one shared pair of electrons. The bond between oxygen atoms has two shared pairs of electrons. The bond between nitrogen atoms has three shared pairs of electrons.

→ When the interacting atoms are non-identical non-metals, there is a difference between their electronegativities and the electron pairs are not equally shared. The element with the higher electronegativity will have a greater share of electron pairs. This leads to charge asymmetry in the covalent bond. Such bonds are called **polar bonds** as the electric charge is not shared equally.

Example:

O:H The covalent bond is polar with the highly electro-negative oxygen atom having a much higher share of the electron pair. The O atom becomes slightly negatively charged (δ^-), and the H atom becomes slightly positively charged (δ^+). This separation of charge is called a **dipole**. Figure 4.2 shows this charge asymmetry.

> **polar bonds:** a covalent bond in which electrons are asymmetrically arranged such that one atom has a greater electron density than the other
> **dipole:** opposite charges separated by a distance

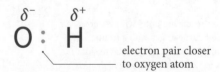

δ^- δ^+
O : H
electron pair closer to oxygen atom

Figure 4.2 Polar O–H bond

Table 4.1 Electronegativities of metals and non-metals

Element	K	Na	Ca	Al	H	C	N	O	F
Electronegativity	0.82	0.93	1.00	1.61	2.20	2.55	3.04	3.44	3.98

➔ When the interacting atoms are a metal and a non-metal there is a very large difference between their electronegativities and electron sharing will not occur. Instead electrons are completely transferred from the outer shell of the metal to the outer shell of the non-metal. This results in the formation of charged atoms called **ions**. The attraction between the positive and negative ions is called an **ionic bond**.

> **ion:** a positively or negatively charged atom or molecule
> **ionic bond:** a chemical bond formed between oppositely charged ions

Example:

NaF When sodium and fluorine react an ionic bond forms when one electron from the outer shell of the sodium atom is transferred to the outer shell of the fluorine atom. The sodium ion (Na^+) that forms attracts the negative fluoride ion (F^-).

➔ KEY QUESTIONS

1 Distinguish between covalent and ionic bonds.

2 Determine which of the following bonds are polar:
S–S; Cl–Cl; H–Br; N–H

3 Identify which of the following compounds contain ionic bonds:
KBr; NCl_3; SrO; P_2O_5

Answers ➲ p. 51

---

2 Ionic and covalent compounds

» Students investigate the differences between ionic and covalent compounds through:
  • using nomenclature, valency and chemical formulae (including Lewis dot diagrams)
  • examining the spectrum of bonds between atoms with varying degrees of polarity with respect to their constituent elements' positions on the periodic table
  • modelling the shapes of molecular substances.

Ionic bonding and ionic compounds

➔ Charged atoms are called ions. Positive ions are called cations. Atoms can form cations by losing one or more electrons. Negative ions are called anions. Atoms can form anions by gaining one or more electrons.

Example:

Magnesium atoms can lose their 2 valence electrons when they react with oxygen. Magnesium ions (Mg^{2+})

are formed. The oxygen atoms gain 2 electrons to form a stable octet in their valence shell. Oxide ions (O^{2-}) are formed.

$$2Mg + O_2 \rightarrow 2Mg^{2+} + 2O^{2-}$$

➔ The magnesium ions and oxide ions attract one another to form an ionic compound called magnesium oxide (MgO). The attractive force between the magnesium ion and the oxide ion is called an ionic bond. Ionic bonds are strong chemical bonds.

➔ Lewis electron dot diagrams can be used to visualise the transfer of electron when atoms react to form ions. Figure 4.3 shows the formation of magnesium ions and oxide ions when magnesium atoms and oxygen atoms react.

| 2 valence electrons | 6 valence electrons | magnesium ion | oxide ion |

Figure 4.3 Lewis electron dot diagram for an ionic compound

Valency rules and nomenclature for ionic compounds

➔ Ionic compounds are composed of simple ions or complex polyatomic ions.

➔ Polyatomic ions, such as ammonium ions (NH_4^+), sulfate ions (SO_4^{2-}), carbonate ions (CO_3^{2-}) and nitrate ions (NO_3^-) consist of groups of atoms with a net positive or negative charge.

➔ The atoms within the polyatomic ion are bound to each other by covalent bonds. Table 4.2 lists the symbols and valencies for some common simple ions and polyatomic ions.

Table 4.2 Valencies of simple and polyatomic ions

Valency	Ion symbol	Ion name
+1	H^+	hydrogen
	Na^+	sodium
	K^+	potassium
	Ag^+	silver
	Cu^+	copper (I)
	NH_4^+	ammonium
+2	Mg^{2+}	magnesium
	Ca^{2+}	calcium
	Ba^{2+}	barium
	Zn^{2+}	zinc
	Fe^{2+}	iron (II)
	Cu^{2+}	copper(II)
+3	Al^{3+}	aluminium
	Fe^{3+}	iron (III)

(continues)

Table 4.2 Valencies of simple and polyatomic ions *(continued)*

Valency	Ion symbol	Ion name
−1	H^-	hydride
	F^-	fluoride
	Cl^-	chloride
	Br^-	bromide
	I^-	iodide
	NO_3^-	nitrate
	OH^-	hydroxide
−2	O^{2-}	oxide
	S^{2-}	sulfide
	CO_3^{2-}	carbonate
	SO_4^{2-}	sulfate
	SO_3^{2-}	sulfite
−3	N^{3-}	nitride
	P^{3-}	phosphide
	PO_4^{3-}	phosphate

→ The net charge on an ionic compound is zero because the total charge of all the cations must equal the total charge of all the anions.

→ The formula of an ionic compound is found by determining the number of each cation and anion required so the sum of their valencies (or charges) is zero.

→ In naming ionic compounds, the cations are named before the anions. Some cations have roman numerals following their names. This identifies the valency where the metal can have a variable valency.

EXAMPLE 1

Use the valency table (Table 4.2) to construct the formulae for the following ionic compounds:

a   silver sulfate

b   zinc hydride

c   iron (III) chloride.

In an ionic compound the sum of the positive and negative valencies is zero

Answer:

a   The silver ion has a valency of +1, and the sulfate ion has a valency of −2. Thus 2 silver ions (total charge = +2) are required to balance the charge of the sulfate ion.
Thus the formula is: Ag_2SO_4

b   The zinc ion has a valency of +2 and the hydride ion has a valency of −1. Thus 2 hydride ions (total charge of −2) will be required to balance the charge of the zinc ion.
Thus the formula is: ZnH_2

c   The iron (III) ion has a valency of +3 and the chloride ion has a valency of −1. Thus 3 chloride ions will have a total charge of −3, which balances the +3 charge of the iron (III) ion.
Thus the formula is: $FeCl_3$

EXAMPLE 2

Use the nomenclature rules to name the following ionic compounds:

a $Mg(NO_3)_2$

b Cu_2S

c $(NH_4)_2SO_3$

Check whether roman numerals may be required

Answer:

Cations are named before anions.

a   magnesium nitrate

b   copper (I) sulfide

c   ammonium sulfite

In Cu_2S, the roman numeral (I) is used because copper can have variable valencies of +1 and +2 in some compounds.

→ KEY QUESTIONS

4   Aluminium reacts with oxygen to form aluminium oxide. What is the formula of aluminium oxide?

5   State the number of valence electrons present in fluorine and identify the formula of its most stable ion.

6   Name the compound that has the formula $(NH_4)_2CO_3$.

7   Determine the valency of X, which forms a compound X_2SO_4.

Answers ⊃ p. 51

Covalent bonding and covalent molecular compounds

→ Molecules are particles that can move independently of each other. Some molecules are composed of single atoms. The noble gases are examples of these monatomic molecules. Other molecules consist of more than one atom as shown in Table 4.3. Molecules with 2 atoms bonded together are called **diatomic molecules**.

diatomic molecule: a particle composed of two atoms chemically bonded together

Table 4.3 Common molecules

Classification	Name	Formula
monatomic	argon	Ar
diatomic	oxygen	O_2
	nitrogen	N_2
	hydrogen chloride	HCl

(continues)

Table 4.3 Common molecules (*continued*)

Classification	Name	Formula
triatomic	ozone	O_3
	water	H_2O
	nitrogen dioxide	NO_2
tetra-atomic	phosphorus	P_4
	ammonia	NH_3
	sulfur trioxide	SO_3

→ The atoms that join together to form molecules are typically non-metals. Non-metal atoms bond with other non-metal atoms by sharing electrons rather than by the formation of ions due to complete electron loss or gain.

→ The sharing of an electron pair results in the formation of a covalent bond. The two atoms that form the bond each donate an electron to form the shared pair.

→ As previously discussed there are single, double and triple covalent bonds. Consider the following examples.

Chlorine molecules (Cl_2)

→ Each chlorine atom has 7 electrons in the valence shell. By each atom contributing one of these electrons to form the shared pair, a single covalent bond is formed, which holds the chlorine atoms together. Each chlorine atom has achieved a stable octet in its valence shell by sharing electrons.

Oxygen molecules (O_2)

→ Oxygen molecules are diatomic. Two oxygen atoms join together to form the oxygen molecule (O_2). Each oxygen atom has 6 electrons in the valence shell. By sharing two pairs of electrons, each oxygen atom achieves a stable octet in its valence shell. A double covalent bond forms.

Nitrogen molecules (N_2)

→ Nitrogen molecules are also diatomic. Two nitrogen atoms join together to form the nitrogen molecule (N_2). However, in this case, three pairs of electrons are shared to form a triple covalent bond. In this way each nitrogen atom achieves a stable octet in its valence shell.

→ Non-metallic elements can combine with other non-metals to form molecular compounds. In these cases, electron pairs are shared to form a covalent bond. Molecular compounds can contain single, double and triple covalent bonds.

Valency rules and nomenclature for covalent molecular compounds

→ The concept of valency can also be used to predict the chemical formulae of covalently bonded molecules. In covalent molecular compounds the valency of an element is equal to the number of electrons needed to be shared to complete its valence shell. Table 4.4 lists the valencies of common non-metals. Some non-metals such as nitrogen have variable valencies.

- In a simple molecular compound composed of two elements the sum of the valencies of one element must match that of the other.
- In writing the chemical formula the first element should be the one which is further to the left in the periodic table or lower in a vertical group if both elements belong to the same group.

Table 4.4 Valencies of non-metals in molecular compounds

Element	Common valencies
H	1
O	2
C	4
N	3,5
S	2,4,6
Cl	1,7

EXAMPLE 3

Show for each example that the valency of each element is consistent with the table of valencies.

a H_2O
b CCl_4

Review the table of valencies before answering this problem

Answer:

a Oxygen has a valency of 2 and each hydrogen has a valency of 1. Thus 2 hydrogen atoms are required to match the valency of the oxygen atom.
$2 = 1 + 1$

b Carbon has a valency of 4 and chlorine has a valency of 1. Thus 4 chlorine atoms are required to match the valency of the carbon atom.
$4 = 1 + 1 + 1 + 1$

→ In naming molecular compounds:
- Greek prefixes are used to indicate the number of each type of atom in the molecule (mono =1; di = 2; tri = 3; etc.)
- The second element in the formula has the suffix '-ide'.

Examples:

NO_2 is named nitrogen *di*oxide
(nitrogen has a valency of 4 and oxygen has its normal valency of 2)

N_2O_3 is named *di*nitrogen *tri*oxide
(nitrogen has a valency of 3 and oxygen has a valency of 2)

SO_3 is named sulfur *tri*oxide
(sulfur has a valency of 6 and oxygen has a valency of 2)

➜ Some common molecular compounds are known only by their common names.

Examples:
- H_2O is water (not *di*hydrogen monoxide)
- NH_3 is ammonia
- CH_4 is methane

➜ Some molecular compounds are known by both their systematic name and their common name.

Examples:
- N_2O is *di*nitrogen oxide or nitrous oxide
- NO is nitrogen *mon*oxide or nitric oxide

➜ KEY QUESTIONS

8 State the number of atoms present in an ammonia molecule.

9 State the formula of dichlorine heptoxide.

10 Determine the valency of A in a molecular compound of formula A_2O_5.

Answers ➾ p. 51

Shapes of molecules and intermolecular forces

➜ The molecular formula of a simple molecule such as water does not provide us with information about the structure of the molecule. Lewis electron dot diagrams help us to understand the chemical bonding in molecules.

➜ Lewis electron dot diagrams show the bonding and non-bonding electrons in the valence shell of the atoms that are linked by a covalent bond. To achieve stability, each hydrogen atom shares an electron pair. Other atoms such as oxygen and nitrogen share two and three electron pairs respectively to achieve a stable octet of electrons in their valence shells. Figure 4.4 shows Lewis electron dot diagrams for hydrogen, oxygen and nitrogen.

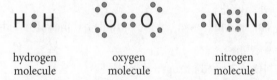

hydrogen   oxygen   nitrogen
molecule   molecule   molecule

Figure 4.4 Lewis electron dot diagrams

➜ Figure 4.5 shows the Lewis electron dot structures of common covalent molecular compounds. Hydrogen chloride molecules have one single covalent bond between the hydrogen and chlorine atoms. The chlorine atom has 7 valence electrons and shares the hydrogen's electron to achieve a stable octet. In carbon dioxide molecules, oxygen atoms share two electron pairs with

the carbon atom. Oxygen has 6 electrons in its valence shell and shares 2 of the carbon's electrons to achieve a stable octet. Carbon has 4 valence shell electrons and shares two pairs from each oxygen atom to achieve a stable octet. In hydrogen cyanide molecules, the carbon and nitrogen atoms share three electron pairs to form a triple covalent bond. The carbon also shares an electron with the hydrogen atom.

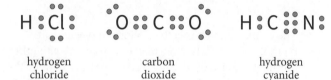

hydrogen   carbon   hydrogen
chloride   dioxide   cyanide

Figure 4.5 Covalent molecular compounds

➜ Another method of showing the covalent bonds in molecules is to use structural formulas in which the electron pairs are shown as a single line (–) that joins the atoms. In a double bond, two lines (=) are drawn and, in a triple bond, three lines (≡) are drawn. Figure 4.6 shows the structural formulas of hydrogen, carbon dioxide and nitrogen molecules.

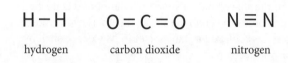

hydrogen   carbon dioxide   nitrogen

Figure 4.6 Structural formulas

➜ Structural formulae do not always show the three-dimensional shapes of molecules. Molecular model kits can be used in schools to help visualise the three-dimensional structures of molecules. Water (H_2O), for example, is a bent molecule with an H−O−H bond angle of 104.5°. Ammonia (NH_3) has a pyramidal shape. Methane (CH_4) has a tetrahedral shape. Figure 4.7 shows the shapes of water, ammonia and methane molecules.

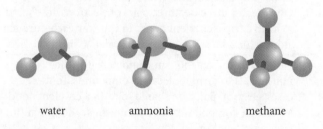

water   ammonia   methane

Figure 4.7 Shapes of molecules

➜ When atoms form a covalent bond their electron atomic orbitals overlap as shown in the following diagram for the formation of water from oxygen and hydrogen atoms. Each hydrogen's electron is in a spherical 's' orbital. The oxygen's 6 valence electrons occupy the 'p' orbitals, with 2 electrons in each orbital. Bonding occurs when the orbitals overlap to form a covalent bond (Figure 4.8). The final angular or bent shape of the water molecule is due to variations in repulsion between the non-bonding orbitals and the bonding orbitals. This simplified view will be extended in the Year 12 course.

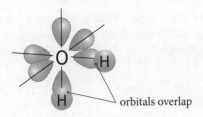

water molecule

Figure 4.8 Orbital overlap when hydrogen and oxygen atoms form water

Polar and non-polar molecules

→ Electron pairs that make up a covalent bond are only shared equally if the atoms are the same. Thus, hydrogen molecules (H_2) consist of 2 hydrogen atoms linked by a single covalent bond. The electron pair in this bond is shared equally by each hydrogen atom. In the case of the hydrogen chloride molecule (HCl), the electron pair is not equally shared as the chlorine atom is much more electronegative than the hydrogen atom. The electronegativity of an element is its electron-attracting ability. Table 4.5 compares the electronegativity of some common non-metals. Fluorine has the highest electronegativity.

> **electronegativity:** a measure of the electron attracting ability of an atom when bonded to another element in a compound

→ In the HCl molecule, this unequal sharing leads to a charge asymmetry, with the chlorine atom slightly negative and the hydrogen atom slightly positive. This charge separation in the bond creates a dipole. Such a molecule is said to be polar. However, hydrogen molecules are non-polar, as they are symmetrical. Hydrogen fluoride, water and ammonia are polar molecules because of their shape and the presence of polar bonds. In the case of water the two O−H bond dipoles combine to give a net **molecular dipole**, with the oxygen atom being slightly negative.

> **molecular dipole:** molecules in which charge asymmetry exists such that one end of the molecule is slightly positive and the other end slightly negative

→ In the HF molecule, the H−F bond is an example of a dipole, and the bond is called a polar bond. Figure 4.9 shows a way of representing a polar bond. The electron pair of the covalent bonds lies closer to the fluorine atom and makes the chlorine slightly negative. In the structural formula the arrow tip represents the negative end of the dipole, and the other end is the positive end of the dipole.

$$\overset{\delta^+}{H} \overset{\delta^-}{:F} \qquad \overset{\longmapsto}{H - F}$$

Figure 4.9 Representation of a bond dipole

→ Not all molecules with polar bonds are necessarily polar. Carbon dioxide, for example, is a non-polar molecule that contains two polar bonds. Its linear shape and symmetry lead to a cancellation of the individual bond dipoles. Generally, molecules are non-polar if the sum of all their bond dipoles is zero in three dimensions. Figure 4.10 shows that the two bond dipoles point in opposite directions.

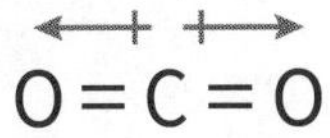

$$\overset{\longleftarrow + \longmapsto}{O = C = O}$$

Figure 4.10 Carbon dioxide is a non-polar molecule with polar bonds

> → **KEY QUESTIONS**
>
> 11 State the shape of each of the following molecules:
>   a methane
>   b carbon dioxide
>   c water.
>
> 12 Explain why methane is a non-polar molecule.
>
> 13 Identify the polarity of the Cl atoms in the non-polar CCl_4 molecule.
>
> 14 HCN is a linear molecule. Predict whether this molecule is polar or non-polar.
>
> Answers ⊃ p. 51

Table 4.5 Electronegativities of some non-metals

Element	F	O	Cl	N	S	C	H
Electronegativity	3.98	3.44	3.16	3.04	2.58	2.55	2.20

3 Allotropy

» Students investigate elements that possess the physical property of allotropy.

➜ The term **allotrope** refers to different structural forms of an element. The element phosphorus can exist in different allotropic forms, as shown in Figure 4.11. The highly reactive white form of phosphorus is a tetra-atomic molecule (P_4), whereas the red allotrope of phosphorus is a polymer of P_4. Polymers are large molecules that consist of many smaller molecules (called monomers) joined together. The black and violet forms of phosphorus are also polymeric, but less common than white or red phosphorus. Each allotrope has different physical properties but similar chemical properties.

allotropes: different structural forms of an element in the same physical state

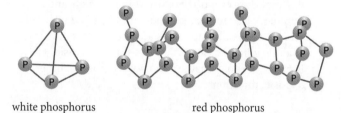

white phosphorus   red phosphorus

Figure 4.11 Phosphorus allotropes

➜ Carbon exists in a wide variety of allotropes. The most well known of these allotropes are diamond and graphite, whose structures are shown in Figure 4.12.
  • Graphite consists of hexagonal layers of carbon atoms. The bonding between carbon atoms in each layer is strong but the intermolecular forces between each layer are quite weak. Shearing forces can move the layers over each other and, as a result, graphite is used as a dry lubricant, as well as the 'lead' in pencils.
  • However, in diamond, the carbon atoms are arranged in interlocking tetrahedrons, which give diamond its great hardness. Graphite and diamond are examples of covalent network solids, which will be studied in the next section.

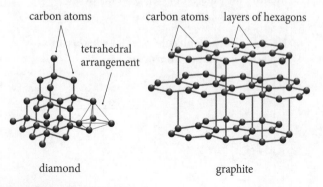

carbon atoms   carbon atoms   layers of hexagons

tetrahedral
arrangement

diamond   graphite

Figure 4.12 Carbon allotropes

➜ Graphite is an electrical conductor, whereas diamond is an insulator. Graphite has mobile electrons that can flow along each layer when a potential difference is applied. Diamond has no mobile electrons.

➜ Graphite and diamond have similar chemical properties. For example, they both burn in excess oxygen to form carbon dioxide.

➜ KEY QUESTIONS

15 Graphene consists of a single layer of hexagonally arranged carbon atoms. Explain whether this substance can be classified as an allotrope of carbon.

16 Alpha sulfur has the molecular formula S_8. These orthorhombic-shaped crystals have a melting point of 113 °C. Needle-shaped crystals called beta sulfur have a melting point of 119 °C. Explain why alpha and beta sulfur can be classified as allotropes of sulfur.

17 Tin exists in alpha and beta forms. Alpha tin has cubic-shaped crystals similar to diamonds, whereas beta tin has tetragonal-shaped crystals. Alpha tin does not conduct electricity, whereas beta tin does conduct. Explain why beta tin is able to conduct electricity.

Answers ➲ p. 51

4 Chemical structures

» Students investigate the different chemical structures of atoms and elements, including but not limited to:
  • ionic networks
  • covalent networks (including diamond and silicon dioxide)
  • covalent molecular
  • metallic structure.

Crystals

➜ Crystalline chemical substances can be classified into four categories based on their physical properties. These categories are:
  • ionic crystals
  • covalent network crystals
  • covalent molecular crystals
  • metallic crystals.

➜ The following dichotomous key illustrates how physical properties can be used to create this classification.

1A.	Crystalline substance has a high melting point	Go to 2.
1B.	Crystalline substance has a low melting point	**Covalent molecular crystal**
2A.	Crystal has a high lustre and is malleable and ductile	**Metallic crystal**
2B.	Crystal has a low lustre and is brittle	Go to 3.
3A.	Crystalline substance does not conduct in solid state but conducts when melted	**Ionic crystal**
3B.	Crystalline substance does not generally conduct in solid or molten state (*)	**Covalent network crystal**

*Graphite is an exception; it conducts in the solid state.

➔ The properties of the four classification groups are summarised in Table 4.6 (see below).

Ionic crystals

➔ Ionic crystals have positive ions and negative ions arranged in fixed **lattice** positions.

> **lattice:** the geometric arrangement of atoms, ions or molecules in a crystal

➔ There are no mobile charge carriers present in the solid state and so the crystal is a non-conductor.

➔ The lattice is hard and the compound has a high melting point due to the strong attractive forces (ionic bonds) holding the ions in the lattice.

➔ The lattice is brittle because any shear force will cause ions of similar charge to come closer together. This will increase the electrostatic repulsion, which leads to the crystal shattering.

➔ When the crystal lattice is heated above its melting point, the ionic bonds are partially broken and the ions become mobile. These mobile charge carriers allow the melted salt to become conductive.

➔ Ionic bonds extend in three dimensions throughout ionic crystals. The cations and anions in an ionic compound are located in fixed positions in the crystal lattice. The geometry of the lattice depends on the charges of the ions present as well as their ionic radii.

Example:

Sodium chloride

The sodium cations and chloride anions are arranged in a cubic lattice. Figure 4.13 shows the positions of the ions in the crystal lattice. It does not show the sizes of the ions. Strong electrostatic attractive forces hold the lattice together.

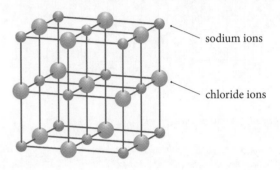

sodium ions

chloride ions

Figure 4.13 Sodium chloride crystal lattice

Covalent network crystals

➔ Covalent network crystals contain neutral non-metal or semi-metal atoms bonded by covalent bonds in three dimensions.

➔ The very high melting points and hardness of substances such as diamond and silicon carbide are explained in terms of strong covalent bonding in three dimensions.

➔ The absence of mobile charge carriers explains why these crystals are insulators.

➔ Graphite is an exception to this, in that its covalent bonds are confined to two-dimensional parallel planes.

Table 4.6 Properties of crystal groups

Property	Ionic crystal	Covalent network crystal	Covalent molecular crystal	Metallic crystal
Chemical bonding	ionic	covalent	covalent	metallic
Melting point	high	very high	low	high
Electrical conductivity	solid—nil liquid—high	solid—nil liquid—nil	solid—nil liquid—nil	solid—high liquid—high
Other properties	hard, brittle	very hard, brittle	soft, brittle	malleable, ductile, lustrous
Examples	sodium chloride zinc oxide calcium sulfide	silicon dioxide silicon carbide diamond	ice sucrose iodine	copper aluminium silver

Delocalised electrons in these planes explain the electrical conductivity of graphite. Weak intermolecular forces between these planes hold the structure together and explain why graphite powder is used as a dry lubricant.

→ The structures of graphite and diamond were shown in Figure 4.12. The covalent network of SiO_2 is shown in Figure 4.14. The silicon and oxygen atoms are arranged tetrahedrally in the lattice.

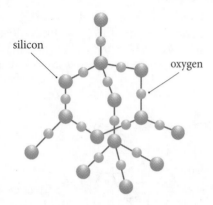

Figure 4.14 Silicon dioxide

Covalent molecular crystals

→ Covalent molecular crystals contain individual molecules arranged in a pattern within the crystal lattice. The atoms within each molecule are bonded covalently but the forces between each molecule involve weak intermolecular attractions.

→ These weak intermolecular forces allow us to explain the soft, brittle nature of these crystals, as well as their low melting points. Soft crystals such as waxes make useful lubricants.

→ The absence of mobile charge carriers explains why covalent molecular substances do not conduct in the solid or liquid state.

→ A number of common non-metallic elements exist as covalent molecular crystals below their melting points. Examples include iodine (I_2), sulfur (S_8) and white phosphorus (P_4). Figure 4.15 shows the lattice structure of iodine molecules.

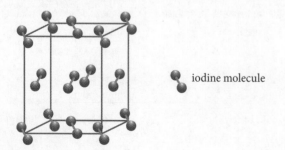

iodine molecule

Figure 4.15 Iodine lattice

Metallic crystals

→ Metals are often described as a three-dimensional lattice of positive metal ions in a 'sea' of electrons. The sea of electrons refers to a delocalised electron cloud. The valence electrons in a metal do not remain with the individual atoms. They exist in a conduction band that permeates the whole crystal lattice.

→ The attraction between the positive metal ions and the delocalised sea of electrons is called the **metallic bond**.

> **metallic bond:** attraction between the positive metal ions and the delocalised sea of electrons

→ Metals have high electrical conductivity. The delocalised sea of electrons move in an electric field due to a potential difference created across the ends of the crystal.

→ Metals are good heat conductors. The mobile electron cloud transfers this heat energy through the crystal.

→ Metals have high malleability and ductility. The ions of the lattice are able to slide over each other when a force is applied and the delocalised electrons are able to stabilise the lattice during this change.

→ Metals have a high lustre. The delocalised electrons at the metal's surface rapidly absorb and release light energy.

→ Mixtures of metals form alloys that have different physical properties compared with the pure metals. For example, when copper is alloyed with tin the alloy called bronze is formed, which is harder than copper. Similarly, silver is a relatively soft metal, but when alloyed with small amounts of copper it retains its silver colour but it is much harder.

→ Figure 4.16 shows two different models of the lattice structure of iron.

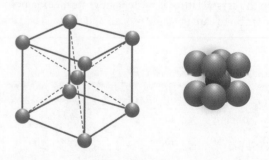

body-centred cubic lattice

Figure 4.16 Models of iron's crystal lattice

Modelling the structures of molecules

» Investigate the differences between ionic and covalent compounds through:
  • modelling the shapes of molecular substances.

Aim

to use a molecular model kit to construct a variety of molecules and classify them according to their three-dimensional shape

Method

1 Use the model kit to construct the following molecules:
  a dichlorine monoxide (Cl_2O)
  b nitrogen trifluoride (NF_3)
  c acetylene (C_2H_2)
  d carbon tetrabromide (CBr_4)
  e carbon disulfide (CS_2).

2 Photograph or draw your completed molecules.

3 Classify the shape of each molecule using the terms: linear; bent; pyramidal; tetrahedral

Answers

The structure of molecules is modelled below.

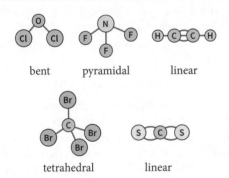

Figure A4.1 Molecular structures

→ **KEY QUESTIONS**

18 Identify the crystal lattice structure of:
  a KCl   b SiO_2 c Au

....

19 Identify the shapes of the following molecules:
  a I_2 b CO_2 c CH_4

....

20 **Describe the shape of a sodium chloride crystal and identify the arrangement of ions in the crystal.**

Answers ⊃ p. 51

5 Physical properties of elements and compounds

» Students explore the similarities and differences between the nature of intermolecular and intramolecular bonds and the strength of the forces associated with each, in order to explain the:
  • physical properties of elements
  • physical properties of compounds.

Strength of chemical bonds

→ Ionic and covalent bonds are strong bonding forces. The strength of covalent bonds varies considerably, as shown in Table 4.7. Bond energies refer to the amount of energy that must be supplied to break the bond during chemical reactions.

Table 4.7 Bond energies (BE) of covalent bonds

Bond	BE (kJ/mol)	Bond	BE (kJ/mol)	Bond	BE (kJ/mol)
H–H	432	C–C	347	C=C	614
H–F	565	C–H	413	O=O	495
H–Cl	427	O–H	467	C≡C	839

→ The strength of ionic bonds is compared in Table 4.8 using lattice energies. Lattice energies refers to the energy required to dissociate an ionic lattice into separate ions.

Table 4.8 Lattice energies of ionic compounds

Ionic compound	Lattice energy (kJ/mol)
NaCl	788
KCl	718
RbCl	693
NaI	700
KI	645
RbI	627
Na_2O	2488
K_2O	2245
Rb_2O	2170

Intermolecular forces

→ All molecules attract one another. These intermolecular forces are not as strong as intramolecular forces, but they are important in maintaining the structure of matter. There are three types of intermolecular forces:
  • dipole–dipole forces

- dispersion forces
- hydrogen bonding.

These forces are explained in the following examples.

Dipole–dipole forces

➜ Polar molecules attract one another or other polar molecules. The slightly positive end of one molecule will attract the slightly negative end of another. The presence of dipole–dipole attraction creates some ordering of molecules in the liquid and solid states. The melting and boiling points of such molecules is higher than similar weight non-polar molecules.

Dispersion forces

➜ Molecules that are non-polar must attract one another, otherwise they could not be condensed to form liquids or solids. All covalent molecular substances attract one another by weak intermolecular forces, called dispersion forces. Dispersion forces arise due to the formation of temporary dipoles between atoms and molecules.

➜ **Temporary dipoles** are caused by fluctuating electron distributions in atoms. The heavier an atom or molecule, the larger the dispersion forces between neighbouring atoms. Molecular shape also influences the strength of dispersion forces. However, for similar-weight molecules, dipole–dipole forces are stronger than dispersion forces. Figure 4.17 shows the steps in the formation of dispersion forces.

> **temporary dipoles:** dipoles that form for short time intervals and then break down

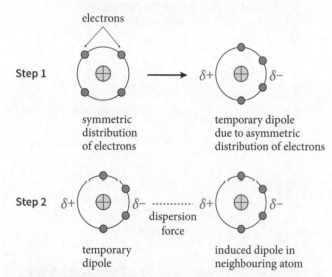

Figure 4.17 Formation of dispersion forces

Hydrogen bonding

➜ Hydrogen bonding is a strong intermolecular force arising from a type of polar attraction. It is the strongest of the intermolecular forces. Hydrogen atoms that are bonded to fluorine, oxygen or nitrogen atoms exhibit this type of attraction. Because F, O and N are very small, highly electronegative elements, a hydrogen atom bonded to them becomes increasingly positive due to a reduced share of the electron pair of the covalent bond. These partially positive hydrogen atoms in one molecule are attracted to the non-bonding electron pairs in F, O or N atoms in neighbouring molecules. This attraction is the basis of the hydrogen bond. Hydrogen bonding is about ten times stronger than dipole–dipole attractions. Figure 4.18 shows the hydrogen bonding between HF molecules.

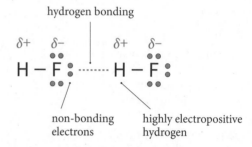

Figure 4.18 Hydrogen bonding

➜ The strength of a hydrogen bond is about 10% of the bond energy of a covalent bond.

Comparison of the physical properties of ionic and covalent molecular compounds

➜ The physical properties of ionic crystals vary according to the ions present and the strength of the ionic bonds in the crystal lattice. Consider the following physical properties.

Melting points of compounds

➜ The melting point of ionic compounds is a measure of the strength of the ionic bonds in the crystal. The higher the melting point, the stronger the bonds. Table 4.9 compares the melting points of some ionic chlorides and oxides. The oxides of these metals have higher melting points than their chlorides, indicating the greater strength of the metal ion-oxide ion bond.

Table 4.9 Melting points

Compound	Melting point (°C)
NaCl	801
$CaCl_2$	772
$FeCl_3$	306
Na_2O	1132
CaO	2927
Fe_2O_3	1565

- Covalent molecular compounds have low melting and boiling points due to weak intermolecular forces between their molecules. Table 4.10 shows that the melting points of covalent molecular compounds are much lower than ionic compounds.

Table 4.10 Melting and boiling points of covalent molecular compounds

Molecule	Melting point (°C)	Boiling point (°C)
ammonia NH_3	−78	−33
hydrogen fluoride HF	−83	20
methane CH_4	−183	−162
water H_2O	0	100

- Covalent network crystals have very high melting points. The three-dimensional arrangement of atoms and covalent bonds requires very high temperatures to melt them, as shown in Table 4.11.

Table 4.11 Melting points of covalent networks

Covalent network	Melting point (°C)
boron (B)	2300
graphite (C)	3974
silicon dioxide (SiO_2)	1713
silicon carbide (SiC)	2986*

* Decomposes.

Electrical conductivity of compounds

- Ionic compounds do not conduct electricity in the solid state as the ions are not free to move to carry the electric current. When soluble ionic compounds are dissolved in water, their ions can carry an electric current through the solution as the ions are free to move between the electrodes. Such solutions are called **electrolytes**. Ionic compounds can also be melted to produce molten electrolytes. Figure 4.19 shows a conductivity circuit with a light bulb. The bulb illuminates when an electrolyte is present in the beaker. The cations move towards the negative electrode and the anions move towards the positive electrode.

> **electrolyte:** solution or melted material that conducts an electric current

- Covalent molecular substances do not conduct electricity in the solid, molten or dissolved states because there are no charged ions to carry the current.
- Covalent network solids generally do not conduct electricity, but graphite is an exception.

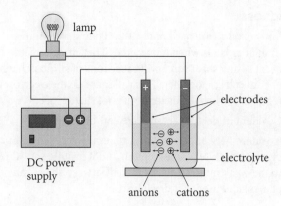

Figure 4.19 Testing for conductivity

Solubility

- Ionic compounds vary in their solubility in water. Some ionic compounds are very soluble and some are very insoluble. Table 4.12 shows the solubility rules for some common ionic compounds classified according to the anion present. All common ionic compounds of group 1 elements are soluble in water. The solubility of an ionic compound in water depends of the relative strength of the ionic bonds in the crystal lattice, and the strength of the attraction between the ions and water dipoles in the dissolved state. Strong ion–water dipole attractions promote the solubility of ionic compounds.

Table 4.12 Solubility rules

Ionic compound	Solubility rule	Common exceptions
Nitrates	all nitrates are soluble	–
Chlorides	most chlorides are soluble	AgCl; $PbCl_2$
Sulfates	most sulfates are soluble	$BaSO_4$; $PbSO_4$
Carbonates	most carbonates are insoluble	all group 1 carbonates

- In most cases the solubility of an ionic compound increases if the water is heated.
- Some covalent molecular compounds (e.g. glucose, acetic acid) are water soluble but most are insoluble. Polar compounds are more soluble in water than non-polar compounds of similar molecular weight, as the polar molecules can interact with water molecules via dipole–dipole interactions. Non-polar hydrocarbons such as hexane (C_6H_{14}) and benzene (C_6H_6) are very insoluble in water, as the intermolecular forces between the water and the hydrocarbons are too weak to assist the dissolution process.
- Covalent network solids are insoluble in water as too much energy is required to break the covalent bonds in the crystal lattice.

Hardness

➔ Ionic crystals are hard but brittle. They shatter into smaller crystals when hammered. The lattice is brittle because any shear force will cause ions of similar charge to come closer together. This will increase the electrostatic repulsion, which leads to the crystal shattering.

➔ Covalent molecular crystals are soft but brittle.

➔ Covalent network crystals are generally very hard but brittle. Graphite is an exception and it is quite soft (due to the weak intermolecular forces between the covalent planes) and used as a dry lubricant.

EXAMPLE 4

A solid substance (A) has the following physical properties. Use this information to classify (A) as an ionic, covalent molecular or covalent network substance.

Properties of A:

> Check conductivity data first

- white, hard crystals
- slightly soluble in water
- melting point = 501 °C
- boiling point = 950 °C
- does not conduct at 25 °C
- conducts at 600 °C.

Answer:

The solid (A) is an ionic crystal because it does not conduct when solid but does conduct when melted. Its other properties (hard crystals; high melting point) are also indicative of an ionic substance.

EXAMPLE 5

Use the supplied data in Table 4.13 to classify crystalline substances X, Y and Z. Justify your conclusions.

> Check melting point and conductivity data first

Table 4.13 Element data

Test	X	Y	Z
Appearance	transparent crystals	white crystals	white crystals
Melting point (°C)	1713	44	963
Effect of heating to 1000 °C (in absence of air)	no visible change	sublimes to form white fumes	solid melts to form a clear liquid

(continues)

Table 4.13 Element data *(continued)*

Test	X	Y	Z
Solubility in water	insoluble	insoluble	soluble
Solubility in non-polar organic solvents	insoluble	soluble	insoluble
Electrical conductivity of solid	nil	nil	nil
Electrical conductivity of molten material	nil	nil	high
Electrical conductivity of aqueous solution	–	–	high

Answers:

X = covalent network solid: very high melting point; non-conductor in solid state; insoluble in water

Y = covalent molecular solid: very low melting point; non-conductor in solid and liquid states; soluble in non-polar organic solvents

Z = ionic solid: high melting point; good conductor when melted or in aqueous solution due to the presence of mobile ions; soluble in water but insoluble in organic solvents

➔ KEY QUESTIONS

21 Compare the melting points of ionic compounds and covalent molecular compounds.

22 Explain why water does not conduct in its solid and liquid states.

23 Use solubility rules to determine whether calcium nitrate is soluble in water.

24 Compare the hardness of covalent molecular and covalent network crystals.

25 Identify the three types of intermolecular forces.

Answers ➲ p. 51

CHAPTER SYLLABUS CHECKLIST

Are you able to answer these questions from the syllabus for this chapter? Tick each question as you go through the checklist if you are able to answer it. If you cannot answer a question, turn to the relevant page in the study guide to find the answer. For NESA key word meanings, go to www.educationstandards.nsw.edu.au and search 'key words'.

	FOR A COMPLETE UNDERSTANDING OF THIS TOPIC:	PAGE NO.	✓
1	Can I explain why covalent bonds are polar or non-polar in terms of electronegativity?	36	
2	Can I explain how positive and negative ions form?	37	
3	Can I draw Lewis electron dot diagrams for ionic compounds?	37	
4	Can I use valency rules to write the chemical formulae of ionic compounds?	37–38	
5	Can I use nomenclature rules to name ionic compounds?	38	
6	Can I use nomenclature rules to name covalent molecular compounds?	39	
7	Can I draw Lewis electron dot diagrams for covalent molecular compounds?	40	
8	Can I state the shapes of water, ammonia and methane molecules?	40	
9	Can I draw structural formulae of covalent molecular compounds?	41	
10	Can I distinguish between polar and non-polar molecules?	41	
11	Can I predict whether molecules are polar or non-polar?	41	
12	Can I explain allotropy and give examples of elements that form allotropes?	42	
13	Can I identify examples of covalent network solids?	43	
14	Can I explain the nature of metallic bonds and explain the physical properties of metallic crystals?	44	
15	Can I compare the strengths of different types of chemical bonds?	45	
16	Can I compare the strengths of intermolecular and intramolecular forces?	46	
17	Can I explain why ionic compounds have much higher melting points than covalent molecular compounds?	46–47	
18	Can I explain why covalent network solids have very high melting points?	47	
19	Can I explain why ionic compounds conduct electricity when melted or dissolved in water?	47	
20	Can I use solubility rules to predict whether an ionic compound dissolves in water?	47	
21	Can I compare the hardness of ionic, covalent molecular and covalent network crystals?	48	

Objective-response questions   (1 mark each)

1   Identify which one of the following compounds is ionic:

   A H_2O **B** PCl_3
   C CuO   **D** CS_2

2   Figure 4.20 shows the arrangement of cations and anions in an ionic crystal. Each cation is surrounded by an octahedral arrangement of anions. Each anion is surrounded by an octahedral arrangement of cations. The ratio of cations to anions in this crystal would be:

   A 1:1   **B** 1:2
   C 6:1   **D** 1:6

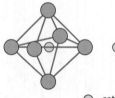

   ○ cation
   ● anion

   Figure 4.20 Cations and anions in a crystal

3   Substance X consists of white, waxy crystals that melt readily at 66 °C. The solid and molten forms do not conduct electricity. Which of the following compounds could have the properties of X?

   A $C_{30}H_{62}$ **B** CO_2
   C NaCl   **D** CaO

4   In Figure 4.21, select the electron dot diagram that correctly shows the electrons in the valence shells of a nitrogen molecule.

   A N $\vdots$ N   **B** N $\vdots\vdots$ N

   C $\vdots$ N $\vdots\vdots$ N $\vdots$ **D** $\vdots$ N $\vdots\vdots$ N $\vdots$

   Figure 4.21 Electron dot diagrams for nitrogen

5   The formula of aluminium sulfide is:

   A AlS   **B** AlS_2
   C Al_2S_3 **D** Al_3S_2

Extended-response questions

6   Use your knowledge of the number of valence electrons in carbon, sulfur, hydrogen and oxygen to draw structural formulae for the following molecules:

   a CS_2 (1 mark)
   b H_2O_2 (1 mark)

7   Draw electron dot diagrams for the following molecules:

   a ethane (C_2H_6—single covalent bonds only)   (1 mark)
   b ethylene (C_2H_4—one double covalent bond present)
                                              (1 mark)
   c acetylene (C_2H_2—one triple covalent bond present)
                                              (1 mark)

8   An unknown substance (R) has the following physical properties. Use the following information to classify (R) as a metallic, ionic or covalent molecular substance.

   Properties of R:
   • white, hard crystals
   • melting point = 373 °C
   • boiling point = 914 °C
   • does not conduct at 25 °C
   • conducts at 700 °C
   • slightly soluble in water.   (1 mark)

9   Sodium sulfate solution is mixed with a barium chloride solution.

   a Identify the ions that are present in the mixed solution prior to reaction.   (2 marks)
   b Use your knowledge of the solubility of ionic compounds to predict whether any ions will combine to form an insoluble ionic compound.   (1 mark)

10 Draw Lewis electron dot diagrams for the following ionic compounds:

   a NaF
   b $GaCl_3$ (2 marks)

ANSWERS

KEY QUESTIONS

Key questions ⊃ p. 37

1. Covalent bonds involve the sharing of electron pairs between neighbouring atoms. Ionic bonds involve the attraction between positive ions and negative ions.

2. H–Br; N–H

3. KBr; SrO

Key questions ⊃ p. 38

4. Al_2O_3

5. There are 7 valence electrons; F^-

6. ammonium carbonate

7. valency of X = +1 (sulfate ions have a valency of −2)

Key questions ⊃ p. 40

8. 4 atoms (formula = NH_3)

9. Cl_2O_7

10. valency = 5

Key questions ⊃ p. 41

11. a tetrahedral b linear c bent

12. The C–H bond dipoles cancel out to give a net zero dipole for the whole tetrahedral molecule.

13. Slightly negative

14. Polar

Key questions ⊃ p. 42

15. Yes, graphene is an allotrope of carbon as its crystalline structure is different but the solid is still composed only of carbon atoms.

16. They are both composed of sulfur atoms that are arranged to produce different-shaped crystals with different physical properties such as melting point. They are allotropes of sulfur.

17. Beta tin's structure includes delocalised electrons that can conduct electricity, whereas alpha tin has a diamond-like structure where no mobile electrons are present.

Key questions ⊃ p. 45

18. a ionic b covalent network c metallic

19. a linear b linear c tetrahedral

20. Cubic crystal; each positive sodium ion is surrounded by 6 negative chloride ions. Each chloride ion is surrounded by 6 sodium ions.

Key questions ⊃ p. 48

21. Ionic compounds have much higher melting points than covalent molecular molecules.

22. Water is a covalent molecular compound that has no charge carriers to conduct a current when melted.

23. Calcium nitrate is soluble, as all nitrates are soluble.

24. Covalent molecular crystals are soft, whereas covalent network crystals are very hard.

25. Dispersion force; dipole–dipole force; hydrogen bonding

YEAR 11 EXAM-TYPE QUESTIONS

Objective-response questions

1. **C.** Ionic compounds form when a metal reacts with a non-metal. **A**, **B** and **D** are incorrect as they are covalent molecular compounds.

2. **A.** 1 : 6 = cations:anions in the first diagram, and 1 : 6 = anions:cations in the second diagram. In the whole crystal, the ratio of cations to anions is 1 : 1. Thus 1 : 2 and 6 : 1 and 1 : 6 make **B**, **C** and **D** incorrect.

3. **A.** The low melting point and the substance does not conduct electricity when melted. **B** is incorrect as it is a gas. **C** is incorrect as molten NaCl conducts electricity as it is ionic. **D** is incorrect as CaO has a high melting point because it is an ionic solid.

4. **D.** Nitrogen molecule has a triple covalent bond; nitrogen atoms have 5 valence electrons. **A** is incorrect as it only shows a single covalent bond, and no non-bonding electrons are shown in the valence shell. **B** is incorrect as no non-bonding electrons are shown in the valence shell. **C** is incorrect as a double covalent bond is shown and nitrogen atoms have 5 valence electrons, not 4.

5. **C.** Aluminium ions have a 3+ valency and sulfide ions have a 2− valency. **A**, **B** and **D** are incorrect as the elements are assigned the incorrect valencies.

Extended-response questions

6. **EM** Students need to remember the number of valence electrons in each atom: C = 4, S = 6, H = 1, O = 6.
   a When C and S bond then two double bonds are required to ensure each atom achieves an octet of electrons in its valence shell.

   b In H_2O_2 only single bonds are required to achieve a stable noble gas configuration for each element.

   Figure A4.2 shows the structural formulae.

   a S=C=S ✓ b H–O–O–H ✓

   Figure A4.2 Structural formulae

7. **EM** Students need to recall that H atoms form one single bond (one electron pair) with carbon atoms, whereas carbon atoms can form single, double or triple covalent bonds with each other.

   Figure A4.3 shows the electron dot diagrams.

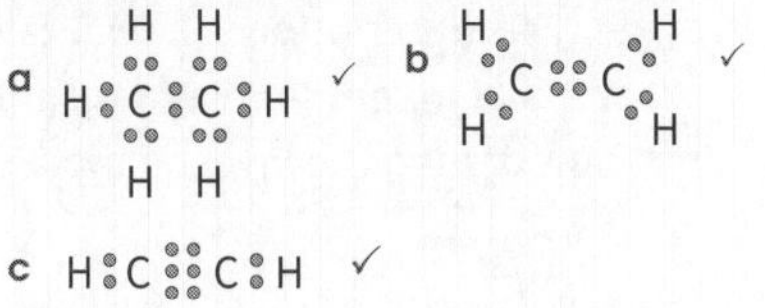

   Figure A4.3 Electron dot diagrams

8. **EM** Students need to determine which pieces of data are most relevant. R is a molten liquid above its melting point. Because it conducts when molten it must be ionic as ions are free to move to carry charge in the circuit.

   Element R is an ionic compound. It has a high melting and boiling point. It conducts when molten as the ions are free to move, but not in the solid state as the ions cannot move. ✓

9. **EM** Students are required to recall the symbol for each ion, including its charge. Students need to recall the solubility rules for sulfate salts, and that calcium sulfate is an exception to the rule that most sulfates are water soluble.
   a Na^+, SO_4^{2-} ✓; Ba^{2+}, Cl^- ✓
   b Barium ions will combine with sulfate ions to form insoluble barium sulfate. ✓

10. **EM** Students are required to recall that electrons from the metal are completely transferred from its valence shell to the valence shell of the non-metal. There is no overlap of valence shells as there is in covalent molecular compounds as separate ions are formed.

    Figure A4.4 shows the electron dot diagrams.

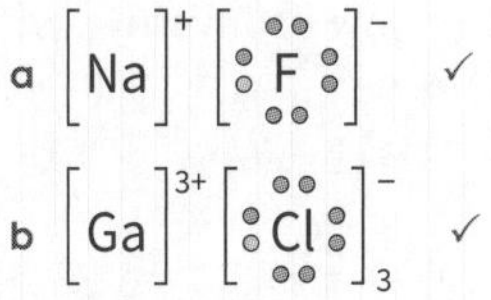

    Figure A4.4 Lewis electron dot diagrams

What happens in chemical reactions?

When magnesium burns in air, a bright white light and considerable heat is produced. The silvery magnesium is converted into a white powder called magnesium oxide. This description is a qualitative observation. If the mass of magnesium and magnesium oxide had been measured, then the investigation is quantitative.

1 Chemical reactions

» Students conduct practical investigations to observe and measure the quantitative relationships of chemical reactions, including but not limited to:
  • masses of solids and/or liquids in chemical reactions
  • volumes of gases in chemical reactions.

Quantitative investigations of chemical reactions

→ Measuring the volume of hydrogen gas evolved at 25 °C when a known mass of magnesium is dissolved in excess hydrochloric acid is an example of a **quantitative investigation**.

→ Observing colour changes when a test tube of yellow sulfur is heated over a Bunsen flame is an example of a **qualitative investigation**.

quantitative investigation: measurements of the quantity of materials involved in a reaction or the amounts of products formed. Measurements of mass or volume are quantitative procedures

qualitative investigation: recording observations, describing trends and identifying materials

→ Some typical student experiments involving quantitative analysis can now be investigated.

FIRSTHAND INVESTIGATION 1

Gas analysis: measuring the volume of hydrogen released in a chemical reaction

» Students conduct investigations to observe and measure the quantitative relationships of chemical reactions, including volumes of gases in chemical reactions.

Aim

to use downward water displacement to measure the volume of hydrogen released per milligram of magnesium when magnesium dissolves in dilute hydrochloric acid

Apparatus

Figure 5.1 shows the equipment needed for this investigation.

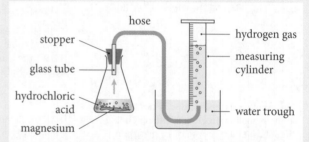

Figure 5.1 Apparatus to measure volume of hydrogen

Method

1 Weigh 75 mg of clean magnesium ribbon on an electric balance.
2 Measure 50 mL of dilute hydrochloric acid using a measuring cylinder and pour the acid into a 250 mL conical flask.
3 Fill a 100 mL measuring cylinder with water and cover the top with plastic wrap. Invert the cylinder and place in a water trough as shown. Remove the plastic wrap. Clamp the cylinder in place.
4 Connect a rubber hose to a small glass tube inserted in a rubber stopper. Place the end of the hose under the cylinder of water.
5 Add the magnesium to the acid and quickly insert the stopper.

6 Ensure all the magnesium dissolves and measure the volume of hydrogen gas collected in the cylinder.

7 Record the temperature using a Celsius thermometer.

Sample results

Consider the following sample data.

mass of magnesium (mg)	75
volume of hydrogen collected (mL)	73
temperature (°C)	25

Calculation

Volume of hydrogen per milligram of Mg
= 73/75 = 0.97 mL/mg

Reliability

The reliability of this experiment could be improved by repeating it a minimum of five times, and calculating the mean of the five measurements.

 FIRSTHAND INVESTIGATION 2

Gravimetric analysis: measuring the mass of water released on the dehydration of a compound

» Students conduct investigations to observe and measure the quantitative relationships of chemical reactions, including masses of solids and/or liquids in chemical reactions.

Aim

to measure the percentage loss in mass as water is removed from hydrated magnesium sulfate

Background

The **hydrated salt** magnesium sulfate is commonly known as Epsom salts. These crystals contain fixed amounts of water molecules in the crystal lattice. The water molecules can be removed by heating.

Apparatus

Figure 5.2 shows the equipment needed for this investigation.

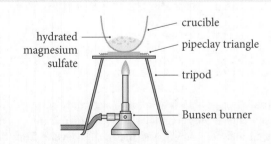

Figure 5.2 Dehydration of hydrated crystals

Method

1 Weigh a clean crucible on an electronic balance.

2 Add about 2 g of hydrated magnesium sulfate crystals to the crucible and reweigh.

3 Place the crucible and contents on a pipeclay triangle supported by a tripod.

4 Heat the crucible slowly with a non-luminous flame to allow water vapour to escape slowly.

5 Continue heating for about 5 to 10 minutes.

6 Turn off the Bunsen and allow the crucible to cool back to room temperature.

7 Reweigh the crucible and contents.

Sample results

Consider the following sample data.

mass of crucible (g)	22.45
mass of crucible + hydrated crystals (g)	24.65
mass of crucible + dehydrated crystals (g)	23.53

Calculation

Mass of hydrated crystals = 24.65 − 22.45
= 2.20 g

Mass of water lost by dehydration = 24.65 − 23.53 g
= 1.12 g

Percentage loss in mass on dehydration = $\frac{1.12}{2.20} \times 100$
= 50.9%

Accuracy

The experimental **accuracy** could be improved by heating the crystals until constant mass is achieved. This is done by repeated heating, cooling and weighing until the mass no longer changes. Cooling should also be done in a vessel called a desiccator, which contains drying crystals that remove all moisture from the air.

accuracy: the accuracy of a quantitative analysis refers to how close the result is to the correct answer

hydrated salts: ionic compounds that crystallise with a fixed number of water molecules (e.g. $CuSO_4 \cdot 5H_2O$)

→ KEY QUESTIONS

1 Classify the measurement of the volume of carbon dioxide released when 2.00 g of calcium carbonate is decomposed as a qualitative or quantitative experiment.

2 Explain how the reliability of a quantitative investigation can be improved.

3 Explain how the accuracy of a gravimetric analysis can be improved.

Answers ⊃ p. 58

2 Mass conservation and equations

» Students relate stoichiometry to the law of conservation of mass in chemical reactions by investigating:
  • balancing chemical equations
  • solving problems regarding mass changes in chemical reactions.

Mass conservation in chemical reactions

→ In a chemical reaction, reactants are converted into products.

→ Consider the following example, in which liquid mercury is heated in a closed vessel with oxygen gas (Figure 5.3). During the heating the silvery-coloured mercury is converted into a red solid. This red solid is mercury oxide, and it is the only product of this reaction. This reaction was performed by Antoine Lavoisier in 1774. Lavoisier observed that the mass of the reaction vessel and its contents did not change during the reaction. Lavoisier went on to perform other reactions of metals with oxygen and, by 1785, he concluded that in a chemical reaction the mass of products was equal to the mass of reactants. This idea is known as the **law** of mass conservation.

law: a scientific law is a statement that describes or predicts various natural phenomena or events

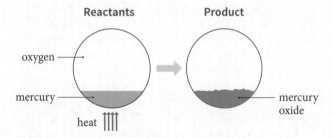

Reactants   **Product**

oxygen

mercury   mercury oxide

heat

Figure 5.3 Oxidation of mercury with oxygen

→ The law of mass conservation is consistent with atom conservation in a chemical reaction.

→ In a chemical reaction, the number of atoms in the reactants does not change when they are converted into products. All that has happened is that the atoms have combined in new patterns. There is also a change in energy between the reactants and products.

→ Figure 5.4 shows that atoms are conserved in a chemical reaction. In this reaction methane burns in oxygen to form carbon dioxide and water. The number of each type of atom has been counted and the number is the same in the products and reactants.

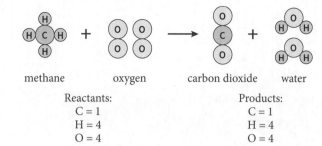

methane   oxygen   carbon dioxide   water

Reactants:	Products:
C = 1	C = 1
H = 4	H = 4
O = 4	O = 4

Figure 5.4 Atom conservation in the combustion of methane

→ In Figure 5.4, we saw a model of a chemical reaction. Using the atomic weights of each element, we can calculate the reacting mass of each substance. The atomic weights of the three elements in the reaction are:

H = 1.008 u; C = 12.01 u; O = 16.00 u

Mass of 1 molecule of methane (CH_4) = 12.01 + 4(1.008)
$$= 16.042 \text{ u}$$

Mass of 2 molecules of oxygen (O_2) = 2 × 2(16.00)
$$= 64.00 \text{ u}$$

Total mass of reactants = 16.042 + 64.00 = 80.042 u

Mass of 1 molecule of carbon dioxide (CO_2)
= 12.01 + 2(16.00) = 44.01 u

Mass of 2 molecules of water (H_2O)
= 2 × [2(1.008) + 16.00] = 36.032 u

Total mass of products = 44.01 + 36.032 = 80.042 u

Thus the total mass of reactant molecules is equal to the total mass of product molecules.

→ The percentage composition of a compound can be calculated from experimental data.

EXAMPLE 1

A known mass sample of mercury oxide was thermally decomposed, and the mass of the mercury formed was measured. The results are tabulated. Calculate the percentage composition of mercury oxide.

mass of mercury oxide (g)	10.55
mass of mercury (g)	9.77

Calculate the mass of oxygen released

Answer:

Mass of oxygen released = 10.55 − 9.77 = 0.78 g

Percentage mercury = $\dfrac{9.77}{10.55} \times 100 = 92.6\%$

Percentage oxygen = $\dfrac{0.78}{10.55} \times 100 = 7.4\%$

All pure compounds have a fixed percentage composition of elements. If the percentage composition of a compound is accurately measured, and the results deviate from the true result, then that sample must be impure.

→ The percentage composition of elements in a compound can be calculated using their atomic weights (from the periodic table).

EXAMPLE 2

Calculate the percentage composition by weight of mercury oxide (HgO).
(Atomic weights: Hg = 200.6 u; O = 16.00 u)

Answer:

$$\%Hg = \frac{200.6}{(200.6+16.00)} \times 100 = 92.613\%$$

$$\%O = \frac{16.00}{(200.6+16.00)} \times 100 = 7.387\%$$

Calculate the total atomic weight of elements in HgO

This result agrees with the experiment described in the previous problem.

→ KEY QUESTIONS

4 State the law of mass conservation in a chemical reaction.

5 A sample of 36.032 g of water can be decomposed using electrolysis. Here 32.00 g of oxygen is formed. Calculate the mass of hydrogen that forms.

6 Use a simple particle diagram to show that atoms are conserved when copper (II) carbonate is thermally decomposed to form copper (II) oxide and carbon dioxide.

Answers ⊃ p. 58

Balancing chemical equations

→ A chemical equation is a symbolic representation of a chemical reaction. The rules for writing a balanced equation are:
  - The formulae of the reactants are written first.
  - The formulae of the products are written last.
  - The arrow between the reactants and products means 'reacts to form'.
  - Ensure the number of atoms of each element are the same in the reactants and products to ensure atom and mass conservation.

→ The ratio of the number of each reactant particle to each product particle is called the reaction **stoichiometry**.

→ The following box provides an example of stoichiometry.

stoichiometry: the ratio of the number of reactant particles to product particles in a balanced chemical equation

Magnesium reacts with silver nitrate solution

Observation
Magnesium is placed in a silver nitrate solution. The magnesium dissolves and a silvery deposit is formed.

Explanation
The magnesium atoms react with the silver nitrate and silver metal is formed. The solution contains magnesium nitrate.

Word equation
magnesium + silver nitrate → magnesium nitrate + silver

Symbolic equation
STEP 1. Write the correct symbols and formulae for each substance using your valency rules.

Magnesium = Mg

Silver nitrate = $AgNO_3$ (Valencies: $Ag^+ = +1$; $NO_3^- = -1$)

Magnesium nitrate = $Mg(NO_3)_2$ (Valencies: $Mg^{2+} = +2$; $NO_3^- = -1$)

Silver = Ag

STEP 2. Replace the words in the word equation by the chemical formulae.

$$Mg + AgNO_3 \rightarrow Mg(NO_3)_2 + Ag$$

STEP 3. Check atom balance.

Reactants: Mg = 1; Ag = 1; N = 1; O = 3

Products: Mg = 1; Ag = 1; N = 2; O = 6

Thus not all the atoms balance.

STEP 4. Place coefficients (integers) in front of the formulae to achieve an atom balance.

$$Mg + 2AgNO_3 \rightarrow Mg(NO_3)_2 + 2Ag$$

STEP 5. Re-check that the atoms now balance.

Reactants: Mg = 1; Ag = 2; N = 2; O = 6

Products: Mg = 1; Ag = 2; N = 2; O = 6

The atoms now balance and so the equation is balanced.

STEP 6. Insert the states of matter for reactants and products.

$$Mg(s) + 2AgNO_3(aq) \rightarrow Mg(NO_3)_2(aq) + 2Ag(s)$$

The reaction stoichiometry in this example is:

$Mg : AgNO_3 : Mg(NO_3)_2 : Ag = 1 : 2 : 1 : 2$

→ KEY QUESTIONS

7 Use atomic weights in the periodic tale to calculate the percentage composition by weight of the elements in barium chloride.

8 Balance the following equations:
  a $C_2H_4(g) + O_2(g) \rightarrow CO_2(g) + H_2O(l)$
  b $Au_2O_3(s) \rightarrow Au(s) + O_2(g)$

9 Zinc metal reacts with the tin (II) nitrate, and tin metal is formed. The solution contains zinc nitrate. Write a balanced equation for this reaction.

Answers ⊃ p. 58

CHAPTER 5: CHEMICAL REACTIONS AND STOICHIOMETRY   55

CHAPTER SYLLABUS CHECKLIST

Are you able to answer these questions from the syllabus for this chapter? Tick each question as you go through the checklist if you are able to answer it. If you cannot answer a question, turn to the relevant page in the study guide to find the answer. For NESA key word meanings, go to www.educationstandards.nsw.edu.au and search 'key words'.

	FOR A COMPLETE UNDERSTANDING OF THIS TOPIC:	PAGE NO.	✓
1	Can I distinguish between qualitative and quantitative investigations?	52	
2	Can I describe an experiment to measure the volume of a gas produced in a chemical reaction?	52	
3	Can I describe an experiment to measure the mass of a product produced in a chemical reaction?	53	
4	Can I explain how to improve experimental accuracy and reliability?	53	
5	Can I use atomic theory to explain the law of mass conservation in a chemical reaction?	54	
6	Can I determine the percentage composition of a compound from gravimetric data?	54	
7	Can I use atomic weights of elements to calculate the percentage by weight of elements in a compound?	55	
8	Can I balance a chemical equation and determine the reaction stoichiometry?	55	

Objective-response questions
(1 mark each)

1   Calculate the mass of water formed when 4 g of hydrogen reacts completely with 32 g of oxygen.

    A   4 g
    B   32 g
    C   28 g
    D   36 g

2   Identify which investigation is not a quantitative experiment:

    A   Measuring the volume of carbon dioxide released when 5.0 g of calcium carbonate is thermally decomposed.
    B   Using the 'pop' test to identify that a gas released when magnesium dissolves in hydrochloric acid is hydrogen.
    C   Determining the change in mass when 2.0 g of magnesium is burnt in air.
    D   Determining the volume of oxygen required to fully combust 4.0 g of methane.

3   The percentage by weight of carbon in carbon dioxide is:

    A   27.3%
    B   42.8%
    C   57.2%
    D   72.7%

4   An experiment was performed to measure the percentage loss in mass when 4.00 g of hydrated cobalt (II) chloride was dehydrated by heating in a crucible. After cooling, the solid remaining was weighed. How could the accuracy of this experiment be improved?

    A   Repeat the experiment five times.
    B   Ensure that the final product is heated and reweighed until there is no further change in weight.
    C   Use 1.00 g of hydrated cobalt (II) chloride.
    D   Heat the hydrated solid in a large evaporating basin instead of a crucible.

5   Identify the set of coefficients a, b, c and d that will balance the following equation:

$$a\,CH_4(g) + b\,O_2(g) \rightarrow c\,CO_2(g) + d\,H_2O(l)$$

    A $a = 1$; $b = 2$; $c = 2$; $d = 2$
    B $a = 2$; $b = 1$; $c = 2$; $d = 1$
    C $a = 1$; $b = 2$; $c = 2$; $d = 1$
    D $a = 1$; $b = 2$; $c = 1$; $d = 2$

Extended-response questions

6   The following data was collected for an experiment in which silver oxide was thermally decomposed in a crucible into silver and oxygen.

mass of crucible (g)	23.85
mass of crucible and solid before heating (g)	28.88
mass of crucible and solid after heating (g)	28.53

    a   Calculate the mass of silver oxide used in the experiment. (1 mark)
    b   Calculate the mass of silver formed in the experiment. (1 mark)
    c   Calculate the percentage composition of silver oxide. (2 marks)

7   Propane has the formula C_3H_8.

    Use the atomic weights in the periodic table to determine the percentage composition of this compound. (3 marks)

8   Barium nitrate has the formula $Ba(NO_3)_2$.

    Use the atomic weights in the periodic table to determine the percentage composition of this compound. (4 marks)

9   Balance the following equations:

    a $S_8(s) + O_2(g) \rightarrow SO_2(g)$
    b $N_2(g) + O_2(g) \rightarrow N_2O_5(s)$
    c $P_4(s) + O_2(g) \rightarrow P_4O_{10}(s)$ (3 marks)

10 Balance the following equations:

    a $K_2CO_3(s) + HCl(aq) \rightarrow KCl(aq) + H_2O(l) + CO_2(g)$
    b $Cu(s) + HNO_3(aq) \rightarrow Cu(NO_3)_2(aq) + H_2O(l) + NO_2(g)$
    c $C_4H_{10}(g) + O_2(g) \rightarrow CO_2(g) + H_2O(l)$ (3 marks)

ANSWERS

Key questions ⊃ p. 53

1 Quantitative as amounts of materials are measured.

2 Repeat the experiment a minimum of five times and take an average.

3 Use more accurate measuring equipment. An electronic balance that weighs to two or three decimal places increases accuracy compared with a one-decimal place balance.

Key questions ⊃ p. 55

4 The mass of reactants is equal to the mass of products.

5 $m(H_2) = 36.032 - 32.00 = 4.032$ g

6 Atoms are conserved. Reactants and products have 1 copper atom, 1 carbon atom and 3 oxygen atoms. This is drawn in Figure A5.1.

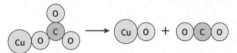

Figure A5.1 Atom conservation

7 For $BaCl_2$:

$$\%Ba = \frac{137.3}{(137.3 + 2 \times 35.45)} \times 100 = 65.95\%$$

$$\%Cl = \frac{2 \times 35.45}{(137.3 + 2 \times 35.45)} \times 100 = 34.05\%$$

8 a $C_2H_4(g) + 3O_2(g) \rightarrow 2CO_2(g) + 2H_2O(l)$

   b $2Au_2O_3(s) \rightarrow 4Au(s) + 3O_2(g)$

9 $Zn(s) + Sn(NO_3)_2(aq) \rightarrow Zn(NO_3)_2(aq) + Sn(s)$

Objective-response questions

1 **D.** $4 + 32 = 36$ g. Therefore **A**, **B** and **C** are incorrect, as the law of mass conservation is not obeyed.

2 **B.** Masses or volumes have not been measured. **A** and **D** are incorrect as measuring gas volume is quantitative. **C** is incorrect as measuring mass changes is quantitative.

3 **A.** $\%C = \frac{\text{mass of C}}{\text{mass of CO}_2} \times 100 = \frac{12.01}{44.01} \times 100 = 27.3\%$. **B**, **C** and **D** are wrong as incorrect calculation methods are used. **D** is the percentage by weight of oxygen. Answers **B** and **C** assume the formula is CO rather than CO_2.

4 **B.** The procedure ensures that all water has been removed. **A** will only improve reliability. **C** will reduce the accuracy as there is a greater percentage error when weighing smaller masses. **D** will not alter the results.

5 **D.** a and c must be the same because the number of C atoms must balance. Therefore **A** and **C** are incorrect. **B** is incorrect as oxygen atoms do not balance.

Extended-response questions

6 **EM** Students need to calculate the mass of silver oxide by subtracting the mass of the crucible. The mass of silver is obtained using the mass conservation law.

   a m(silver oxide) = $28.88 - 23.85 = 5.03$ g ✓

   b m(silver) = $28.53 - 23.85 = 4.68$ g ✓

   c % silver = $\frac{4.68}{5.03} \times 100 = 93.0\%$ ✓

   % oxygen = $100 - 93.0 = 7.0\%$ ✓

7 **EM** Students need to first calculate the total mass of each element. The sum of these atomic weights gives the total mass of the compound.

   Mass of 3 carbon atoms = $3 \times 12.01 = 36.03$ u

   Mass of 8 hydrogen atoms = $8 \times 1.008 = 8.064$ u

   Total mass = $36.03 + 8.064 = 44.094$ u ✓

   $\%C = \frac{36.03}{44.094} \times 100 = 81.71\%$ ✓ $\%H = \frac{8.064}{44.094} \times 100 = 18.29\%$ ✓

8 **EM** Students must first calculate the total mass of each element. The sum of these atomic weights gives the total mass of the compound.

   Mass of 1 barium atom = 137.3 u

   Mass of 2 nitrogen atoms = $2 \times 14.01 = 28.02$ u

   Mass of 6 oxygen atoms = $6 \times 16.00 = 96.00$ u

   Total mass = $137.3 + 28.02 + 96.00 = 261.32$ u ✓

   $\%Ba = \frac{137.3}{261.32} \times 100 = 52.54\%$ ✓ $\%N = \frac{28.02}{261.32} \times 100 = 10.72\%$ ✓

   $\%O = \frac{96.00}{261.32} \times 100 = 36.74\%$ ✓

9 **EM** Students need to demonstrate a facility to balance equations. In (a), 8 molecules of SO_2 are needed to balance the sulfur atoms. Eight molecules of oxygen will then rebalance the oxygen atoms. In (b), 5 molecules of oxygen and 2 molecules of product will balance oxygen atoms. Two molecules of nitrogen will then rebalance the nitrogen atoms. In (c), 5 molecules of oxygen will balance the oxygen atoms.

   a $S_8(s) + 8O_2(g) \rightarrow 8SO_2(g)$ ✓

   b $2N_2(g) + 5O_2(g) \rightarrow 2N_2O_5(s)$ ✓

   c $P_4(s) + 5O_2(g) \rightarrow P_4O_{10}(s)$ ✓

10 **EM** This is a question in which part (b) is a more difficult equation to balance. In (a), 2 molecules of HCl will balance the H and Cl atoms. In (b), 4 molecules of HNO_3 and 2 molecules of water will balance the H atoms. Two molecules of NO_2 rebalance the nitrogen and oxygen atoms. In (c), the C atoms are balanced first and then the H atoms are balanced second. This creates a fraction to balance the oxygen atoms. The fraction $(\frac{13}{2})$ is removed by multiplying the whole equation by 2.

   a $K_2CO_3(s) + 2HCl(aq) \rightarrow 2KCl(aq) + H_2O(l) + CO_2(g)$ ✓

   b $Cu(s) + 4HNO_3(aq) \rightarrow Cu(NO_3)_2(aq) + 2H_2O(l) + 2NO_2(g)$ ✓

   c $2C_4H_{10}(g) + 13O_2(g) \rightarrow 8CO_2(g) + 10H_2O(l)$ ✓

CHAPTER 6
THE MOLE CONCEPT

How are measurements made in chemistry?

Chemists measure the amount of substances involved in chemical reactions. In a laboratory the masses of reactants and products are measured in grams using electronic balances. The amount of a substance can also be expressed in a new unit called the 'mole'. This is a convenient quantity as it directly relates to the stoichiometry of a chemical equation.

1 Avogadro's constant and the mole

» Students explore the concept of the mole and relate this to Avogadro's constant to describe, calculate and manipulate masses, chemical amounts and numbers of particles in:
  - moles of elements and compounds $n = \dfrac{m}{M}$.
    (n = chemical amount in moles, m = mass in grams, M [or MM] = molar mass in g mol^{-1})

Atomic weight standard

➔ The atomic weights of the elements are based on a standard. This standard is the carbon-12 isotope. Its mass is set at 12 atomic mass units (or 12 u) exactly. One atomic mass unit (or 1 u) is equal to one-twelfth $\left(\dfrac{1}{12}\right)$ of the mass of a carbon-12 atom. The mass of single carbon-12 atoms has been measured using a mass spectrometer and found to be equal to 1.9927×10^{-23} g.

Thus $1\text{ u} = \dfrac{1.9927 \times 10^{-23}}{12} = 1.661 \times 10^{-24}$ g

➔ Such small masses are not useful for chemists working in a laboratory on a daily basis. Another method is used to establish a convenient scale to measure the amount of material in a substance.

➔ Consider the following calculations in which the elements oxygen (O) and bismuth (Bi) are compared. The periodic table shows that the relative atomic weight of oxygen is 16.00 u and for bismuth it is 209.0 u. If the chemist weighs out 16.00 g of oxygen and 209.0 g of bismuth, we can calculate the number of atoms of each element in the sample.

Oxygen sample:

mass of 1 atom of O = $16.00 \times 1.661 \times 10^{-24}$ g
$= 2.6576 \times 10^{-23}$ g

number of O atoms in 16.00 g $= \dfrac{16.00}{2.6576 \times 10^{-23}}$
$= 6.02 \times 10^{23}$

Bismuth sample:

mass of 1 atom of Bi = $209.0 \times 1.661 \times 10^{-24}$ g
$= 3.4715 \times 10^{-22}$ g

number of Bi atoms in 209.0 g $= \dfrac{209.0}{3.4715 \times 10^{-22}}$
$= 6.02 \times 10^{23}$

➔ These calculations show that the number of atoms in 16.00 g of oxygen is the same as the number of atoms in 209.0 g of bismuth. Similar calculations for other elements show that 6.02×10^{23} atoms of any element have a weight equal to their atomic weights expressed in grams. This number of atoms is referred to as the **Avogadro constant** (N_A), named in honour of the Italian physicist Amadeo Avogadro. The more accurate value of N_A is:

$$N_A = 6.022 \times 10^{23}$$

➔ Thus 12 g of C-12 will contain 6.022×10^{23} atoms of C-12. This number of atoms is called the mole. The unit called the **mole** is a measure of the number of particles present in a sample. Using this definition of the mole we can compare the masses of an Avogadro number (i.e. 1 mole) of any element to the C-12 standard. Thus 1 mole of copper contains 6.022×10^{23} atoms of copper and this amount of copper has a mass of 63.55 g.

Avogadro constant (N_A): the number of atoms in 12 grams of C-12 isotope

mole: the amount of a substance that contains an Avogadro number of elementary particles

1 Identify the isotope that is the atomic weight standard.

2 Calculate the mass of one atom of sodium.

3 Compare the number of atoms in 5.00 g of lithium and 5.00 g of aluminium.

Answers ⊃ p. 69

Molar mass

Table 6.1 compares the atomic weight of various elements and their molar mass (M). The molar mass of an element is the mass of one mole of the element. The abbreviation for mole is mol. The molar mass of an element has the units of g/mol.

Table 6.1 Molar mass

Element	Atomic weight (u)	Molar mass (M) (g/mol)
Sodium	22.99	22.99
Zinc	65.38	65.38
Uranium	238.0	238.0

→ This molar mass unit is very convenient for chemists. If they weigh out 65.38 g of zinc, for example, they know that they have weighed out an Avogadro number of atoms of zinc.

→ Using the mole unit, the amount of an element (n) can be calculated from its mass (m) and its molar mass (M). For elements, the molar mass is equal to its molar atomic weight. (Note that the symbol MM is sometimes used for molar mass, but M is the accepted IUPAC symbol.)

Key formula

$$n = m/M$$

→ Figure 6.1 shows that 1 mole of zinc and uranium have very different masses. Zinc has a much lower density than uranium and the volume of 1 mole of each element is different.

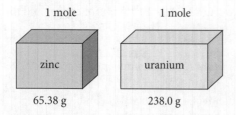

Figure 6.1 One mole of zinc and magnesium

EXAMPLE 1

Calculate the number of moles of oxygen present in 100.0 g of the gas.

Answer:

Oxygen is a diatomic gas (O_2).

> Calculate the molar mass of gaseous oxygen

$$M(O_2) = 2 \times 16.00$$
$$= 32.00 \text{ g/mol}$$

$$n(O_2) = m/M$$
$$= \frac{100.0}{32.00}$$
$$= 3.125 \text{ mol}$$

→ KEY QUESTIONS

4 Calculate the molar mass of:
   a dinitrogen pentoxide
   b iron (III) sulfate.

5 Calculate the number of moles of ozone (O_3) in 20.0 g of the gas.

6 Calculate the mass of 4.50 moles of cobalt (II) chloride.

Answers ⊃ p. 69

→ The number of atoms or molecules (N) present in a sample of an element can be calculated using the Avogadro constant (N_A).

Key formula

$$N = n.N_A$$

EXAMPLE 2

Calculate the number of molecules of hydrogen gas present in 0.15 moles of the gas.

Answer:

$$N(H_2) = n.N_A$$
$$= (0.15)(6.022 \times 10^{23})$$
$$= 9.03 \times 10^{22} \text{ molecules}$$

> Use the Avogadro constant in this calculation

→ The mole concept can also be applied to compounds. The molar mass of a compound is the sum of the molar masses of its constituent atoms.

EXAMPLE 3

Calculate the molar mass of sodium sulfate.

Answer:

Formula of sodium sulfate = Na_2SO_4

[Use the valency rules to write the correct formula]

The atomic weights of each element can be extracted from the periodic table.

$M(Na_2SO_4) = 2(22.99) + 32.07 + 4(16.00)$
$= 142.05$ g/mol

➡ The amount of compound in moles can be calculated using the equation:

$n = m/M$

EXAMPLE 4

Calculate the number of moles of water present in 50.0 g of water.

Answer:

Formula of water = H_2O

[Calculate the molar mass of water]

$M(H_2O) = 2(1.008) + 16.00$
$= 18.016$ g/mol

$n(H_2O) = m/M$
$= \dfrac{50.0}{18.016}$
$= 2.78$ mol

➡ The number of molecules of a molecular compound can be calculated knowing the number of moles of the compound.

EXAMPLE 5

Calculate the number of:

a   molecules of methane present in 1.25 moles of methane.

b   hydrogen atoms present in 1.25 moles of methane.

Answer:

a $N(CH_4) = n.N_A$

[Recall the formula of methane]

$= (1.25)(6.022 \times 10^{23})$
$= 7.53 \times 10^{23}$ molecules

b   Each methane molecule contains 4 atoms of hydrogen (Figure 6.2).

$N(H) = 4 \times N(CH_4)$
$= 4 \times 7.53 \times 10^{23}$
$= 3.01 \times 10^{24}$ atoms

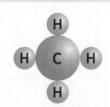

Figure 6.2 Methane

1 molecule of methane contains 4 hydrogen atoms

➡ The number of ions in an ionic compound can also be calculated using mole theory. Consider the following example.

EXAMPLE 6

Barium chloride is an ionic compound. 2.60 g of barium chloride crystals was weighed out into a beaker.

Calculate the number of:

[Determine the formula of barium chloride using valency rules]

a   moles of barium chloride

b   moles of chloride ions

c   chloride ions in the sample.

Answer:

a $M(BaCl_2) = 137.3 + 2(35.45)$
$= 208.2$ g/mol

$n(BaCl_2) = m/M$
$= \dfrac{2.60}{208.2}$
$= 0.0125$ mol

b   In $BaCl_2$, the ratio of $Ba^{2+} : Cl^- = 1 : 2$

$n(Cl^-) = 2 \times 0.0125$
$= 0.0250$ mol

c $N(Cl^-) = n.N_A$
$= (0.0250)(6.022 \times 10^{23})$
$= 1.51 \times 10^{22}$ chloride ions

Reaction stoichiometry and mole calculations

➡ Mole theory can be used to calculate the amount of each reactant required to react in a chemical reaction. Mole theory can also be used to calculate the amounts of products that will form if the reaction goes to completion.

➡ It is important to ensure that the correct formulae are used and that the equation is correctly balanced before any calculation is performed. The term stoichiometry refers to the mole ratio of reactants and products in a reaction. In the following example the stoichiometry of reactants to product is $4 : 3 : 2$:

$$4Al(s) + 3O_2(g) \rightarrow 2Al_2O_3(s)$$

EXAMPLE 7

When magnesium burns in oxygen gas, a white powder called magnesium oxide forms.

[Use the stoichiometry of the balanced equation to determine the amount of oxygen]

a   Write the balanced equation for this reaction.

b   Calculate the mass of oxygen required to fully react with 3.50 g of magnesium metal.

Answer:

a Magnesium oxide has the formula MgO

$$2Mg(s) + O_2(g) \rightarrow 2MgO(s)$$

b The balanced equation shows that 2 moles of magnesium react with 1 mole of oxygen gas to form 2 moles of magnesium oxide. The ratio $2:1:2$ is called the **stoichiometric ratio** for the reactants and products in this reaction.

Calculate the number of moles of magnesium:

$$n(Mg) = m/M$$
$$= \frac{3.50}{24.31}$$
$$= 0.144 \text{ mol}$$

The $Mg:O_2$ stoichiometric ratio is $2:1$.

Thus the number of moles of O_2 required is:

$$n(O_2) = \frac{0.144}{2}$$
$$= 0.0720 \text{ mol}$$

Calculate the mass of 0.0720 mol of O_2:

$$m(O_2) = n.M$$
$$= (0.0720)(32.00)$$
$$= 2.30 \text{ g}$$

stoichiometric ratio: the mole ratio of the reactants and products in the balanced equation

➔ The reaction stoichiometry can also be used to determine the amount of products that will form. In some calculations an excess of one reactant is added to ensure that all the other reactants are completely converted into the products. For example, when zinc reacts with dilute hydrochloric acid to form zinc chloride and hydrogen gas, an excess of hydrochloric acid is added to ensure all the zinc metal dissolves.

EXAMPLE 8

a Write a balanced equation for the reaction of 4.50 g of zinc in excess dilute hydrochloric acid.

b Calculate the mass of each product formed.

Use the reaction stoichiometry to calculate the amounts of each product

Answer:

a $Zn(s) + 2HCl(aq) \rightarrow ZnCl_2(aq) + H_2(g)$

b The stoichiometry of the reaction is:

$Zn:HCl:ZnCl_2:H_2 = 1:2:1:1$

The acid is added in excess and so 1 mole of zinc will form 1 mole of zinc chloride and 1 mole of hydrogen.

Calculate the number of moles of zinc:

$$n(Zn) = m/M$$
$$= \frac{4.50}{65.38}$$
$$= 0.0688 \text{ mol}$$

Therefore $n(ZnCl_2) = 0.0688 \text{ mol}$
$n(H_2) = 0.0688 \text{ mol}$

$$m(ZnCl_2) = n.M$$
$$= (0.0688)(65.38 + 2(35.45))$$
$$= 9.38 \text{ g}$$
$$m(H_2) = n.M$$
$$= (0.0688)(2 \times 1.008)$$
$$= 0.137 \text{ g}$$

➔ KEY QUESTIONS

7 **0.20 mol of a gaseous diatomic element has a mass of 7.60 g. Identify this element.**

8 **Calculate the number of atoms present in 3.41 g of ammonia (NH_3).**

9 **Calculate the mass of oxygen required to completely react with 4.033 g of hydrogen.**

Answers ➲ p. 69

2 Percentage composition and empirical formulae

» Students explore the concept of the mole and relate this to Avogadro's constant to describe, calculate and manipulate masses, chemical amounts and numbers of particles in:
  • percentage composition calculations and empirical formulae.

➔ Gravimetric analysis allows chemists to determine the percentage composition by weight of each element in a compound. Using this information the chemist can then determine the number of moles of each element and the mole ratio of elements present. From this information the **empirical formula of the compound** is calculated.

empirical formula of a compound: the formula in which the proportions of each element are expressed in the simplest mole ratio

Examples:

• Ethane
  The mole ratio of carbon to hydrogen in ethane $= 1:3$.
  The empirical formula of ethane is CH_3.

- Sulfur dioxide
  The S : O mole ratio is 1 : 2.
  The empirical formula of sulfur dioxide is SO_2.

EXAMPLE 9

A compound was gravimetrically analysed and the percentage by weight of each element determined. The results of the analysis are:

70.0% iron; 30.0% oxygen.

> Calculate the number of moles of each element

Use this data to determine the empirical formula of the compound.

Answer:

In each 100 g of the compound, there will be 70.0 g of iron and 30.0 g of oxygen. Use this information to calculate the number of moles of each element and the mole ratio.

Iron: $n(Fe) = m/M$
$$= \frac{70.0}{55.85}$$
$$= 1.253 \text{ mol}$$

Oxygen: $n(O) = m/M$
$$= \frac{30.0}{16.0}$$
$$= 1.875 \text{ mol}$$

Mole ratio of iron to oxygen:

$Fe : O = 1.253 : 1.875$
$\qquad = 1 : 1.496$
$\qquad = 1 : 1.5$
$\qquad = 2 : 3$

Empirical formula = Fe_2O_3

Molecular formulae

→ Gravimetric analysis provides information that allows chemists to calculate the empirical formula of a compound. In the case of ionic compounds, the empirical formula is the same as the chemical formula since these compounds consist of vast ionic arrays.

→ However, in covalent molecular compounds the empirical formula may not necessarily correspond to the molecular formula. Hydrogen peroxide, for example, has a molecular formula of H_2O_2 but the 2 : 2 ratio can be simplified to 1 : 1 and thus the empirical formula is HO.

Example:
- Octene
  Molecular formula (MF) = C_8H_{16}
  Empirical formula (EF) = CH_2

→ Chemists have developed methods (e.g. mass spectrometry) for determining the molar mass of a molecule and this information together with the empirical formula can be used to determine the **molecular formula** of the compound.

molecular formula: the true chemical formula of a covalent molecular compound; the molecular formula is a multiple of the empirical formula

EXAMPLE 10

Use the following data to determine the empirical formula and molecular formula of a binary compound of phosphorus and oxygen.
- Percentage composition by weight:
  56.34 %P; 43.66 %O
- Molar mass = 219.88 g/mol

> Calculate the number of moles of each element

Answer:

In each 100 g of the compound there is 56.34 g of P and 43.66 g of O.

$n(P) = m/M$
$$= \frac{56.34}{90.97}$$
$$= 1.819 \text{ mol}$$

$n(O) = m/M$
$$= \frac{43.66}{16.00}$$
$$= 2.729 \text{ mol}$$

Mole ratio: $P : O = 1.819 : 2.729$
$\qquad\qquad = 1 : 1.5$
$\qquad\qquad = 2 : 3$

Empirical formula = P_2O_3

The molar empirical mass of P_2O_3 is found by summing the molar atomic weights.

Molar empirical mass = 2(30.97) + 3(16.00)
$\qquad\qquad\qquad = 109.94 \text{ g/mol.}$

This molar empirical mass is exactly half the molar mass and therefore the molecular formula of this compound must be twice the empirical formula.

Molecular formula = 2(EF)

Molecular formula = P_4O_6

Figure 6.3 shows the structure of P_4O_6.

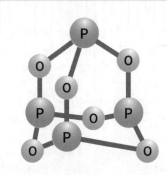

Figure 6.3 Structure of P_4O_6

10 Calculate the percentage by weight of elements in aluminium oxide.

11 Determine the empirical formula and molecular formula of a hydrocarbon that is 88.81% by mass of carbon and a molar mass of 54.09 g/mol.

12 The percentage composition (by weight) of acetic acid is: carbon: 40.01%; hydrogen: 6.72%; oxygen: 53.27%. Calculate the empirical formula of acetic acid.

Answers ⟳ p. 69

3 Reacting mole ratios

» Students conduct an investigation to determine that chemicals react in simple whole number ratios by moles.

→ The stoichiometry of a reaction can be experimentally investigated using gravimetric analysis.

 FIRSTHAND INVESTIGATION 1

Gravimetric analysis: Combustion of magnesium

» Students conduct an investigation to determine that chemicals react in simple whole number ratios by moles.

Aim

to investigate mass changes in the combustion of magnesium in air (oxygen) and to determine the reaction stoichiometry

Method

1 Clean about 50 cm of magnesium ribbon so that it is free of corrosion. Weigh the magnesium (m1) using an electric balance.

2 Weigh a clean porcelain crucible and lid (m2).

3 Place the magnesium ribbon in the crucible which is supported on a tripod using a pipe-clay triangle.

4 Heat the crucible with a hot blue Bunsen flame until ignition of the magnesium begins. Place the lid on the crucible and allow the reaction to go to completion (Figure 6.4).

5 Remove the heat source and allow the crucible to cool to room temperature. Reweigh to determine the mass of the crucible/lid and contents (m3).

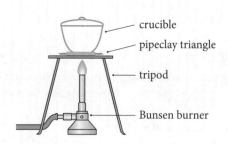

Figure 6.4 Combustion of magnesium in a crucible

Safety

1 Do not look at the burning magnesium as the bright white light can cause eye damage.

2 Wear safety glasses.

3 Do not touch the crucible while it is hot.

Sample results

m1 (mass of magnesium) (g)	0.459
m2 (mass of crucible/lid) (g)	30.245
m3 (mass crucible/lid + product) (g)	31.001

Analysis

• The sample results are used to calculate the mass of magnesium oxide.

mass of reactant (magnesium) (g)	0.459
mass of product (magnesium oxide) (m3 − m2) (g)	0.756

magnesium + oxygen → magnesium oxide

• Calculate moles of magnesium and magnesium oxide.

» $n(\text{Mg}) = m/M$
$$= \frac{0.459}{24.31}$$
$$= 0.0189 \text{ mol}$$

» $n(\text{MgO}) = m/M$
$$= \frac{0.756}{24.31 + 16.00}$$
$$= 0.0188 \text{ mol}$$

• Mole ratio Mg : MgO = 0.0189 : 0.0188 = 1 : 1

This mole ratio is consistent with the stoichiometry of the reaction: 2 : 1 : 2

This stoichiometric ratio is shown in the following equation:

$$2\text{Mg}(s) + O_2(g) \rightarrow 2\text{MgO}(s)$$

Accuracy and reliability

- **Reliability** of the analysis can be improved by repeating the experiment (at least five times) or combining group results from at least five groups and calculating a mean.

- Accuracy can be improved by ensuring that all the magnesium has burnt to form magnesium oxide. The crucible and lid should be pre-heated and cooled to constant weight before the experiment. Cooling should be done in a dry atmosphere in a desiccator to prevent absorption of moisture.

reliability: the reliability of a quantitative experiment refers to how close repeated experiments are to the mean value. Reliability is a measure of the size of the standard deviation from the mean. Outlier values should be excluded

4 Investigating stoichiometry

» Students conduct a practical investigation to demonstrate and calculate the molar mass (mass of one mole) of:
- an element
- a compound.

→ Due to differences in densities and molar masses one mole of elements have quite different masses and volumes.

 FIRSTHAND INVESTIGATION 2

Molar quantities of elements and compounds

» Students conduct a practical investigation to demonstrate and calculate the molar mass (mass of one mole) of:
- an element
- a compound.

Aim

to compare the masses of molar quantities of various elements and compounds

Method

1 The following elements and compounds will be investigated:
- Elements: magnesium, copper
- Compounds: water (H_2O; sodium chloride (NaCl); sucrose ($C_{12}H_{22}O_{11}$)

2 Use the table of atomic weights to calculate the molar mass of each substance.

3 Calculate the mass of 0.100 mol of each substance.

4 Use an electronic balance to weigh the calculated amount of each substance based on the calculated quantities in (3). Weigh each sample into a small beaker. Add additional quantities to the beaker until the correct mass is present. For water, use a dropper to add further quantities.

5 Take a photo of each sample for your report.

Sample calculations

Water:
$$M(H_2O) = 2 \times 1.008 + 16.00$$
$$= 18.016 \text{ g/mol}$$

$$n = 0.10 \text{ mol}$$
$$m(H_2O) = nM$$
$$= (0.10)(18.016)$$
$$= 1.80 \text{ g (3 significant figures)}$$

Magnesium:
$$M(Mg) = 24.31 \text{ g/mol}$$
$$m(Mg) = (0.10)(24.31)$$
$$= 2.43 \text{ g}$$

Copper:
$$M(Cu) = 64.55 \text{ g/mol}$$
$$m(Cu) = (0.10)(63.55)$$
$$= 6.36 \text{ g}$$

Sodium chloride:
$$M(NaCl) = 22.99 + 35.45$$
$$= 58.44 \text{ g/mol}$$
$$m(NaCl) = (0.10)(58.44)$$
$$= 5.84 \text{ g}$$

Sucrose:
$$M(C_{12}H_{22}O_{11}) = 12 \times 12.01 + 22 \times 1.008 + 11 \times 16.00$$
$$= 342.296 \text{ g/mol}$$
$$m(C_{12}H_{22}O_{11}) = (0.10)(342.296)$$
$$= 34.2 \text{ g}$$

5 Limiting reagent reactions

» Students explore the concept of the mole and relate this to Avogadro's constant to describe, calculate and manipulate masses, chemical amounts and numbers of particles in limiting reagent reactions.

→ In some calculations the reactants are mixed together but not in the correct stoichiometric ratio. In these examples one reactant will be in excess and the other in a limiting amount. It is the limiting reactant that determines the amount of products that form. Consider the following example.

EXAMPLE 11

10.0 g of carbon monoxide gas and 10.0 g of oxygen gas are mixed together. The mixture is ignited with a flame and carbon dioxide is formed.

a   Write a balanced equation for this reaction.

b   Calculate the mass of carbon dioxide gas that will form.

> Calculate the number of moles of each reactant

Answer:

a $2CO(g) + O_2(g) \rightarrow 2CO_2(g)$

b   The stoichiometry of this reaction is:

$CO : O_2 : CO_2 = 2 : 1 : 2$

Calculate the number of moles of each reactant:

$n(CO) = m/M$

$= \dfrac{10.0}{12.01 + 16.00}$

$= 0.357$ mol

$n(O_2) = m/M$

$= \dfrac{10.0}{32.00}$

$= 0.313$ mol

In order for all the oxygen to react there would need to be $2(0.313) = 0.626$ mol of CO present. But only 0.357 mole of CO is present.

Therefore the limiting reactant is CO and O_2 is in excess. Thus the number of moles of CO will determine the number of moles of CO_2 formed. Therefore $n(CO_2) = n(CO)$.

$n(CO_2) = 0.357$ mol

$m(CO_2) = n.M$

$= (0.357)(12.01 + 2(16.00))$

$= 15.7$ g

→ **KEY QUESTIONS**

13   20 moles of sulfur are mixed with 10 moles of oxygen and the mixture heated until ignition began The product is sulfur dioxide. Calculate the mass of sulfur dioxide formed.

14   30.0 g of white phosphorus (P_4) is burnt in 60.0 g of oxygen gas to form a white solid (P_4O_{10}). Determine the mass of P_4O_{10} formed.

15   25.00 g of copper (II) oxide was mixed with 5.00 g of hydrogen, the mixture was heated, and copper and water formed. Calculate the mass of water formed.

Answers ⊃ p. 69

CHAPTER SYLLABUS CHECKLIST

Are you able to answer these questions from the syllabus for this chapter? Tick each question as you go through the checklist if you are able to answer it. If you cannot answer a question, turn to the relevant page in the study guide to find the answer. For NESA key word meanings, go to www.educationstandards.nsw.edu.au and search 'key words'.

	FOR A COMPLETE UNDERSTANDING OF THIS TOPIC:	PAGE NO.	✓
1	Can I recall the isotope that is used as the atomic weight standard?	59	
2	Can I recall the value of the Avogadro constant?	59	
3	Can I recall the definition of the *mole*?	59	
4	Can I calculate the molar mass of compounds from their formula?	60	
5	Can I calculate the number of moles of an element or compound from their mass and molar mass?	61	
6	Can I calculate the number of atoms in a compound from the number of moles of the compound?	61	
7	Can I determine the stoichiometry of a reaction from the balanced equation?	61–62	
8	Can I calculate the percentage composition of a compound?	62	
9	Can I calculate the empirical formula of a compound from its percentage composition?	62	
10	Can I calculate the molecular formula using the empirical formula and molar mass?	63	
11	Can I determine the limiting reagent in a chemical reaction?	65	

Objective-response questions
(1 mark each)

1 The mass in grams of 1 molecule of nitrogen is:

   A 2.33×10^{-23} g

   B 4.65×10^{-23} g

   C 14.01 g

   D 28.02 g

2 The molar mass of iron (III) oxide is:

   A 71.85 g/mol

   B 183.55 g/mol

   C 159.7 g/mol

   D 103.85 g/mol

3 Calculate the number of molecules in 96 g of ozone (O_3).

   A 2

   B 1.20×10^{24}

   C 6.02×10^{23}

   D 3

4 Calculate the number of chloride ions in 5.0 g of calcium chloride.

   A 6.02×10^{23}

   B 2

   C 2.71×10^{22}

   D 5.43×10^{22}

5 Calculate the mass of oxygen required to completely react with 8.00 g of zinc.

$$2Zn(s) + O_2(g) \rightarrow 2ZnO(s)$$

   A 3.91 g

   B 1.96 g

   C 8.00 g

   D 4.00 g

Extended-response questions

6 Use the following data to determine the empirical formula and molecular formula of a binary compound of nitrogen and oxygen.

   • Percentage composition by weight: 36.86% N; 63.14% O

   • Molar mass = 76.02 g/mol   (5 marks)

7 3.00 g of potassium carbonate reacts with excess nitric acid (HNO_3) to form potassium nitrate, carbon dioxide and water.

   a Write a balanced equation for this reaction.   (1 mark)

   b Calculate the mass of carbon dioxide evolved.   (3 marks)

8 25.00 g of calcium carbonate was decomposed to form calcium oxide and carbon dioxide using a high-temperature furnace.

   a Write a balanced equation for the reaction.   (1 mark)

   b Calculate the mass of calcium oxide formed.   (3 marks)

   c The calcium oxide was then hydrated with water to form calcium hydroxide. Calculate the mass of water required to fully hydrate the calcium oxide.   (2 marks)

9 20.0 g of carbon monoxide gas and 10.0 g of oxygen gas are mixed together. The mixture is ignited with a flame and carbon dioxide is formed. Calculate the mass of carbon dioxide gas that will form.   (5 marks)

10 Diphosphorus pentoxide solid reacts with water to form phosphoric acid (H_3PO_4).

   a Write a balanced equation for this reaction.   (1 mark)

   b 1.41 g of diphosphorus pentoxide and 0.50 g of water are mixed together. Calculate the maximum mass of phosphoric acid that will form.   (3 marks)

ANSWERS

KEY QUESTIONS

Key questions ⊃ p. 60

1 carbon-12

2 22.99 g of sodium contains 6.022×10^{23} atoms.

Therefore 1 atom has a mass of $\dfrac{22.99}{6.022 \times 10^{23}}$ g = 3.818×10^{-23} g.

3 $n(\text{Li}) = \dfrac{5.00}{6.941} = 0.720$ mol; $N(\text{Li}) = 0.720 \times 6.022 \times 10^{23}$
$= 4.34 \times 10^{23}$ lithium atoms

$n(\text{Al}) = \dfrac{5.00}{26.98} = 0.185$ mol; $N(\text{Al}) = 0.185 \times 6.022 \times 10^{23}$
$= 1.11 \times 10^{23}$ aluminium atoms

The number of lithium atoms is much greater than the number of aluminium atoms.

4 a $M(\text{N}_2\text{O}_5) = 2 \times 14.01 + 5 \times 16.00 = 108.02$ g/mol
   b $M(\text{Fe}_2(\text{SO}_4)_3) = 2 \times 55.85 + 3 \times 32.07 + 12 \times 16.00$
   $= 399.91$ g/mol

5 $n(\text{O}_3) = m/M = \dfrac{20.0}{3 \times 16.00} = 0.417$ mol

6 $m(\text{CoCl}_2) = nM = (4.50)(58.93 + 2 \times 35.45) = 584$ g

Key questions ⊃ p. 62

7 $M = m/n = \dfrac{7.60}{0.20} = 38.0$ g/mol

The gas is diatomic. Therefore the atomic weight is $\dfrac{1}{2} \times 38.0 = 19.0$ u. The element is fluorine. (Check the periodic table.)

8 $M(\text{NH}_3) = 14.01 + (3 \times 1.008) = 17.034$ g/mol

$n(\text{NH}_3) = m/M = \dfrac{3.41}{17.034} = 0.200$ mol

$N(\text{NH}_3) = 0.200 \times 6.022 \times 10^{23} = 1.204 \times 10^{23}$ molecules

Each ammonia molecule consists of 4 atoms.

Therefore the number of atoms present in 3.41 g of ammonia $= 4 \times 1.204 \times 10^{23} = 4.82 \times 10^{23}$ atoms.

9 $2\text{H}_2(\text{g}) + \text{O}_2(\text{g}) \rightarrow 2\text{H}_2\text{O}(\text{l})$

2 mol of hydrogen requires 1 mol of oxygen.

$n(\text{H}_2) = m/M = \dfrac{4.033}{2 \times 1.008} = 2.000$ mol

$n(\text{O}_2) = \dfrac{1}{2} \times 2.000 = 1.000$ mol

$m(\text{O}_2) = nM = (1.000)(32.00) = 32.00$ g

Key questions ⊃ p. 64

10 $M(\text{Al}_2\text{O}_3) = 2 \times 26.98 + 3 \times 16.00 = 101.96$ g/mol

$\%\text{Al} = \dfrac{2 \times 26.98}{101.96} \times 100 = 52.92\%$

$\%\text{O} = \dfrac{3 \times 16.00}{101.96} \times 100 = 47.08\%$

11 In 100 g of hydrocarbon: $m(\text{C}) = \dfrac{88.81}{100} \times 100 = 88.81$ g

$m(\text{H}) = \dfrac{11.19}{100} \times 100 = 11.19$ g

$n(\text{C}) = \dfrac{88.81}{12.01} = 7.395$ mol

$n(\text{H}) = \dfrac{11.19}{1.008} = 11.10$ mol

C : H mole ratio = $7.395 : 11.10 = 1 : 1.50 = 2 : 3$

$\text{EF} = \text{C}_2\text{H}_3$

$M = 54.09$ g/mol

Empirical mass $(\text{C}_2\text{H}_3) = 2 \times 12.01 + 3 \times 1.008$
$= 27.044$
$= \dfrac{1}{2} \times 54.09$

Therefore $\text{MF} = 2 \times \text{EF} = \text{C}_4\text{H}_6$

12 In 100 g of acetic acid: $m(\text{C}) = 40.01$ g; $m(\text{H}) = 6.72$ g; $m(\text{O}) = 53.27$ g

$n(\text{C}) = \dfrac{40.01}{12.01} = 3.33$ mol; $n(\text{H}) = \dfrac{6.72}{1.008} = 6.67$ mol;

$n(\text{O}) = \dfrac{53.27}{16.00} = 3.33$ mol

C : H : O mole ratio = $3.33 : 6.67 : 3.33 = 1 : 2 : 1$

$\text{EF} = \text{CH}_2\text{O}$

Key questions ⊃ p. 66

13 $\text{S}(\text{s}) + \text{O}_2(\text{g}) \rightarrow \text{SO}_2(\text{g})$

Mole ratio $\text{S} : \text{O}_2 : \text{SO}_2 = 1 : 1 : 1$

10 moles of S will react with 10 mol O_2. 10 mol of S is in excess.

10 moles of SO_2 will form.

$m(\text{SO}_2) = nM = (10 \times 32.07) + (2 \times 16.00) = 640.7$ g

14 $\text{P}_4(\text{s}) + 5\text{O}_2(\text{g}) \rightarrow \text{P}_4\text{O}_{10}(\text{s})$

$n(\text{P}_4) = \dfrac{30.0}{4 \times 30.97} = 0.242$ mol; $n(\text{O}_2) = \dfrac{60.0}{2 \times 16.00} = 1.875$ mol

Stoichiometry $\text{P}_4 : \text{O}_2 = 1 : 5$.

Therefore oxygen is in excess and all the P_4 reacts. Thus $n(\text{P}_4\text{O}_{10})$ formed $= 0.242$ mol, as $\text{P}_4 : \text{P}_4\text{O}_{10} = 1 : 1$.

$m(\text{P}_4\text{O}_{10}) = nM = (0.242)(4 \times 30.97 + 10 \times 16.00) = 68.7$ g

15 $\text{H}_2(\text{g}) + \text{CuO}(\text{s}) \rightarrow \text{Cu}(\text{s}) + \text{H}_2\text{O}(\text{l})$

Stoichiometry $= 1 : 1 : 1 : 1$

$n(\text{CuO}) = \dfrac{25.00}{63.55 + 16.00} = 0.3143$ mol

$n(\text{H}_2) = \dfrac{5.00}{2 \times 1.008} = 2.480$ mol

Hydrogen is in excess and all the CuO reacts.

$n(\text{H}_2\text{O})$ formed $= n(\text{CuO}) = 0.3143$ mol

$m(\text{H}_2\text{O}) = nM = (0.3143)(2 \times 1.008 + 16.00) = 5.662$ g

YEAR 11 EXAM-TYPE QUESTIONS

Objective-response questions

1 **B.** $M(\text{N}_2) = 2(14.01) = 28.02$ g/mol

6.022×10^{23} molecules have a mass of 28.02 g

1 molecule has a mass of $\dfrac{28.02}{6.022 \times 10^{23}} = 4.65 \times 10^{-23}$ g

A, **C** and **D** are incorrect. **C** is the mass of 1 mole of nitrogen atoms and **D** is the mass of 1 mole of nitrogen molecules.

2 **C.** $M(Fe_2O_3) = 2(55.85) + 3(16.00) = 159.7$ g/mol

A, **B** and **D** are incorrect. **A** is wrong because it is incorrectly based on FeO.

---

3 **B.** $M(O_3) = 3(16.00) = 48.00$ g/mol

$$n = m/M = \frac{96}{48.00} = 2.0 \text{ mol}$$

$$N = n.N_A = 2.0 \times 6.022 \times 10^{23} = 1.20 \times 10^{24}$$

A, **C** and **D** are incorrect. **A** is incorrect as 2 is the number of moles not the number of molecules. **D** is incorrect as this is the number of moles of oxygen atoms in 1 mole of ozone.

---

4 **D.** $n(CaCl_2) = m/M = \dfrac{5.0}{40.08 + 2(35.45)} = 0.04505 \text{ mol}$

$$n(Cl^-) = 2n(CaCl_2) = 0.0901 \text{ mol}$$

$$N(Cl^-) = n.N_A = 0.0901 \times 6.022 \times 10^{23} = 5.43 \times 10^{22}$$

A, **B** and **C** are incorrect. **B** is the number of moles of chloride ions in 1 mole of calcium chloride.

---

5 **B.** $n(Zn) = m/M = \dfrac{8.0}{65.41} = 0.122 \text{ mol}$

$$n(O_2) = \frac{0.122}{2} = 0.0612 \text{ mol}$$

$$m(O_2) = n.M(O_2) = (0.0612)(32.00) = 1.96 \text{ g}$$

A, **C** and **D** are incorrect. The 2 : 1 stoichiometry must be taken into account. **A** does not take this into account. **C** and **D** have not been calculated using mole theory.

Extended-response questions

6 **EM** This is a question in which mass data must be converted to moles in order to determine mole ratios. Marks are awarded for this key step. In this question the empirical molar mass equals the molar mass of the compound. A binary compound has two elements bonded together.

In each 100 g of the compound there is 36.86 g of N and 63.14 g of O.

$$n(N) = m/M = \frac{36.86}{14.01} = 2.630 \text{ mol } \checkmark$$

$$n(O) = m/M = \frac{63.14}{16.00} = 3.946 \text{ mol } \checkmark$$

Mole ratio: N : O = 2.630 : 3.946 = 1 : 1.5 = 2 : 3

Empirical formula = N_2O_3 ✓

The molar empirical mass of N_2O_3 is found by summing the molar atomic weights.

Molar empirical mass = $2(14.01) + 3(16.00) = 76.02$ g/mol ✓

This molar empirical mass is equal to the molar mass and therefore the molecular formula of this compound is the same as the empirical formula.

MF = EF

Molecular formula = N_2O_3 ✓

---

7 **EM** This is a question in which knowledge of valencies and the principles of balancing equations are essential to gain full marks. If the equation is incorrect then the wrong answer will be obtained in (b).

a $K_2CO_3(s) + 2HNO_3(aq) \rightarrow 2KNO_3(aq) + CO_2(g) + H_2O(l)$ ✓

b $n(K_2CO_3) = m/M = \dfrac{3.00}{(2 \times 39.10) + 12.01 + (3 \times 16.00)}$

$$= \frac{3.00}{138.21}$$

$$= 0.02171 \text{ mol } \checkmark$$

$$n(CO_2) = n(K_2CO_3) = 0.02171 \text{ mol } \checkmark$$

$$m(CO_2) = n.M = (0.02171)(12.01 + (2 \times 16.00)) = 0.955 \text{ g } \checkmark$$

---

8 **EM** This question needs students to ensure that the equations in (a) and (c) are correctly balanced. Marks are awarded for balanced equations. The formulae used to calculate moles should be written and the substitutions must be shown, not just the final answer.

a $CaCO_3(s) \rightarrow CaO(s) + CO_2(g)$ ✓

b $M(CaCO_3) = 40.08 + 12.01 + 3(16.00) = 100.09$ g/mol ✓

$$n(CaCO_3) = m/M = \frac{25.00}{100.09} = 0.2498 \text{ mol}$$

$$n(CaO) = n(CaCO_3) = 0.2498 \text{ mol } \checkmark$$

$$M(CaO) = 40.08 + 16.00 = 56.08 \text{ g/mol}$$

$$m(CaO) = (0.2498)(56.08) = 14.01 \text{ g } \checkmark$$

c $CaO(s) + H_2O(l) \rightarrow Ca(OH)_2(s)$ ✓

1 mol CaO reacts with 1 mol H_2O

Therefore 0.2498 mol CaO reacts with 0.2498 mol H_2O.

$$m(H_2O) = n.M(H_2O) = (0.2498)((2 \times 1.008) + 16.00) = 4.500 \text{ g } \checkmark$$

---

9 **EM** This question needs students to identify a limiting reactant. The moles of the limiting reactant determine the amount of products formed. Students should clearly show how they determined the limiting reactant.

$2CO(g) + O_2(g) \rightarrow 2CO_2(g)$ ✓

The stoichiometry of this reaction is: $CO : O_2 : CO_2 = 2 : 1 : 2$

The number of moles of each reactant:

$$n(CO) = m/M = \frac{20.0}{28.01} = 0.7143 \text{ mol } \checkmark$$

$$n(O_2) = m/M = \frac{10}{32.00} = 0.3125 \text{ mol } \checkmark$$

In order for all the carbon monoxide to react there would need to be $\frac{1}{2}(0.7143) = 0.3572$ mol of O_2 present—but only 0.3125 moles of O_2 is present.

Therefore the limiting reactant is O_2 and CO is in excess. Thus not all the CO burns.

The amount of CO that reacts is $2 \times 0.3125 = 0.625$ mol. ✓

Therefore 0.625 mol of CO_2 forms.

$$m(CO_2) = n.M = 0.625 \times (12.01 + 32.00) = 27.5 \text{ g } CO_2 \checkmark$$

---

10 **EM** This question needs students to show that the limiting reactant in this question is water and this governs the amount of phosphoric acid formed. The correct stoichiometry is then essential to determine the correct mass of phosphoric acid formed.

a $P_2O_5(s) + 3H_2O(l) \rightarrow 2H_3PO_4(aq)$ ✓

b $n(P_2O_5) = m/M = \dfrac{1.41}{(2 \times 30.07) + (5 \times 16.00)} = \dfrac{1.41}{140.14} = 0.0101$ mol

$$n(H_2O) = m/M = \frac{0.50}{(2 \times 1.008) + 16.00} = \frac{0.50}{18.016} = 0.0278 \text{ mol } \checkmark$$

From the balanced equation, 1 mol of P_2O_5 reacts with 3 mol of water (1 : 3 ratio).

The water is the limiting reagent in this process as the ratio = 0.0101 : 0.0278 = 1 : 2.75.

Thus the amount of water will determine the amount of phosphoric acid that forms. ✓

Thus 0.00927 mol of P_2O_5 will react with 0.0278 mol water to form 0.0185 mol H_3PO_4 (1 : 3 : 2 mol ratio).

$$m(H_3PO_4) = n.M = (0.0185)(3 \times 1.008 + 30.97 + 4 \times 16.00)$$

$$= (0.0185)(97.994) = 1.81 \text{ g} = 1.8 \text{ g (2 s.f.) } \checkmark$$

CHAPTER 7 CONCENTRATION AND MOLARITY

How are chemicals in solutions measured?

When a solute is dissolved in a solvent the final solution is a homogeneous mixture. Terms such as *dilute* and *concentrated* are often used to describe the proportion of solute to solvent. Chemists have developed various quantitative methods to determine the amount of solute in a given volume of solution.

1 Concentration of solutions

» Students conduct practical investigations to determine the concentrations of solutions and investigate the different ways in which concentrations are measured.
» Students manipulate variables and solve problems to calculate concentration, mass or volume using $c = n/V$ (molarity formula).

Solution concentration

→ The concentration of a solution is a measure of the amount of solute that is dissolved in a fixed volume of solution. Solutions can be described as concentrated or dilute. A concentrated solution can be diluted by adding more solvent.

Example:

100 mL of a concentrated NaCl solution may contain 30 g of NaCl. If more water is now added to obtain a solution that has a total volume of 10 000 mL, then the resulting solution is said to be **dilute** as it contains 30 g of salt in a much larger volume of solution. Mathematically:

Concentrated solution: concentration = 30 g/100 mL
                                     = 0.30 g/mL

Diluted solution: concentration = 30 g/10 000 mL
                                = 0.0030 g/mL

dilute: a solution containing a larger volume of water so that its concentration has been reduced

Molarity

→ One of the more useful measures of solution concentration is the **molarity** of a solution.

$$\text{Molarity} = \frac{\text{moles solute}}{\text{litres solution}}$$

molarity: the concentration of a solution expressed as the number of moles of solute per litre of solution

→ The molarity of a solution can be calculated using the following key formula.

Key formula

$$c = n/V$$

where c = concentration or molarity (mol/L or mol.L^{-1})
        n = moles of solute (mol)
        V = volume of solution (L)

→ Figure 7.1 shows hydrochloric acid solutions with decreasing molarities. 11 mol/L HCl is concentrated hydrochloric acid. The 1 mol/L and 0.1 mol/L solutions are created by diluting the concentrated acid with water.

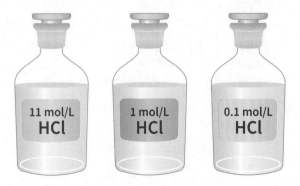

Figure 7.1 Solutions of hydrochloric acid of different molarities

EXAMPLE 1

Calculate the molarity of a solution that contains 0.25 mol of magnesium sulfate in 5000 mL of solution.

Answer:

$n = 0.25$ mol

$V = \dfrac{5000}{1000} = 5.0$ L

Recall the formula for molarity

$c = n/V = \dfrac{0.25}{5.0} = 0.050$ mol/L

EXAMPLE 2

Calculate the mass of glucose ($C_6H_{12}O_6$) that is needed to prepare 2.0 L of a 0.20 mol/L solution.

Answer:

1 Calculate the molar mass (M) of glucose.

$M = 6(12.01) + 12(1.008) + 6(16.0)$
$\quad = 180.156$ g/mol

2 Calculate the number of moles of glucose required using $c = n/V$.

Calculate the number of moles of glucose using the molarity formula

$c = 0.20$ mol/L

$V = 2.0$ L

$n = c.V = (0.20)(2.0) = 0.40$ mol

3 Calculate the mass of glucose using $n = m/M$.

$n = 0.40$ mol

$M = 180.156$ g/mol

$m = n.M = (0.40)(180.156) = 72$ g (2 s.f.)

EXAMPLE 3

All the iodide ions in a 10 mL solution of potassium iodide were precipitated by the addition of excess silver nitrate. The silver iodide formed was collected, washed, dried and weighed, and found to have a mass of 0.2125 g. Calculate the molarity of potassium iodide in the original solution.

Answer:

Calculate the number of moles of silver iodide

1 Write the balanced equation for the precipitation reaction.

$KI(aq) + AgNO_3(aq) \rightarrow AgI(s) + KNO_3(aq)$

2 Calculate the molar mass of silver iodide.

$M(AgI) = 107.9 + 126.9 = 234.8$ g/mol

3 Calculate the number of moles of silver iodide formed using $n = m/M$

$n(AgI) = \dfrac{0.2125}{234.8} = 9.050 \times 10^{-4}$ mol

4 Interpret the balanced equation in terms of moles.

1 mole of KI forms 1 mole of AgI

$n(KI) = n(AgI) = 9.050 \times 10^{-4}$ mol

5 Calculate the concentration of the KI solution using $c = n/V$

$c(KI) = n/V = \dfrac{9.050 \times 10^{-4}}{10 \times 10^{-3}} = 0.0905$ mol/L

→ KEY QUESTIONS

1 A student is supplied with 500 mL of a 4.0 mol/L KOH solution. How many moles of potassium hydroxide are present in the solution?

2 Calculate the molarity of 250 mL solution which contains 0.20 moles of glucose.

3 Determine the volume of a 0.12 mol/L solution that contains 3.0×10^{-2} moles of sodium chloride.

Answers ⊃ p. 78

Alternative concentration units

→ Other concentration units are commonly used in chemistry and in industry. They are often more convenient than using molarity as a unit as the concentration can be quickly calculated on a weight or volume basis.

Percent by volume (%v/v)

→ Alcoholic drinks and various liquid medications often list the concentration of a liquid component as a percentage by volume (%v/v).

Key formulas

$$c = \dfrac{\text{volume of liquid solute}}{\text{volume of solution}} \times 100$$

$$c = \dfrac{V(\text{solute})}{V(\text{solution})} \times 100$$

EXAMPLE 4

Calculate the volume of ethanol in 1500 mL of wine with an ethanol content of 12%v/v.

Answer:

$c = 12$%v/v

$V(\text{wine}) = 1500$ mL

Recall the definition of %v/v

$12 = \dfrac{V(\text{ethanol})}{1500} \times 100$

$V(\text{ethanol}) = 1500 \times \dfrac{12}{100}$
$\qquad\qquad = 180$ mL

Percent by weight (%w/w)

→ Solid mixtures or pastes (e.g. toothpaste) may express the concentration of a component as a percentage by weight (%w/w). This measure of concentration or percentage composition can be used even if the mixture is not a solution.

Key formulas

$$c = \frac{\text{mass of component}}{\text{mass of mixture}} \times 100$$

$$c = \frac{m(\text{component})}{m(\text{mixture})} \times 100$$

EXAMPLE 5

Calculate the concentration of carbon in a sample of steel if 2.80 tonnes of steel contained 58.0 kilograms of carbon.

Answer:

$m(\text{carbon}) = 58.0 \text{ kg}$

$m(\text{steel}) = 2.80 \text{ t}$
$\quad\quad\quad\quad = 2800 \text{ kg}$

Recall the definition of %w/w

$c = \frac{m(\text{carbon})}{m(\text{steel})} \times 100$

$c = \frac{58.0}{2800} \times 100$
$\quad = 2.07 \text{ \%w/w}$

Parts per million (ppm)

→ When the concentration of a component in a solution or mixture is very low then the unit of parts per million (ppm) is useful. The concentration of atmospheric and water pollutants can be reported this way. Parts per million can be expressed on a weight/weight, volume/volume or weight/volume basis.

Key formulas

weight/weight basis: $c = \frac{\text{mg(solute)}}{\text{kg(mixture)}}$

volume/volume basis: $c = \frac{\text{mL(solute)}}{\text{kL(mixture)}}$

weight/volume basis: $c = \frac{\text{mg(solute)}}{\text{L(water)}}$

EXAMPLE 6

Calculate the concentration of the specified solute in each example:

a 100 g of dried prawns contained 0.60 mg of mercury. Calculate the mercury concentration in parts per million.

b 20 L of high altitude dried air was analysed and found to contain 4.2 microlitres (μL) of ozone at the same temperature and pressure. Calculate the ozone concentration in parts per million.

c 200 L of creek water contained 1.10 g of cadmium ions. Calculate the concentration of cadmium in the water in parts per million.

Answer:

a $m(\text{Hg}) = 0.60 \text{ mg}$

$m(\text{prawn}) = 100 \text{ g}$
$\quad\quad\quad\quad\quad = \frac{100}{1000}$
$\quad\quad\quad\quad\quad = 0.10 \text{ kg}$

$c = \frac{0.60}{0.10} = 6.0 \text{ ppm}$

Recall the alternative definitions of 'parts per million'

b $V(\text{ozone}) = 4.2 \text{ }\mu\text{L}$
$\quad\quad\quad\quad\quad = \frac{4.2}{1000}$
$\quad\quad\quad\quad\quad = 0.0042 \text{ mL}$

$V(\text{air}) = 20 \text{ L}$
$\quad\quad\quad\quad = \frac{20}{1000}$
$\quad\quad\quad\quad = 0.020 \text{ kL}$

$c = \frac{0.0042}{0.020}$
$\quad = 0.21 \text{ ppm}$

c $m(\text{Cd}^{2+}) = 1.10 \text{ g}$
$\quad\quad\quad\quad\quad = 1100 \text{ mg}$

$V(\text{water}) = 200 \text{ L}$

$c(\text{Cd}^{2+}) = \frac{1100}{200}$
$\quad\quad\quad\quad = 5.50 \text{ ppm}$

→ KEY QUESTIONS

4 25 g of zinc and 70 g of copper are mixed and melted to form a homogeneous mixture. The mixture was cooled to form solid brass. Calculate the percentage by weight of zinc in the brass.

5 15 L of polluted water contained 45 mg of mercury ions. Determine the concentration of mercury in parts per million.

Answers ⊃ p. 78

2 Standard solutions and dilutions

» Students conduct an investigation to make a standard solution and perform a dilution.
» Students manipulate variables and solve problems to calculate concentration, mass or volume using dilutions (*number of moles before dilution = number of moles of sample after dilution*).

Standard solutions

→ A standard solution will either be a primary standard or a secondary standard.

→ A primary standard solution is one that has been prepared from highly stable, pure solids of known composition. They must be readily soluble. In the school laboratory, anhydrous sodium carbonate is a common standard base. Sodium hydroxide is unsuitable as a primary standard as its crystals absorb water from the atmosphere during the weighing process. Hydrochloric acid is not a primary standard as it is made by dissolving hydrogen chloride gas in water. Weighing a gas is not a simple procedure.

→ A secondary standard solution is one that has had its concentration previously established by reaction with the primary standard. For example, the concentration of a hydrochloric acid solution can be determined by a volumetric experiment with a standard sodium carbonate solution.

standard solution: a solution of accurately known concentration

primary standard: a pure solid of known composition which is used to prepare a standard solution

secondary standard: a solution whose concentration has been determined by titration with a primary standard or other standardised solution

FIRSTHAND INVESTIGATION 1

Preparation of a primary standard solution

» Students conduct an investigation to make a standard solution.

Aim

to prepare a 0.0500 mol/L standard sodium carbonate solution

Method

1 Dry the anhydrous sodium carbonate in a drying oven and then in a desiccator.

2 Calculate the mass of Na_2CO_3 required to prepare 500 mL of a 0.0500 mol/L solution.

$$\begin{aligned} m(Na_2CO_3) &= nM \\ &= cVM \\ &= (0.0500)(0.500)(105.99) \\ &= 2.65 \text{ g} \end{aligned}$$

3 Weigh 2.65 g of anhydrous sodium carbonate accurately into a small, clean and dry beaker using an electronic balance (Figure 7.2).

4 Clean a 500 mL volumetric flask thoroughly with water and then rinse with distilled water.

5 Dissolve the solid in a little distilled water and quantitatively transfer the solution to the volumetric flask. Repeatedly rinse the beaker with water from a wash bottle and add all rinses to the volumetric flask. Add water to the engraved mark on the flask so that the bottom of the meniscus is on the line. Stopper and mix thoroughly. Label the flask with the name and concentration of the solution.

anhydrous: a crystalline substance containing no water

volumetric flask: a glass flask used to accurately prepare a standard solution

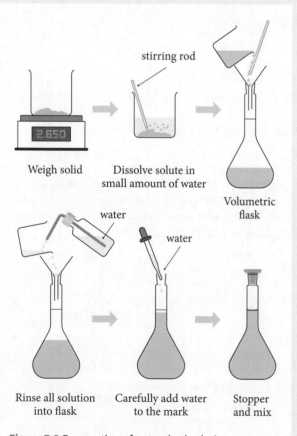

Weigh solid   Dissolve solute in small amount of water

stirring rod

Volumetric flask

water   water

Rinse all solution into flask   Carefully add water to the mark   Stopper and mix

Figure 7.2 Preparation of a standard solution

6 5.00 g of potassium chloride is placed in a beaker and water was added until the total volume is 200 mL. Determine the molarity of the resulting solution.

7 4.50 g of barium chloride is dissolved in water and the total volume of the solution is adjusted to 150 mL. Calculate the molarity of the chloride ions in the solution.

Answers ⊃ p. 78

Dilution calculations

→ When a solution is diluted the number of moles of solute (n) does not change. Only the total solution volume changes. As $n = c.V$ (from the molarity formula), then the value of ($c.V$) is a constant when diluting solutions.

$$c.V = \text{constant}$$

→ This expression can be more usefully written as the following formula.

Key formula

$$c_1 V_1 = c_2 V_2$$

where the subscripts 1 and 2 represent the concentrated and dilute solutions

EXAMPLE 7

Calculate the final molarity of a sulfuric acid solution which is prepared by diluting 250 mL of a 5.0 mol/L solution with sufficient water to make 1.0 L.

Answer:

$c_1 = 5.0$ mol/L
$V_1 = 250$ mL $= 0.250$ L
$V_2 = 1.0$ L

Ensure that units of volume are the same

$$c_1 V_1 = c_2 V_2$$
$$(5.0)(0.250) = c_2(1.0)$$
$$c_2 = 1.25 \text{ mol/L} = 1.3 \text{ mol/L (2 s.f.)}$$

FIRSTHAND INVESTIGATION 2

Diluting a standard solution

» Students conduct an investigation to perform a dilution.

Aim

to accurately dilute a 0.0500 mol/L sodium carbonate solution by a factor of ten

Method

1 Clean a 25 mL pipette with small volumes of the 0.0500 mol/L sodium carbonate solution. Discard the washings (Figure 7.3).

2 Fill the pipette with the sodium carbonate solution so the base of the meniscus is on the line.

3 Transfer the 25.00 mL of the Na_2CO_3 solution into a clean 250 mL volumetric flask.

4 Allow the tip of the burette to drain for 10 seconds against the inside wall of the volumetric flask.

5 Add distilled water to the volumetric flask until the base of the meniscus is on the engraved line.

6 Stopper the volumetric flask and mix the contents.

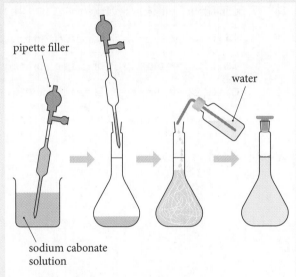

pipette filler

water

sodium cabonate solution

Figure 7.3 Accurately diluting a solution

Calculation

The new diluted concentration can be calculated:

$$c_1 V_1 = c_2 V_2$$
$$(0.0500)(0.02500) = c_2(0.2500)$$
$$c_2 = 0.00500 \text{ mol/L}$$

→ KEY QUESTIONS

8 Explain why sodium hydroxide crystals are not suitable to accurately prepare a standard solution.

9 50 mL of 0.15 mol/L copper (II) sulfate solution is mixed with 400 mL of water. Calculate the final molarity of the solution.

Answers ⊃ p. 78

CHAPTER SYLLABUS CHECKLIST

Are you able to answer these questions from the syllabus for this chapter? Tick each question as you go through the checklist if you are able to answer it. If you cannot answer a question, turn to the relevant page in the study guide to find the answer. For NESA key word meanings, go to www.educationstandards.nsw.edu.au and search 'key words'.

	FOR A COMPLETE UNDERSTANDING OF THIS TOPIC:	PAGE NO.	✓
1	Can I define the terms *solute*, *solvent* and *solution*?	71	
2	Can I explain the difference between a concentrated and dilute solution?	71	
3	Can I define the term *molarity*?	71	
4	Can I state the formula to calculate the molarity of a solution?	71–72	
5	Can I recall alternative concentration units used in chemistry?	72–73	
6	Can I define the term *standard solution*?	74	
7	Can I distinguish between primary standard solutions and secondary standard solutions?	74	
8	Can I describe the steps in preparing a primary standard solution?	74–75	
9	Can I describe the steps in accurately diluting a standard solution?	75	
10	Can I recall the formula to calculate the concentration of a diluted solution?	75	

Objective-response questions
(1 mark each)

1 A bottle of nitric acid (HNO_3) is labelled: 4.0 mol/L.

   Select the correct statement about this solution.

   A 1 litre of the nitric acid solution contains 4 grams of solute.

   B 4 litres of the nitric acid solution contains 1 mole of solute.

   C 1 litre of the solution contains 252 grams of solute.

   D 1 litre of the solution contains 63 grams of solute.

2 Calculate the number of moles of potassium nitrate in 25.00 mL of a 0.020 mol/L solution.

   A 0.020 moles

   B 0.500 moles

   C 0.0008 moles

   D 0.00050 moles

3 Calculate the molarity of the solution formed by dissolving 10 g of sodium bromide in sufficient water to make 200 mL of solution.

   A 0.49 mol/L

   B 50 mol/L

   C 0.050 mol/L

   D 0.00049 mol/L

4 Calculate the molarity of the diluted solution formed when 25 mL of 0.40 mol/L HCl is diluted with 75 mL of water.

   A 0.10 mol/L

   B 0.20 mol/L

   C 0.13 mol/L

   D 1.20 mol/L

5 100 mL of 10 mol/L hydrochloric acid is added to water and the final volume adjusted to 2.5 L. Calculate the molarity of the diluted hydrochloric acid.

   A 0.40 mol/L

   B 40.0 mol/L

   C 0.040 mol/L

   D 4.0 mol/L

Extended-response questions

6 Calculate the volume to which 30.0 mL of a standardised 0.500 mol/L sulfuric acid solution must be diluted so that the new concentration is 0.100 mol/L.
   (2 marks)

7 Calculate the volume of water that is required to produce a 0.10 mol/L sulfuric acid solution from 5.0 mL of concentrated (18.0 mol/L) sulfuric acid.   (2 marks)

8 Element (E) forms a bromide with the formula EBr_2.

   20.0 g of EBr_2 is dissolved in water and the volume adjusted to 500 mL. The molarity of this solution was 0.200 mol/L. Calculate the molar mass of element (E).
   (3 marks)

9 Calculate the volume of 0.20 mol/L barium chloride solution that needs to be added to 200 mL of 0.15 mol/L sodium sulfate solution to completely precipitate all the sulfate ions.   (4 marks)

10 100 mL of 0.100 mol/L sodium chloride is mixed with 100 mL of 0.100 mol/L silver nitrate. Calculate the mass of silver chloride precipitate that will form.   (5 marks)

ANSWERS

KEY QUESTIONS

Key questions ⊃ p. 72

1 $n(KOH) = cV = (4.0)(0.500) = 2.0$ mol

2 $c(glucose) = n/V = \dfrac{0.20}{0.250} = 0.80$ mol/L

3 $V(NaCl) = n/c = \dfrac{3\times10^{-2}}{0.12} = 0.25$ L

Key questions ⊃ p. 73

4 $c(Zn) = \dfrac{25}{25+70} \times 100 = 26$ %w/w

5 $c(Hg^{2+}) = \dfrac{45}{15} = 3.0$ mg/L = 3.0 ppm

Key questions ⊃ p. 75

6 $M(KCl) = 39.10 + 35.45 = 74.55$ g/mol

$n(KCl) = m/M = \dfrac{5.00}{74.55} = 0.06707$ mol

$c = n/V = \dfrac{0.06707}{0.200} = 0.335$ mol/L

7 $M(BaCl_2) = 137.3 + (2 \times 35.45)$
$= 208.2$ g/mol

$n(BaCl_2) = m/M = \dfrac{4.50}{208.2} = 0.0216$ mol

$n(Cl^-) = 2n(BaCl_2) = 0.0432$ mol

$c(Cl^-) = n/V = \dfrac{0.0432}{0.150} = 0.288$ mol/L

8 NaOH absorbs water from the atmosphere so its mass changes during the weighing.

9 $c_1V_1 = c_2V_2$

$(0.15)(0.050) = c_2(0.450)$
$c_2 = 0.0167$ mol/L

YEAR 11 EXAM-TYPE QUESTIONS

Objective-response questions

1 C. The molar mass of nitric acid is 63 g/mol; thus 4 moles weigh 252 g.

A is incorrect as 4.0 mol is not equivalent to 4 g. B is incorrect as 4.0 mol/L means 1 L of the solution contains 4.0 moles of solute. D is incorrect as 63 g is only 1 mole.

2 D. $n(KNO_3) = cV = (0.020)(0.025) = 0.00050$ mol

A is incorrect as 0.020 mole is present in 1 L, not 25 mL. B is incorrect as conversion of mL to L has been inverted. C is wrong as an incorrect multiplication has been performed.

3 A. $M(NaBr) = 102.9$ g/mol; $n = m/M = \dfrac{10}{102.9} = 0.0972$ mol;

$c(NaBr) = n/V = \dfrac{0.0972}{0.200} = 0.49$ mol/L

B is incorrect as the mass has not been converted to moles. C is incorrect as mass rather than moles has been used. D is incorrect as mL has not been converted to litres.

4 A. $c_2 = c_1V_1/V_2 = \dfrac{(0.40)(25)}{100} = 0.10$ mol/L

B, C and D are wrong as incorrect substitutions have been performed.

5 A. $c_1V_1 = c_2V_2$; $(10)(0.1) = c_2(2.5)$; $c_2 = 0.40$ mol/L HCl

B, C and D are wrong as incorrect substitutions have been performed or mL has not been converted to litres.

Extended-response questions

6 EM In this question students need to write the formula and then show substitution into the formula. When the volume V_1 is given in mL then V_2 is in mL. V_2 is the final volume and consequently $V_2 - V_1$ is the volume of water that needs to be added, so the final volume is V_2.

$c_1V_1 = c_2V_2$
$(0.500)(30.0) = (0.100)V_2$ ✓
$V_2 = 150$ mL

Dilute the solution until the total volume is 150 mL. ✓

7 EM In this question students need to use the dilution formula and 1 mark is awarded for a correct substitution. In this case $V_2 - V_1$ is the answer for 1 mark.

$c_1V_1 = c_2V_2$
$(18.0)(5.0) = (0.10)V_2$
$V_2 = 900$ mL ✓

Thus the volume of water that needs to be added is $900 - 5 = 895$ mL. ✓

8 EM In this question students need to understand that an algebraic expression has to be written as the molar mass of E(x) is not known. Thus the number of moles of the bromide is written in terms of x. A mark is awarded for this expression. The molar concentration formula can then be used to solve for x.

Let the molar mass of element E = x.

$M(EBr_2) = x + 2(79.9) = x + 159.8$ g/mol

$n(EBr_2) = m/M = \dfrac{20.0}{x+159.8}$ mol ✓

$c = n/V$

$0.20 = \dfrac{n}{0.500}$

$= \dfrac{20.0}{(x+159.8)(0.500)}$ ✓

Solve for x:

$x = 40.2$

The molar mass of E is 40.2 g/mol. ✓

9 EM In this question students need to understand that a balanced equation worth 1 mark is essential to obtain the correct stoichiometry. The number of moles of sodium sulfate must be calculated using the molarity formula. The stoichiometry can then be used to determine the moles of barium chloride required.

$BaCl_2(aq) + Na_2SO_4(aq) \rightarrow BaSO_4(s) + 2NaCl(aq)$ ✓

Calculate the number of moles of sodium sulfate used.

$n = cV = (0.15)(0.200)$
$= 0.0300$ mol ✓

From the balanced equation, for complete precipitation of barium sulfate, 1 mole of barium chloride is needed to react with each mole of sodium sulfate. As 0.0300 moles of sodium sulfate is used, then 0.0300 mol of barium chloride must be added. ✓

Calculate the volume of the barium chloride solution.

$V(BaCl_2) = n/c = \dfrac{0.0300}{0.20} = 0.15$ L (2 s.f.) ✓

10 **EM** In this question students need to understand that a balanced equation worth 1 mark is essential to obtain the correct stoichiometry. The number of moles of silver nitrate and sodium chloride must be calculated using the molarity formula. This shows that there is no limiting reagent in this case. Thus the mass of AgCl is determined by the stoichiometry.

$AgNO_3(aq) + NaCl(aq) \rightarrow AgCl(s) + NaNO_3(aq)$ ✓

Calculate the number of moles of silver nitrate and sodium chloride used.

$n(AgNO_3) = cV = (0.100)(0.100) = 0.0100$ mol

$n(NaCl) = cV = (0.100)(0.100) = 0.0100$ mol ✓

Thus, the reactants are added in a 1 : 1 mole ratio as is required by the balanced equation for complete reaction.

From the balanced equation, 1 mole of silver chloride is formed from 1 mole of silver nitrate. Thus the number of moles of silver chloride formed in this experiment is 0.0100 mol. ✓

Calculate the molar mass of AgCl.

$M(AgCl) = 107.9 + 35.45$
$= 143.35$ g/mol ✓

Calculate the mass of silver chloride precipitate formed.

$m(AgCl) = nM = (0.0100)(143.35)$
$= 1.43$ g ✓

CHAPTER 8
THE GAS LAWS

MODULE 2 INTRODUCTION TO QUANTITATIVE CHEMISTRY

INQUIRY QUESTION:

How does the Ideal gas law relate to all other gas laws?

The particles in gases are far apart and moving randomly. The attractive forces between gaseous particles is quite small compared with particles in solids and gases. The gaseous particles can collide with each other as well as the sides of their container. Gases fill their container. Gases are fluids as they can be poured from one container into another. In the 18th and 19th centuries chemists investigated gases and established various gas laws.

1 Gas laws

» Students conduct investigations and solve problems to determine the relationship between the Ideal gas law and Gay-Lussac's law (temperature), Boyle's law, Charles' law and Avogadro's law.

Gay-Lussac's law

➜ The French chemist Joseph Gay-Lussac (1778–1850) experimented with gases and determined the volume ratio in which they combined. Gay-Lussac soon discovered that gases always combine in simple whole-number volume ratios.

Example:

hydrogen gas + chlorine gas → hydrogen chloride gas

   100 mL +   100 mL →   200 mL

Volume ratio:

hydrogen : chlorine : hydrogen chloride = 1 : 1 : 2

➜ His work led to the formulation of Gay-Lussac's law of combining gas volumes.

Gay-Lussac's law: the volumes of gases involved in a chemical reaction can be expressed as a ratio of simple, whole numbers (at constant temperature/pressure)

EXAMPLE 1

When 200 mL of hydrogen and 200 mL of oxygen were mixed and reacted at elevated temperatures, 300 mL of gaseous product was formed. Excess oxygen and water vapour were detected in the final mixture. After removal of the water vapour the volume of excess oxygen was found to be 100 mL. Show that this data is consistent with Gay-Lussac's law of combing gas volumes.

Determine the volume of oxygen that reacted

Answer:

The final volume of gaseous product (300 mL) is composed of 100 mL of excess oxygen and 200 mL of water vapour.

hydrogen(200 mL) + oxygen(200 mL)
   → water vapour (200 mL) + excess oxygen(100 mL)

Subtract the volume of the unreacted oxygen (100 mL) from the initial volume of oxygen (200 mL) to find the volume of reacting oxygen.

hydrogen(200 mL) + oxygen(100 mL)
          → water vapour(200 mL)

Volume ratio:

hydrogen : oxygen : water vapour = 200 : 100 : 200
                  = 2 : 1 : 2

This is a simple whole-number ratio, which is in accordance with Gay-Lussac's law.

FIRSTHAND INVESTIGATION

Reacting gases

» Students conduct investigations and solve problems to determine the relationship between the ideal gas law and Gay-Lussac's law (temperature).

Aim

to measure the volumes of oxygen required to react with a fixed volume of nitrogen monoxide gas

Background

Nitrogen monoxide gas reacts with oxygen gas to form brown nitrogen dioxide gas. The product is water soluble.

Method

1   A 100 mL sample of nitrogen monoxide gas was placed in a gas syringe. A rubber hose was attached to the end of the syringe.

2   A measuring cylinder was filled with water and inverted in a trough of water.

3   The NO gas was injected into the inverted cylinder through the hose. The gas was collected by displacement of the water.

4   In a series of experiments various volumes of oxygen gas were injected into the NO gas and allowed to react. Once the product (NO_2) had dissolved in the water the volume of unreacted (excess) oxygen gas was measured using the scale on the measuring cylinder (Figure 8.1).

Apparatus

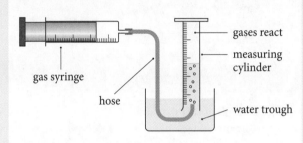

Figure 8.1 Measuring volumes of reacting gases

Sample results

Volume O_2 injected (mL)	100	90	80	70	60	50
Volume excess O_2 (mL)	50	40	30	20	10	0

Questions

1   Use the tabulated data to determine the volume of oxygen which reacts with 100 mL of nitrogen monoxide.

2   Explain how a chemist could prove that the remaining gas in the cylinder was oxygen and not nitrogen monoxide.

3   Explain why the experiment was performed six times to determine the reacting gas volumes.

Answers

1   Volume of reacting oxygen = 50 mL (This is obtained by subtracting the excess oxygen volume from the volume injected.)

2   Test the gas with a glowing splint of wood. If it relights and a flame is formed then the gas is oxygen.

3   Repeating an experiment improves reliability.

Boyle's law

➔ Robert Boyle (1627–1691) discovered the relationship between the volume (V) of a gas of given mass and its pressure (P). This relationship is expressed by Boyle's law.

> **Boyle's law:** the pressure of a gas, at constant temperature, is inversely proportional to its volume

Key formula

$$P.V = \text{constant}$$
$$\text{or } P_1V_1 = P_2V_2$$

where P_1 = initial gas pressure
         V_1 = initial gas volume
         P_2 = final gas pressure
         V_2 = final gas volume

➔ In a vessel of gas at a constant temperature, the particles move about randomly and collide with other particles or the walls of the vessel. If the volume of the vessel is now reduced at constant temperature, the gas becomes compressed. The number of collisions on the vessel walls per second increases and thus the pressure of the gas increases (Figure 8.2). This explains Boyle's law.

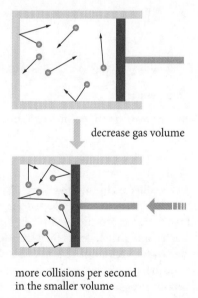

decrease gas volume

more collisions per second in the smaller volume

Figure 8.2 Compressing a gas causes a pressure increase

EXAMPLE 2

Use the tabulated data to determine the final volume of the gas sample at a constant temperature of 27 °C.

Example 2 continued

Initial volume = 1.45 L	Initial pressure = 102 kPa
Final volume = ?	Final pressure = 204 kPa

Answer:

$$P_1V_1 = P_2V_2$$
$$(102)(1.45) = (204)(V_2)$$
$$V_2 = 0.725 \text{ L}$$

> Recall Boyle's law equation

This calculation demonstrates that doubling the gas pressure halves the gas volume.

→ Gases that are insoluble in water may be collected by the downward displacement of water (Figure 8.3). In such cases the total pressure of the collected gas includes the **vapour pressure** of the water at that temperature. For example, at 25 °C the vapour pressure of water is 3 kPa. The vapour pressure of water rises with increasing temperature and at 100 °C the water's vapour pressure equals 100 kPa and the water boils.

> **vapour pressure:** the pressure caused by the presence of a vapour such as water when present in other gases including air

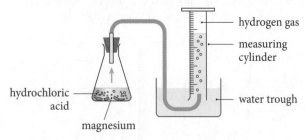

Figure 8.3 Collecting hydrogen by downward displacement of water

EXAMPLE 3

Hydrogen gas is collected by the downward displacement of water at 25 °C. The volume of collected gas was 80 mL and the total gas pressure was 102 kPa. The gas was collected and dried. It was then transferred to a container with a volume of 180 mL. Calculate the pressure of the dried hydrogen gas in the new container at 25 °C. (Vapour pressure of water at 25 °C = 3 kPa.)

Answer:

Initially:

$$P_{total} = P_{hydrogen} + P_{water\ vapour}$$
$$102 = P_{hydrogen} + 3$$
$$P_{hydrogen} = 102 - 3 = 99 \text{ kPa}$$
Thus $P_1 = 99$ kPa
$$V_1 = 80 \text{ mL}$$

> The total pressure is the sum of the gas pressure and the vapour pressure

Finally:

$$V_2 = 180 \text{ mL}$$
$$P_1V_1 = P_2V_2$$
$$(99)(80) = P_2(180)$$
$$P_2 = 44 \text{ kPa}$$

EXAMPLE 4

The following table shows the vapour pressure of methanol as a function of temperature.

Temperature (°C)	Vapour pressure (kPa)
10	7.2
20	13.2
30	21.3
40	34.2
50	55.3
60	82.9
70	122.4

a Plot a graph of this data and draw the line of best fit.

> Ensure a suitable scale is used to ensure the graph occupies at least 80% of the grid area

b The boiling point of a liquid is the temperature where its vapour pressure equals standard air pressure (100 kPa). Use your graph to estimate the boiling point of methanol.

Answer:

a Figure 8.4 represents the vapour pressure of methanol.

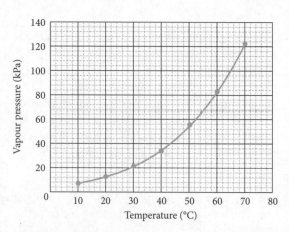

Figure 8.4 Methanol vapour pressure

b From Figure 8.4, the boiling point equals 65 °C at 100 kPa.

1 State Gay-Lussac's law.

2 10 mL of nitrogen gas reacts with 15 mL oxygen gas to form 10 mL of dinitrogen trioxide gas. Show that this data is consistent with Gay-Lussac's law.

3 At 27 °C, a sample of nitrogen gas occupies 750 mL at a pressure of 100 kPa. Calculate the volume of nitrogen at the same temperature if the pressure is increased to 250 kPa.

Answers ⊃ p. 88

Charles' law

→ Jacques Charles (1746–1823) discovered the relationship between the volume (V) of a fixed mass of gas and its temperature (T) at constant pressure. This relationship is expressed by Charles' law.

Charles' law: the volume of a fixed mass of gas is directly proportional to its absolute temperature, at constant pressure

Key formulae

$$V/T = \text{constant}$$
$$\text{or } V_1/T_1 = V_2/T_2$$

where V_1 = initial volume
T_1 = initial absolute temperature
V_2 = final volume
T_2 = final absolute temperature

→ Each division on the absolute temperature scale is the same as each degree on the Celsius scale. The Kelvin absolute temperature scale is named after Lord Kelvin (1724–1907).

→ Figure 8.5 compares the Celsius and Kelvin temperatures scales. Kelvin temperature = Celsius temperature + 273.

absolute temperature scale: a temperature scale based on the lowest possible temperature which has been shown to be –273 °C (or more accurately –273.16 °C) or zero Kelvin

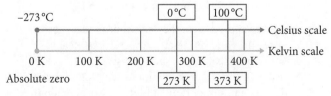

Figure 8.5 Temperature scales

→ In a vessel of a gas at a constant pressure the kinetic energy of the gas particles depends on the temperature of the gas. If the gas is now heated the particles gain kinetic energy. The heated particles move further in the same time than the cooler particles. In order to keep the pressure constant on the vessel walls the vessel has to increase in volume so that the number of collisions of the gas particles per second with the walls is the same. This explains Charles' law (Figure 8.6).

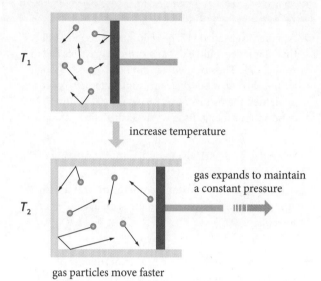

Figure 8.6 Increasing the temperature of a gas

EXAMPLE 5

Determine the temperature that a fixed mass of nitrogen gas at 25 °C must be heated in order to double its volume at a constant pressure.

Answer:

$V_2 = 2V_1$; $T_1 = 25 + 273 = 298$ K; $T_2 = ?$

$V_1/T_1 = V_2/T_2$

$$\frac{V_1}{298} = \frac{2V_1}{T_2}$$

$$\frac{1}{298} = \frac{2}{T_2}$$

> Remember to convert temperature data to absolute temperatures

$T_2 = 2 \times 298$
  $= 596$ K
  $= 323$ °C

4 At 27 °C, a fixed mass of oxygen gas occupies a volume of 900 mL at 100 kPa. Calculate the volume of the gas at 100 kPa if the temperature is raised to 227 °C.

5 50 mL of oxygen gas collected at 30 °C over water had a total gas pressure of 105.2 kPa. Following drying the gas was transferred to a 200 mL container. Calculate the pressure of the dried oxygen gas in the new container. (Vapour pressure of water at 30 °C = 4.2 kPa.)

Answers ➲ p. 88

Avogadro's law

➜ Amadeo Avogadro (1776–1856) proposed in 1811 that elements could exist as atomic aggregates called **molecules**. Thus oxygen gas did not consist of single atoms of oxygen but diatomic molecules (O_2). Avogadro explained the results of Gay-Lussac's gas volume experiments using his law, **Avogadro's law**.

molecule: an electrically neutral entity consisting of more than one atom
Avogadro's law: at constant temperature and pressure, equal volumes of all gases contain equal numbers of molecules

➜ According to Avogadro, the gas experiments of Gay-Lussac made sense if the particles that reacted were molecules rather than atoms, and that a gas with twice the volume of another gas contained twice as many molecules. Thus the reaction between hydrogen and chlorine to form hydrogen chloride gas could be expressed as:

hydrogen + chlorine → hydrogen chloride
volume ratio: 1   :   1   :   2

Assuming that hydrogen and chlorine consisted of diatomic molecules then a balanced symbolic equation could be written in which the coefficients were in the 1 : 1 : 2 molecule ratio:

$$H_2(g) + Cl_2(g) \rightarrow 2HCl(g)$$

EXAMPLE 6

A hydrocarbon (C_aH_b) is vapourised and reacted with oxygen so that it burnt completely to form carbon dioxide and water vapour. The table shows the volumes of gaseous reactants and products at the same temperature and pressure. Use the table data to determine the molecular formula of the hydrocarbon.

Gas/vapour	Volume (L)
C_aH_b	1.5
O_2	13.5
CO_2	9.0
H_2O	9.0

Convert volume data to a simple ratio of whole numbers

Answer:

The volume ratio of gaseous reactants and products is:

$C_aH_b : O_2 : CO_2 : H_2O = 1.5 : 13.5 : 9.0 : 9.0 = 1 : 9 : 6 : 6$

As the volumes are measured at the same temperature and pressure, the molecule ratio is equal to the volume ratio (Avogadro's law).

Molecule ratio:

$C_aH_b : O_2 : CO_2 : H_2O = 1 : 9 : 6 : 6$

These whole numbers represent the coefficients in the balanced equation.

$$C_aH_b(g) + 9O_2(g) \rightarrow 6CO_2(g) + 6H_2O(g)$$

The values of a and b that satisfy the atom balance in this equation are $a = 6$ and $b = 12$.

Thus the molecular formula of the hydrocarbon is C_6H_{12}.

Ideal gas law

➜ In 1834 Emil Clapeyron (1799–1864) developed a particle model of a gas based on the theory that the kinetic energy of gas molecules depended on the temperature of the gas. This model is called the **ideal gas** model. In this model the features of an ideal gas are:
• the gas molecules behave as point particles with zero atomic volume
• the gas molecules have no intermolecular attractions
• the average distance between gas molecules is very great
• the collisions of the gas molecules are elastic (no loss of kinetic energy)
• there is a statistical distribution of velocities of the gas molecules.

ideal gas: a gas composed of molecules of negligible volume that has no intermolecular forces between the molecules. The molecules collide elastically and no energy is lost on collision

➜ Ideal gases obey the ideal gas law, which is expressed mathematically in the following formula.

Key formula

$$PV = nRT$$

where P = gas pressure (kPa)
V = gas volume (L)
n = moles of gas (mol)
R = ideal gas constant (= 8.314 J/K/mol)
T = absolute temperature (K)

➜ Real gases approximate the behaviour of ideal gases at low pressures and moderate temperatures. Real gases deviate from ideal behaviour because:
• real gases have significant molecular volumes and this becomes important at high pressures when the molecules are close together

- real gases experience intermolecular attractions and this becomes significant at low temperatures and high pressures.

→ Noble gases exhibit near-ideal behaviour. The intermolecular forces that exist between gas molecules explains why real gases can be liquefied on compression. Water vapour shows non-ideal behaviour. Water molecules are polar and in the gaseous state they attract each other, particularly at high pressure or low temperatures. At high pressure the molecules are closer together and at low temperatures the molecules have less kinetic energy. As a result the molecules move closer together due to hydrogen bonding and the volume of the water vapour is less than it would be for an ideal gas.

→ Figure 8.7 shows a graph of PV/RT versus temperature for nitrogen gas and carbon dioxide. For an ideal gas the PV/RT ratio for $n = 1$ (1 mole) has a constant value of 1 as pressure increases.

→ However, the value of PV/RT for real gases such as nitrogen and carbon dioxide deviates from 1 as the pressure increases. Intermolecular attractions are dominant when PV/RT is <1, and molecular volume effects are dominant when PV/RT is >1. At normal atmospheric pressure (100 kPa) these real gases approximate ideal gas behaviour.

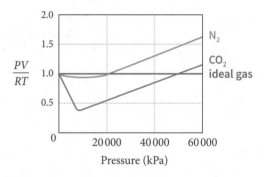

Figure 8.7 Real gases versus ideal gas

→ Boyle's law and Charles' law are consistent with the ideal gas law only when pressures are not too high or when temperatures are not too low compared with the standard pressure (100 kPa) and standard temperature (298 K).

EXAMPLE 7

Calculate the volume of 10.0 g of helium gas at 250 kPa and 25 °C.

Answer:

$n(\text{He}) = m/M = 10.0/4.003 = 2.50$ mol

Calculate the number of moles of helium

$T = 25\,°C = (273 + 25) = 298$ K

$$PV = nRT$$
$$(250)(V) = (2.50)(8.314)(298)$$
$$V = 24.8 \text{ L}$$

EXAMPLE 8

Figure 8.8 compares ammonia gas with an ideal gas. The graph is a plot of PV/RT versus pressure for each gas. The temperature of each gas is constant.

Consider the features of real gases which differ from ideal gases

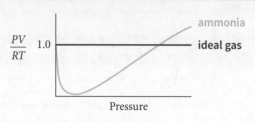

Figure 8.8 PV/RT versus P graph

a An ideal gas obeys the ideal gas equation ($PV = nRT$) at all temperatures and pressures. What is the value of n in this graph?

b Ammonia is a non-ideal gas.

  i Explain what property of ammonia leads to the PV/RT ratio being less than 1 as the pressure increases.

  ii Explain what property of ammonia leads to the PV/RT ratio being greater than 1 at extremely high pressures.

Answer:

a $n = 1$, as the intercept on the vertical axis is 1.

b i The volume of the gas (at constant temperature) is lower than that of an ideal gas as attractive intermolecular forces (hydrogen bonding) cause the gas to become more compressible.

  ii The molecular volumes of the gas molecules become significant at very high pressures and so the gas is less compressible.

→ KEY QUESTIONS

6   20 L of nitrogen and 20 L of hydrogen react at a high temperature and pressure to form a gaseous hydride. After the reaction 16 L of nitrogen, 8 L of hydrogen and 8 L of the gaseous hydride are present. Determine the molecular formula of the gaseous hydride.

7   Use the ideal gas equation to calculate the pressure of 8.006 g of helium in a 5.0 L vessel at 127 °C. (R = universal gas constant = 8.314 J/K/mol)

8   Use the ideal gas equation to calculate the pressure of 4.00 g of argon in a 3.0 L vessel at 25 °C. (R = universal gas constant = 8.314 J/K/mol)

Answers ⊃ p. 88

CHAPTER SYLLABUS CHECKLIST

Are you able to answer these questions from the syllabus for this chapter? Tick each question as you go through the checklist if you are able to answer it. If you cannot answer a question, turn to the relevant page in the study guide to find the answer. For NESA key word meanings, go to www.educationstandards.nsw.edu.au and search 'key words'.

	FOR A COMPLETE UNDERSTANDING OF THIS TOPIC:	PAGE NO.	✓
1	Can I state Gay-Lussac's law (temperature)?	80	
2	Can I solve problems using Gay-Lussac's law (temperature)?	80	
3	Can I state Boyle's law?	81	
4	Can I solve problems using Boyle's law?	82	
5	Can I state Charles' law?	83	
6	Can I solve problems using Charles' law?	83	
7	Can I state Avogadro's law?	84	
8	Can I solve problems using Avogadro's law?	84	
9	Can I state the Ideal gas law?	84	
10	Can I solve problems using the Ideal gas law?	85	
11	Can I explain the differences between real and ideal gases?	85	

Objective-response questions

(1 mark each)

1 10 L of helium gas at 25 °C and 100 kPa is compressed to a volume of 2 L at 25 °C. Calculate the pressure of the compressed gas.

   A 500 kPa **B** 50 kPa **C** 200 kPa **D** 2 kPa

2 20.0 L of neon gas at 0 °C and 100 kPa is heated to a temperature of 25 °C at 100 kPa. Calculate the volume of the gas at 25 °C.

   A 18.3 L **B** 183 L **C** 218 L **D** 21.8 L

3 A sample of argon gas at 20 °C and 150 kPa occupies a volume of 12.0 L. Calculate the number of moles of gas present.

   A 10.8 mol   **B** 1.35 mol
   C 0.739 mol   **D** 0.0926 mol

4 Samples of hydrogen gas and helium gas were placed in separate vessels of the same volume. The vessels had the same pressures and temperatures. Determine the masses of each gas that would satisfy these conditions.

   A 20.16 g hydrogen; 40.03 g helium
   B 10.08 g hydrogen; 40.03 g helium
   C 20.16 g hydrogen; 20.02 g helium
   D 10.08 g hydrogen; 20.02 g helium

5 Identify the graph in Figure 8.9 that correctly shows the relationship between the pressure and volume of a gas according to Boyle's law.

A 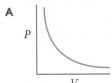   **B**

C 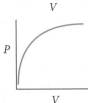   **D**

Figure 8.9 Boyle's law

Short-answer questions

6 Methane (CH_4) burns in oxygen (O_2) to form carbon dioxide gas and water vapour. 40 mL of methane was mixed with 100 mL of oxygen (an excess) at 120°C and 100 kPa pressure. The mixture was ignited and the gases allowed to react. When the system was returned to the original conditions of temperature and pressure, the final mixture had the following composition:

methane (0 mL); oxygen (20 mL); carbon dioxide (40 mL); water vapour (80 mL)

Demonstrate that this data is consistent with Gay-Lussac's law of combining gas volumes. (3 marks)

7 The following data was collected for an experiment in which the volume of a gas was measured as a function of temperature.

Temperature (°C)	0	20	40	60	80
Temperature (K)					
Volume (mL)	22.7	24.4	26.0	27.7	29.3

   a Copy and complete the table by calculating the absolute temperature in Kelvin units. (1 mark)
   b Plot a line graph of volume versus the absolute temperature. (4 marks)
   c Explain whether or not the graph is consistent with Charles' law. (1 mark)

8 A sample of neon gas and a sample of argon gas are placed in different sized containers under different conditions, as shown in the table.

Gas	n (mol)	V (L)	P (kPa)	T (K)
neon	0.044	1.0	100	273
argon	0.040	2.0	?	298

Use *both* sets of data to calculate the gas pressure in the argon container. (3 marks)

9 A molecular gas A_x reacts with chlorine gas to form a gaseous chloride of A, which has the formula ACl_y.

10 mL of the gaseous A_x is mixed with 50 mL of chlorine gas and the reaction was allowed to reach completion. The table summarises the results.

Gas	Initial volume (mL)	Volume after reaction (mL)
A_x	10	0
Cl_2	50	20
ACl_y	0	30

   a Determine the reacting volumes of A_x and Cl_2. (2 marks)
   b Use Gay-Lussac's law and Avogadro's law to determine the:
   i molecular formula of A_x
   ii molecular formula of ACl_y. (4 marks)

10 20 mL of sulfur vapour at 1000 °C reacts with 40 mL of oxygen gas to form 40 mL of sulfur dioxide gas. Determine the number of atoms in the molecule of sulfur in the vapour state at this temperature. (3 marks)

ANSWERS

Key questions ⊃ p. 83

1 The volumes of gases involved in a chemical reaction can be expressed as a ratio of simple, whole numbers (at constant T/P).

2 The volume ratio is:
$N_2 : O_2 : N_2O_3 = 10 : 15 : 10 = 2 : 3 : 2$
This is a simple whole number ratio.

3 $P_1 = 100$ kPa; $V_1 = 750$ mL; $P_2 = 250$ kPa
$$P_1V_1 = P_2V_2$$
$$(100)(750) = (250)(V_2)$$
$$V_2 = 300 \text{ mL}$$

Key questions ⊃ pp. 83–84

4 $V_1 = 900$ mL
$T_1 = 27 + 273 = 300$ K
$T_2 = 227 + 273 = 500$ K
$$V_1/T_1 = V_2/T_2$$
$$\frac{900}{300} = \frac{V_2}{500}$$
$$V_2 = 1500 \text{ mL} = 1.50 \text{ L (3 s.f.)}$$

5 Initially:
$$P_{total} = P_{oxygen} + P_{water\ vapour}$$
$$105.2 = P_{oxygen} + 4.2$$
$$P_{hydrogen} = 105.2 - 4.2 = 101 \text{ kPa}$$

Thus $P_1 = 101$ kPa
$V_1 = 50$ mL

Finally:
$V_2 = 200$ mL
$$P_1V_1 = P_2V_2$$
$$(101)(50) = P_2(200)$$
$$P_2 = 50.75 \text{ kPa} = 51 \text{ kPa (2 s.f.)}$$

Key questions ⊃ p. 85

6 Reacting volume of nitrogen = 20 − 16 = 4 L
Reacting volume of hydrogen = 20 − 8 = 12 L
Volume of hydride formed = 8 L
Volume ratio = 4 : 12 : 8 = 1 : 3 : 2
Molecule ratio = 1 : 3 : 2. These integers are used to create a balanced equation.
Equation:
$$N_2(g) + 3H_2(g) \rightarrow 2(\text{gaseous hydride})$$
Thus formula of hydride = NH_3
$$N_2(g) + 3H_2(g) \rightarrow 2NH_3(g) \text{ (equation is balanced)}$$

7 $n(\text{He}) = m/M = \dfrac{8.006}{4.003} = 2.00$ mol
$P = nRT/V$
$$= \frac{(2.00)(8.314)(127 + 273)}{5.0}$$
$$= 1330 \text{ kPa} = 1.3 \times 10^3 \text{ kPa (2 s.f.)}$$

8 $n(\text{Ar}) = m/M = \dfrac{4.00}{39.95} = 0.100$ mol
$P = nRT/V$
$$= \frac{(0.100)(8.314)(25 + 273)}{3.0}$$
$$= 82.6 \text{ kPa}$$

Objective-response questions

1 **A.** $P_1V_1 = P_2V_2$; $(100)(10) = (P_2)(2)$; $P_2 = \dfrac{100 \times 10}{2} = 500$ kPa

B, **C** and **D** are incorrect calculations. When the gas volume is reduced by a factor of 5 then the pressure rises by a factor of 5.

2 **D.** $T_1 = 273$ K, $T_2 = 298$ K; $V_1/T_1 = V_2/T_2$; $\dfrac{20.0}{273} = \dfrac{V_2}{298}$;
$V_2 = 20.0 \times \dfrac{298}{273} = 21.8$ L

A, **B** and **C** are incorrect. Temperatures must be converted to Kelvin units.

3 **C.** $PV = nRT$; $n = PV/RT$; $T = 20 + 273 = 293$ K;
$$n = \frac{(150)(12.0)}{(8.314)(293)} = 0.739 \text{ mol}$$

A, **B** and **D** are incorrect. Temperatures must be converted to Kelvin units.

4 **A.** $n(H_2) = m/M = \dfrac{20.16}{2.016} = 10$ mol; $n(\text{He}) = \dfrac{40.03}{4.003} = 10$ mol

B, **C** and **D** are incorrect. Hydrogen gas is diatomic and helium is monatomic.

5 **A.** Boyle's law plot is a hyperbola as P is inversely proportional to V.

B is incorrect as the graph is not hyperbolic. **C** and **D** are incorrect as the volume of a gas does not increase as the pressure increases.

Extended-response questions

6 **EM** This question requires students to calculate the volumes of the reactants that combined by subtracting the initial and final volumes. A statement about simple, whole number ratios is required to score full marks.

Volumes of combining gases:
$$CH_4 : O_2 : CO_2 : H_2O = (40 - 0) : (100 - 20) : 40 : 80$$
$$= 40 : 80 : 40 : 80 \checkmark$$
$$= 1 : 2 : 1 : 2 \checkmark$$

This is a simple, whole number ratio as required by Gay-Lussac's law. ✓

7 **EM** This question requires students to understand that Kelvin temperatures are obtained by adding 273 to the Celsius temperature. In drawing a graph marks are awarded for correct axes, scales and units, graph title and plotted data. The line of best fit is linear and passes through the plotted points. The linear graph shows that volume is directly proportional to the absolute temperature.

a

Temperature (°C)	0	20	40	60	80
Temperature (K)	273	293	313	333	353
Volume (mL)	22.7	24.4	26.0	27.7	29.3	✓

b

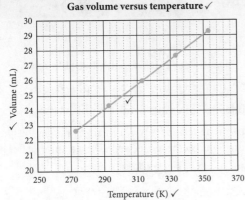

Figure A8.1 Gas volume versus temperature

c The graph is consistent with Charles' law as the gas volume is directly proportional to the absolute temperature. This is shown by the linearity of the graph. ✓

8 **EM** This question needs students to understand that neon and argon gases are almost ideal under these conditions and therefore the PV/nT quotient will be the same for each gas. Equations and substituted data must be shown as well as the final answer and its units.

Use the ideal gas equation: $PV = nRT$

Make R the subject: $R = PV/nT$

R is the same for both gases.

$[PV/nT]_{neon} = [PV/nT]_{argon}$ ✓

$$\frac{(100)(1.0)}{(0.044)(273)} = \frac{(P_{argon})(2.0)}{(0.040)(298)}$$ ✓

$P_{argon} = 49.6$ kPa ✓

9 **EM** This question needs students to understand that reacting volumes are obtained by subtraction of volume data. Students should equate the volume ratios to the mole ratios.

a Reacting volumes: $A_x = 10$ mL ✓ $Cl_2 = 30$ mL ✓

b Volume ratio of reactants and product:

$A_x : Cl_2 : ACl_y = 10 : 30 : 30 = 1 : 3 : 3$

Thus mole ratio = $1 : 3 : 3$ ✓

Equation: $A_x + 3Cl_2 \rightarrow 3ACl_y$

Thus $x = 3$, $y = 2$ ✓

i $A_x = A_3$ ✓

ii $ACl_y = ACl_2$ ✓

10 **EM** This question needs students to understand that the number of atoms in the molecule is an integer (x). The volume ratios determine the mole ratios and therefore the stoichiometry of the equation. The value of x can then be determined from this stoichiometry.

Let S_x be the formula of sulfur vapour.

Volume ratios: $S_x : O_2 : SO_2 = 20 : 40 : 40$

$= 1 : 2 : 2$

$=$ mole ratio ✓

$S_x + 2O_2 \rightarrow 2SO_2$

Thus $x = 2$ ✓

Sulfur vapour = S_2 ✓

CHAPTER 9
CHEMICAL REACTIONS

What are the products of a chemical reaction?

In a chemical reaction, reactants are converted into products. This chapter investigates the indicators of chemical change, a variety of simple chemical reactions, and writing balanced equations for each reaction.

1 Chemical change indicators

» Students investigate a variety of reactions to identify possible indicators of a chemical change.

→ When a chemical change occurs, one or more of the following observations often can be made:
- a new substance is formed (e.g. a gas is evolved or a precipitate forms when solutions are mixed)
- a large change in temperature may occur
- visible light or sound is emitted
- a change in colour occurs
- a new odour is produced.

→ A chemical change is often not reversible. For example, the combustion of petrol to form carbon dioxide and water cannot be reversed. Physical changes such as dissolving salt in water or the condensation of a vapour are easily reversible.

Examples:
- Gas evolution

When a marble chip is added to a tube of dilute hydrochloric acid, the marble dissolves and bubbles of a colourless gas are formed on the marble surface.

$$CaCO_3(s) + 2HCl(aq) \rightarrow CaCl_2(aq) + H_2O(l) + CO_2(g)$$

- Formation of a precipitate

When a colourless solution of lead (II) nitrate is mixed with a colourless solution of potassium iodide, a bright yellow precipitate of lead (II) iodide forms.

$$Pb(NO_3)_2(aq) + 2KI(aq) \rightarrow PbI_2(s) + 2KNO_3(aq)$$

- Large temperature rise

When 2 mol/L solutions of sodium hydroxide and hydrochloric acid are mixed the temperature rises significantly during the neutralisation reaction.

$$NaOH(aq) + HCl(aq) \rightarrow NaCl(aq) + H_2O(l)$$

- Production of visible light

When magnesium is burnt in air or oxygen bright white light is emitted as well as large amounts of heat.

$$2Mg(s) + O_2(g) \rightarrow 2MgO(s)$$

- Production of sound

When a mixture of hydrogen gas and oxygen gas is ignited there is a large 'popping' sound.

$$2H_2(g) + O_2(g) \rightarrow 2H_2O(g)$$

- Colour change occurs

When a purple solution of permanganate ions is mixed with an acidified solution of iron (II) ions the mixture rapidly decolourises.

$$MnO_4^-(aq) + 5Fe^{2+}(aq) + 8H^+(aq) \rightarrow Mn^{2+}(aq) + 4H_2O(l) + 5Fe^{3+}(aq)$$

- A new odour forms

When hydrochloric acid is added to solid sodium sulfide, the mixture fizzes and the gas evolved smells like rotten eggs. As this gas is poisonous the reaction is performed in a fume cupboard.

$$Na_2S(s) + 2HCl(aq) \rightarrow 2NaCl(aq) + H_2S(g)$$

2 Modelling chemical change

» Students use modelling to demonstrate:
- the rearrangement of atoms to form new substances
- the conservation of atoms in a chemical reaction.

→ Ball-and-stick molecular models are very useful in understanding chemical reactions as these models are three-dimensional and the breaking and reforming of chemical bonds can be visualised. Such models cannot show the rate of a reaction or the way in which real molecules collide and new products form.

→ An example of modelling is now described. Students can use these diagrams and their own model kit to simulate the chemical reaction. The rearrangement of atoms during a chemical change is evident when the modelling is performed.

Example:

- Reaction of bromine molecules with cyclohexene molecules (Figure 9.1)

The reaction equation is:

$$C_6H_{10} + Br_2 \rightarrow C_6H_{10}Br_2$$

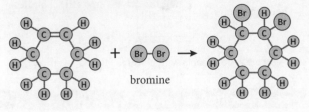

cyclohexene   1,2-dibromocyclohexane

Figure 9.1 Bromine reacts with cyclohexene

→ Figure 9.1 shows that atoms are conserved in the chemical reaction. In this case, 6 carbon atoms, 10 hydrogen atoms and 2 bromine atoms are present in both the reactants and product.

→ Steps in modelling the reaction in Figure 9.1 are:
  - Construct the cyclohexene and bromine molecules using a modelling kit.
  - Check whether all or some of the atoms in cyclohexene are in the same plane
  - Check whether or not the C=C double bond is the same length as the single bonds between carbon atoms.
  - To form the product remove the C=C double bond and replace it by a single bond. Remove the single bond between the bromine atoms and join each bromine atom to the carbon atoms where the double bond had been.

Example:

- Complete combustion of pentane (Figure 9.2)

The reaction equation is:

$$C_5H_{12}(g) + 8O_2(g) \rightarrow 5CO_2(g) + 6H_2O(l)$$

→ It is important when using atomic model kits to model the combustion reaction shown in Figure 9.2 to understand that simple models of reactants and products cannot show the steps in the chemical change. Where the steps are known then computer animation is preferable in observing bond breaking and reforming.

3 Detoxifying poisonous food components

» Students investigate the chemical processes that occur when Aboriginal and Torres Strait Islander peoples detoxify poisonous food items.

→ Over thousands of years Indigenous Australians collected plant foods as part of their diet. However, some of these plant foods contained poisonous compounds that needed to be removed prior to eating.

→ The detoxifying procedures varied somewhat but often included:
  - pounding and grinding the plant fibres followed by soaking and washing in water (often for several days or weeks) to leach out toxins from the fibres
  - roasting in a fire to decompose the toxins
  - fermentation of seed kernels (e.g. from *Macrozamia* cycad fruits) with fungal moulds over several months.

→ Using these different processes Indigenous Australians could remove the toxic components. The steps of the detoxification processes ensure that the toxic compounds are removed from the food prior to consumption. If these toxic compounds are ingested they are chemically converted by gut bacteria into carcinogenic compounds that lead to liver cancer.

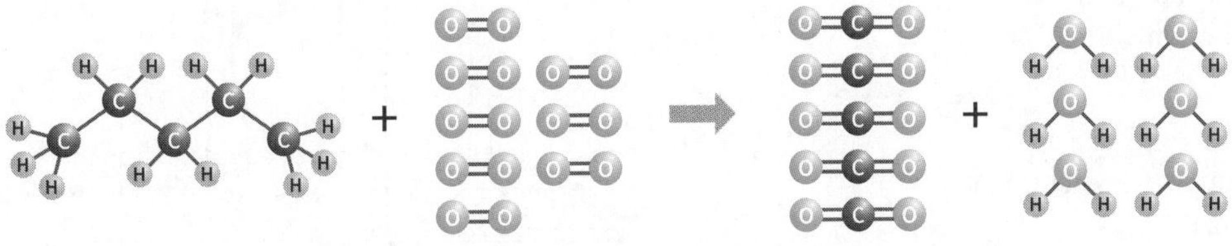

pentane   oxygen   carbon dioxide   water

Figure 9.2 Combustion of pentane

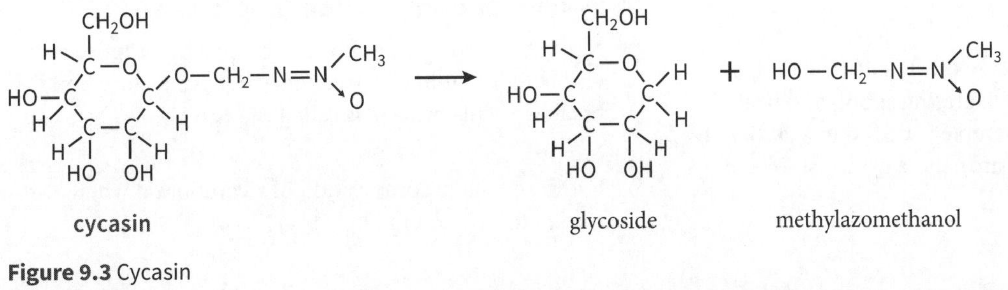

cycasin   glycoside   methylazomethanol

Figure 9.3 Cycasin

→ A toxic molecule called cycasin is found in the fruits of cycad plants. The toxicity of these fruits in humans is due to microbes in the intestine breaking the cycasin into methylazomethanol that is then converted in the liver to a carcinogenic compound. The reaction is shown in Figure 9.3 (previous page).

4 Investigating chemical reactions

» Students conduct investigations to predict and identify the products of a range of reactions; for example, synthesis, decomposition, combustion, precipitation, acid–base reactions and acid–carbonate reactions.
» Students construct balanced equations to represent chemical reactions.

Synthesis reactions

→ Synthesis reactions involve the formation of a new compound from simpler reactants, which may be elements or compounds.

Examples:

- Synthesis of calcium carbonate by the reaction of calcium oxide and carbon dioxide

  $CaO(s) + CO_2(g) \rightarrow CaCO_3(s)$

- Synthesis of iron (III) chloride by the reaction of iron wool in chlorine

  $2Fe(s) + 3Cl_2(g) \rightarrow 2FeCl_3(s)$

→ Figure 9.4 shows this synthesis experiment. The sample of iron wool is placed in a deflagrating spoon and heated in a Bunsen flame. The hot sample is placed in a gas jar of chlorine (in a fume cupboard) and a brown smoke of iron (III) chloride forms.

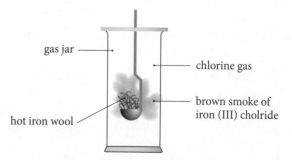

Figure 9.4 Iron reacts with chlorine

Decomposition reactions

→ Compounds can be decomposed into simpler compounds or elements in a number of ways. Energy in the form of heat, light and electricity can be used.

Thermal decomposition

→ Compounds differ in the amount of heat required to decompose them.

→ In a school laboratory, green copper (II) carbonate can be readily thermally decomposed using the heat from a Bunsen burner flame. A sample of copper (II) carbonate is placed in a test tube as shown in Figure 9.5. The solid turns black as copper (II) oxide forms. A positive limewater test confirms that carbon dioxide gas is also formed.

$$CuCO_3(s) \rightarrow CuO(s) + CO_2(g)$$

thermal decomposition (thermolysis): the decomposition of a compound by the application of heat

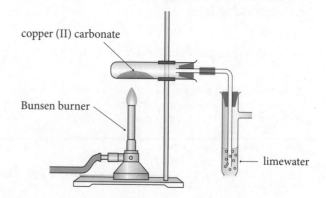

Figure 9.5 Thermal decomposition of copper (II) carbonate

Photolytic decomposition (photolysis)

→ Most chemical compounds are stable when exposed to visible light but higher frequency light can cause bond breakage. This process is called photolysis.

photolysis: the decomposition of a compound when exposed to high energy light

- Some compounds can be decomposed by ultraviolet light.

- Various silver compounds such as silver bromide will darken in sunlight. The rate of reaction increases if UV light is used. The darkening is caused by the formation of silver.

$$2AgBr(s) \rightarrow 2Ag(s) + Br_2(g)$$

- This reaction was used originally in photography where the photographic film was coated with a gelatine emulsion containing silver bromide. Exposure to light darkened the film due to the formation of silver grains.

 FIRSTHAND INVESTIGATION

Effect of light on silver salts

» Students conduct investigations to predict and identify the products of a range of reactions; for example, decomposition.

Aim

to determine the effect of light on silver chloride and silver bromide

Method

1 Prepare precipitates of white silver chloride and cream silver bromide by mixing silver nitrate solution with sodium chloride solution and sodium bromide solution respectively.

2 Filter each mixture to obtain samples of each precipitate on a filter paper.

3 Place the open papers on watch glasses either in the sun or under a UV lamp.

4 Compare the colour changes with a control sample not exposed to light.

Sample results

The silver salts will darken quickly when exposed to light (especially in UV light). The dark grains are due to the formation of silver. The control samples did not darken.

Electrolytic decomposition

- Chemical compounds vary in their thermal stability. The compounds formed by active metals are more thermally stable than compounds formed by less-active metals. In order to decompose very stable compounds, electrical decomposition is performed. This process is called **electrolysis**.

electrolytic decomposition (electrolysis): the decomposition of a compound by the application of an electric current

- Electrical energy is used to decompose chemical compounds or mixtures in various industries. Electrolysis is used to decompose aluminium oxide to form aluminium metal. It is also used to decompose salt water (brine) to produce chlorine, hydrogen and sodium hydroxide.

Example:

- Electrolysis of molten sodium chloride

When sodium chloride is melted and electrolysed at inert platinum electrodes, the sodium ions gain electrons to form sodium metal. The chloride ions lose electrons and form chlorine gas.

Net reaction: $2Na^+(l) + 2Cl^-(l) \rightarrow 2Na(l) + Cl_2(g)$

→ KEY QUESTIONS

4 Sulfur trioxide gas can be synthesised by heating sulfur dioxide gas and oxygen in the presence of a vanadium (V) oxide catalyst. Write a balanced equation for this reaction.

5 Copper (II) carbonate is thermally decomposed. Name the two reaction products.

6 Water is electrolytically decomposed. Identify the products of the reaction and name a standard laboratory test to identify each product.

Answers ⊃ p. 99

Combustion reactions

- **Combustion** is an important chemical process. The burning of fuels such as coal, oil and natural gas provides heat to keep us warm and to power machines. Combustion of fuels requires oxygen. When the oxygen supply is restricted then pollution of the environment can occur due to the release of gases such as carbon monoxide. Figure 9.6 demonstrates the effect of a limited air supply during the combustion of natural gas (mainly methane) using a Bunsen burner. The yellow flame indicates the formation of solid carbon particles.

combustion: the chemical reaction of a substance with an oxidising agent such as oxygen in which a large amount of heat is evolved

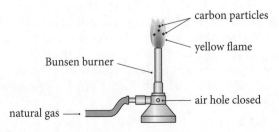

Figure 9.6 Incomplete combustion of natural gas

- Volatile, low-molecular-weight liquid fuels (such as petrol) readily vaporise to produce combustible mixtures with air. Depending on the ratio of fuel vapour to air, the mixture when sparked will burn completely or incompletely in the engine of the car.

- Modern fuel injection systems in cars ensure the optimum fuel–air ratio for maximum power and reduced pollution by carbon monoxide emissions. Catalytic converters in the exhaust system also reduce carbon monoxide emissions by converting the CO to CO_2. Octane (C_8H_{18}) is a major petrol component. The following equations illustrate complete and incomplete combustion:

  - Complete combustion

    $$2C_8H_{18}(l) + 25O_2(g) \rightarrow 16CO_2(g) + 18H_2O(l)$$

  - Incomplete combustion

    $$2C_8H_{18}(l) + 17O_2(g) \rightarrow 16CO(g) + 18H_2O(l)$$

    (CO_2, CO and C are all commonly produced in incomplete combustion reactions of carbon compounds.)

- Elements such as sulfur and phosphorus also undergo combustion when heated in air or oxygen. Sulfur burns in air with a mauve flame. Poisonous sulfur dioxide is formed. Red phosphorus burns with a yellow-white flame in excess oxygen to form a white smoke of tetraphosphorus decaoxide. These reactions are also synthesis reactions.

  $$S_8(s) + 8O_2(g) \rightarrow 8SO_2(g)$$
  $$P_4(s) + 5O_2(g) \rightarrow P_4O_{10}(s)$$

Precipitation reactions

- Precipitation is a chemical reaction in which a solid forms when liquids, solutions or gases are mixed. In the case of aqueous solutions, the formation of a precipitate depends on the solubility of the product in water. If the product is soluble then no precipitate forms and the ions remain dissolved.

- Consider the reaction when colourless silver nitrate solution and colourless sodium chloride solution are mixed. A white precipitate of silver chloride forms as silver chloride is insoluble in the water. The whole formula equation is:

  $$AgNO_3(aq) + NaCl(aq) \rightarrow AgCl(s) + NaNO_3(aq)$$

- This equation shows that aqueous sodium nitrate is present in the final mixture. In fact the ions are not associated but are moving independently in the solution, just like the ions in the original electrolyte solutions that were mixed. This can be shown by the next equation (an ionic equation) where all dissolved salts are shown as independent ions. Only the silver chloride precipitate is shown as associated ions.

  $$Ag^+(aq) + NO_3^-(aq) + Na^+(aq) + Cl^-(aq)$$
  $$\rightarrow AgCl(s) + Na^+(aq) + NO_3^-(aq)$$

- It can be seen that sodium ions and nitrate ions appear on both sides of the equation. They can be cancelled out, as they are only **spectator ions**. They are not involved in the precipitation process. These ions only associate again if the filtered solution is crystallised. After cancelling the spectator ions we are left with the **net ionic equation** for precipitation.

  $$Ag^+(aq) + Cl^-(aq) \rightarrow AgCl(s)$$

spectator ions: ions that do not participate in the chemical reaction

net ionic equation: the ionic equation in which spectator ions are not shown

EXAMPLE 1

When colourless lead (II) nitrate and potassium iodide solutions are mixed, a bright yellow precipitate of lead (II) iodide forms. Write a word equation, whole formula balanced equation and a net ionic equation for this precipitation reaction.

Answer:

In the net ionic equation cancel out like terms

- The word equation is:

  lead (II) nitrate (aq) + potassium iodide (aq)
  $\rightarrow$ lead (II) iodide (s) + potassium nitrate (aq)

- The whole formula balanced equation is constructed by inserting the correct formula for each compound. The equation is then balanced as usual by inserting coefficients:

  $$Pb(NO_3)_2(aq) + 2KI(aq) \rightarrow PbI_2(s) + 2KNO_3(aq)$$

- Convert this equation into ionic form and then cancel the spectator ions:

  $$Pb^{2+}(aq) + 2NO_3^-(aq) + 2K^+(aq) + 2I^-(aq)$$
  $$\rightarrow PbI_2(s) + 2K^+(aq) + 2NO_3^-(aq)$$

- Net ionic equation:

  $$Pb^{2+}(aq) + 2I^-(aq) \rightarrow PbI_2(s)$$

Figure 9.7 illustrates the process.

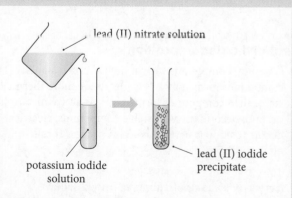

lead (II) nitrate solution

potassium iodide solution

lead (II) iodide precipitate

Figure 9.7 Precipitation of lead (II) iodide

7 Solutions of iron (III) ions are typically yellow or orange-brown in colour. When drops of sodium hydroxide solution are added to the solution of iron (III) ions, a brown precipitate of iron (III) hydroxide forms. Classify this reaction and write a net ionic equation for the reaction.

8 20.0 mL of potassium iodide solution was mixed with excess silver nitrate solution. The mass of the silver iodide formed was 3.459 g. Calculate the molar concentration of potassium iodide in the original solution.

9 A solution of sodium bromide and a solution of silver nitrate are mixed together in a beaker. Classify the type of reaction occurring and write a balanced symbolic equation for the reaction.

10 Write a balanced equation for the complete combustion of butane (C_4H_{10}) in air.

Answers ➲ p. 99

Acid–base reactions

➜ Solutions such as hydrochloric acid (HCl), nitric acid (HNO_3) and sulfuric acid (H_2SO_4) are acidic because they contain hydrogen ions ($H^+(aq)$), which can turn blue litmus indicator red. Solutions such as sodium hydroxide and potassium hydroxide are basic (or alkaline) because they contain hydroxide ions ($OH^-(aq)$), which turn red litmus blue.

• When an acidic solution and a basic solution are mixed a neutralisation reaction occurs and the properties of the acid and base are destroyed as new products form. The products of such acid–base reactions are water and an ionic compound called a 'salt'. The water is formed when the hydrogen ions and hydroxide ions react together.

neutralisation: the reaction between acids and bases in which the final mixture contains an ionic compound called a salt

EXAMPLE 2

Sulfuric acid (H_2SO_4) solution is slowly added to potassium hydroxide solution containing litmus. The indicator suddenly turns from blue to purple when neutralisation is complete. Write a word equation, whole formula balanced equation and a net ionic equation for this acid–base reaction.

> Recall the formula of sulfuric acid

Answer:

• Word equation

   sulfuric acid(aq) + potassium hydroxide(aq)
       → potassium sulfate(aq) + water(l)

• Whole formula equation

   $H_2SO_4(aq) + 2KOH(aq) \rightarrow K_2SO_4(aq) + 2H_2O(l)$

• Ionic equation

   $2H^+(aq) + SO_4{}^{2-}(aq) + 2K^+(aq) + 2OH^-(aq)$
       $\rightarrow 2K^+(aq) + SO_4{}^{2-}(aq) + 2H_2O(l)$

   Cancel out the spectator ions (K^+, $SO_4{}^{2-}$) and simplify the remainder by dividing by 2.

• Net ionic equation

   $H^+(aq) + OH^-(aq) \rightarrow H_2O(l)$

Figure 9.8 illustrates this process.

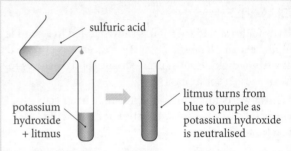

Figure 9.8 Potassium hydroxide solution neutralised with sulfuric acid

➜ Acids also neutralise and dissolve solid samples of basic metal oxides and metal hydroxides. For example, black copper (II) oxide is neutralised by sulfuric acid to form a blue solution of copper (II) sulfate:

   $CuO(s) + H_2SO_4(aq) \rightarrow CuSO_4(aq) + H_2O(l)$

Acid–carbonate reactions

➜ The reaction of a carbonate compound and an acid is also an example of an acid–base reaction.

➜ Some carbonate compounds (such as sodium carbonate) are water soluble and so the acid–base reaction occurs between ions in solution. Some carbonates (e.g. nickel carbonate) are insoluble and in these cases the hydrogen ions of the acid attack the solid at its surface

EXAMPLE 3

Nitric acid (HNO_3) solution is slowly added to a sodium carbonate solution. An effervescence is observed as carbon dioxide gas is evolved. Write a word equation, whole formula-balanced equation and a net ionic equation for this acid–base reaction.

> Recall the formula of nitric acid

Answer:

- Word equation

  nitric acid(aq) + sodium carbonate(aq)
  $\rightarrow$ sodium nitrate(aq) + water(l) + carbon dioxide(g)

- Whole formula equation

  $2HNO_3(aq) + Na_2CO_3(aq)$
  $$\rightarrow 2NaNO_3(aq) + H_2O(l) + CO_2(g)$$

- Ionic equation

  $2H^+(aq) + 2NO_3^-(aq) + 2Na^+(aq) + CO_3^{2-}(aq)$
  $$\rightarrow 2Na^+(aq) + 2NO_3^-(aq) + H_2O(l) + CO_2(g)$$

  Cancel out the spectator ions (Na^+, NO_3^-) to obtain the net ionic equation.

- Net ionic equation

  $2H^+(aq) + CO_3^{2-}(aq) \rightarrow H_2O(l) + CO_2(g)$

EXAMPLE 4

Hydrochloric acid solution is slowly added to a sample of nickel carbonate solid. An effervescence is observed as carbon dioxide gas is evolved. The solid dissolves to form a green solution.

Write a word equation, whole formula balanced equation and a net ionic equation for this acid–base reaction.

Answer:

> Check the valency of nickel ions and carbonate ions

- Word equation

  hydrochloric acid(aq) + nickel carbonate(s)
  $\rightarrow$ nickel chloride(aq) + water(l) + carbon dioxide(g)

- Whole formula equation
  $2HCl(aq) + NiCO_3(s) \rightarrow NiCl_2(aq) + H_2O(l) + CO_2(g)$

- Ionic equation

  $2H^+(aq) + 2Cl^-(aq) + NiCO_3(s)$
  $$\rightarrow Ni^{2+}(aq) + 2Cl^-(aq) + H_2O(l) + CO_2(g)$$

  Cancel out the spectator ion (Cl^-) to obtain the net ionic equation.

- Net ionic equation

  $2H^+(aq) + NiCO_3(s) \rightarrow Ni^{2+}(aq) + H_2O(l) + CO_2(g)$

Figure 9.9 illustrates this process.

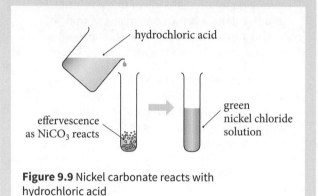

Figure 9.9 Nickel carbonate reacts with hydrochloric acid

→ **KEY QUESTIONS**

11 Classify the reaction type shown in the following word equation:

  magnesium oxide(s) + sulfuric acid(aq)
  $$\rightarrow \text{magnesium sulfate(aq)} + \text{water(l)}$$

12 Identify the salt formed when a $Ca(OH)_2$ solution is neutralised by H_2SO_4 solution.

13 Zinc carbonate reacts with hydrobromic acid (HBr). Write the formula of the salt that forms.

14 When sulfuric acid is added to a sample of blue-green copper(II) carbonate the solid effervesces and dissolves in the acid to form a clear, blue solution of copper(II) sulfate. Write a word equation and a balanced symbolic equation for this reaction.

Answers ⊃ p. 99

Are you able to answer these questions from the syllabus for this chapter? Tick each question as you go through the checklist if you are able to answer it. If you cannot answer a question, turn to the relevant page in the study guide to find the answer. For NESA key word meanings, go to www.educationstandards.nsw.edu.au and search 'key words'.

	FOR A COMPLETE UNDERSTANDING OF THIS TOPIC:	PAGE NO.	✓
1	Can I identify the indicators of chemical change?	90	
2	Can I use model kits to demonstrate the rearrangement and conservation of atoms in a chemical reaction?	90–91	
3	Can I recall that Indigenous Australians use chemical and physical processes to detoxify poisonous food items?	91	
4	Can I recall examples and write equations for synthesis reactions?	92	
5	Can I recall examples and write equations for decomposition reactions?	92–93	
6	Can I recall examples and write equations for combustion reactions?	93	
7	Can I recall examples and write equations for precipitation reactions?	94	
8	Can I recall examples and write equations for acid–base reactions?	95	
9	Can I recall examples and write equations for acid–carbonate reactions?	95	

Objective-response questions
(1 mark each)

1 Identify the synthesis reaction.

   A $2HgO(s) \rightarrow 2Hg(l) + O_2(g)$

   B $2H_2(g) + O_2(g) \rightarrow 2H_2O(l)$

   C $CH_4(g) + 2O_2(g) \rightarrow CO_2(g) + 2H_2O(l)$

   D $BaCO_3(s) \rightarrow BaO(s) + CO_2(g)$

2 Identify the decomposition reaction.

   A $2AgCl(s) \rightarrow 2Ag(s) + Cl_2(g)$

   B $BaO(s) + CO_2(g) \rightarrow BaCO_3(s)$

   C $Na_2S(s) + 2HBr(aq) \rightarrow 2NaBr(aq) + H_2S(g)$

   D $AgNO_3(aq) + KI(aq) \rightarrow AgI(s) + KNO_3(aq)$

3 Identify the combustion reaction.

   A $2Na^+(l) + 2Cl^-(l) \rightarrow 2Na(l) + Cl_2(g)$

   B $2Ag(s) + Br_2(g) \rightarrow 2AgBr(s)$

   C $C_6H_{10}(l) + Br_2(g) \rightarrow C_6H_{10}Br_2(s)$

   D $2C_6H_{14}(l) + 19O_2(g) \rightarrow 12CO_2(g) + 14H_2O(l)$

4 Identify the balanced equation.

   A $C_9H_{18}(l) + 18O_2(g) \rightarrow 9CO(g) + 9H_2O(l)$

   B $C_7H_{14}(l) + 14O_2(g) \rightarrow 7CO(g) + 7H_2O(l)$

   C $2C_9H_{18}(l) + 18O_2(g) \rightarrow 18CO(g) + 18H_2O(l)$

   D $2C_7H_{14}(l) + 21O_2(g) \rightarrow 14CO_2(g) + 14H_2O(l)$

5 Identify an indicator of a chemical change.

   A White salt dissolves in water.

   B Vapour condenses into a liquid when cooled.

   C A foul-smelling gaseous substance is formed when a solid reacts with an acid.

   D Blue solution crystallises when the water evaporates.

Extended-response questions

6 Propane (C_3H_8) gas undergoes complete combustion in excess oxygen to form carbon dioxide and water. Write a balanced equation for this reaction. (1 mark)

7 Magnesium carbonate is converted into magnesium oxide when the white solid is heated over a Bunsen flame.

   a Identify the type of chemical reaction described. (1 mark)

   b A colourless gas is also evolved. Identify a simple test that indicates this gas is carbon dioxide. (1 mark)

   c Write a word equation and a balanced symbolic equation for this reaction. (2 marks)

8 Figure 9.10 shows an experiment in which a student passes an electric current (via platinum electrodes) into water containing a small amount of sulfuric acid to make the water conductive. Colourless gases collect by the downward displacement of water.

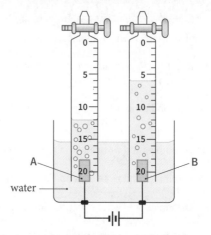

Figure 9.10 Electrolysis of water

   a Identify the type of reaction occurring. (1 mark)

   b Use the diagram to determine the volume of gas released from the negative electrode (A) to the volume of gas from the positive electrode (B). (1 mark)

   c The gases were tested. The gas evolved from (A) gave a positive 'pop' test. The gas evolved from (B) relights a glowing splint of wood. Identify these gases. (2 marks)

   d Write a balanced symbolic equation for this reaction. Relate your equation to the volumes of gases released in part (b). (2 marks)

9 5.0 g of ethane gas (C_2H_6) is mixed with 30.0 g of oxygen and the mixture ignited with a spark.

   a Write a balanced equation for the combustion reaction assuming the ethane burns completely. (1 mark)

   b Calculate the number of moles of ethane and oxygen used and determine if there is sufficient oxygen for complete combustion to occur. (4 marks)

10 2.00 g of sodium metal is heated until it forms a pool of molten sodium. The hot sodium is placed in a gas jar of yellow-green chlorine gas. A white smoke of very fine crystals is seen to form.

   a Identify the compound formed. (1 mark)

   b Classify the type of reaction occurring. (1 mark)

   c Write the balanced equation for the reaction. (1 mark)

   d Calculate the mass of chlorine required to completely react with the sodium. (3 marks)

ANSWERS

KEY QUESTIONS

Key questions ⊃ p. 92

1 Loud explosion; water droplets condense on the inside wall of the gas jar.

2 $2CO + O_2 \rightarrow 2CO_2$
Reactant atoms:
2 carbon atoms + 4 oxygen atoms
Product atoms:
2 carbon atoms + 4 oxygen atoms

3 Chemical change as the toxins are decomposed.

Key questions ⊃ p. 93

4 $2SO_2(g) + O_2(g) \rightarrow 2SO_3(g)$

5 Copper (II) oxide; carbon dioxide

6 Hydrogen and oxygen; 'pop' test for hydrogen; 'relighting a glowing wooden splint' test for oxygen

Key questions ⊃ p. 95

7 Precipitation reaction:
$Fe^{3+}(aq) + 3OH^-(aq) \rightarrow Fe(OH)_3(s)$

8 $AgNO_3(aq) + KI(aq) \rightarrow AgI(s) + KNO_3(aq)$
$M(AgI) = 107.9 + 126.9$
$= 234.8$ g/mol
$n(AgI) = m/M = \dfrac{3.459}{234.8}$
$= 1.473 \times 10^{-2}$ mol
$n(KI) = n(AgI)$ (1 : 1 stoichiometry)
$n(KI) = 1.473 \times 10^{-2}$ mol/L
$c(KI) = n/V = \dfrac{1.473 \times 10^{-2}}{0.0200}$
$= 0.737$ mol/L

9 Precipitation reaction
$NaBr(aq) + AgNO_3(aq)$
$\rightarrow AgBr(s) + NaNO_3(aq)$

10 $2C_4H_{10}(g) + 13O_2(g)$
$\rightarrow 8CO_2(g) + 10H_2O(l)$

Key questions ⊃ p. 96

11 acid–base reaction

12 calcium sulfate $(CaSO_4)$

13 $ZnBr_2$

14 copper (II) carbonate (s)
+ sulfuric acid (aq)
$\rightarrow$ copper (II) sulfate (aq) + water (l)
+ carbon dioxide (g)
$CuCO_3(s) + H_2SO_4(aq)$
$\rightarrow CuSO_4(aq) + H_2O(l) + CO_2(g)$

YEAR 11 EXAM-TYPE QUESTIONS

Objective-response questions

1 **B.** Compounds are formed in a synthesis reaction. **A** and **D** are incorrect as they are decomposition reactions. **C** is incorrect as it is a combustion reaction.

2 **A.** Compound is broken down into elements. **B** is incorrect as this is a synthesis reaction. **C** is incorrect as this is an acid–base reaction. **D** is incorrect as it is a precipitation reaction.

3 **D.** Reaction with oxygen. **A**, **B** and **C** are incorrect as oxygen is not a reactant.

4 **D.** Atoms of each element are conserved. **A** and **B** are incorrect as oxygen atoms do not balance. **C** is incorrect as the equation needs to be divided by 2.

5 **C.** A new substance has formed. **A**, **B** and **D** are incorrect as these are all physical changes.

Extended-response questions

6 **EM** In this question students should recall that the atoms should be balanced in the order C : H : O.
$C_3H_8(g) + 7O_2(g) \rightarrow 3CO_2(g) + 8H_2O(l)$ ✓

7 **EM** This question needs students to understand that the magnesium carbonate is converted to simpler compounds and so it is a thermal decomposition reaction. Students need to recall the limewater test and state what is observed to score this mark. Check the atom balance in the equation.
a Thermal decomposition ✓
b Limewater test. The limewater turns white if the gas is carbon dioxide. ✓
c magnesium carbonate (s)
$\rightarrow$ magnesium oxide (s)
+ carbon dioxide(g) ✓
$MgCO_3(s) \rightarrow MgO(s) + CO_2(g)$ ✓

8 **EM** This question needs students to recall the following facts: electrical energy is used to decompose the water; read the volumes from the bottom of the meniscus; recall the standard tests for hydrogen and oxygen; and state the balanced equation shows a 2 : 1 mole ratio, consistent with Gay-Lussac's law.
a electrolysis ✓
b $V(A) = 12$ mL, $V(B) = 6$ mL;
ratio A : B = 12 : 6 = 2 : 1 ✓
c A = hydrogen ✓
B = oxygen ✓

d $2H_2O(l) \rightarrow 2H_2(g) + O_2(g)$ ✓
The mole ratio of H_2 to O_2 is 2 : 1. This is consistent with the gas volume ratio of 12 : 6 = 2 : 1 ✓

9 **EM** This is a question in which students should balance the atoms in the order C : H : O. A fraction is initially used to balance the oxygen. This fraction is then removed by multiplying the whole equation by 2. The correctly balanced equation will ensure the stoichiometry is correct for (b).
a $2C_2H_6(g) + 7O_2(g)$
$\rightarrow 4CO_2(g) + 6H_2O(l)$ ✓

b $n(C_2H_6) = m/M$
$= \dfrac{5.0}{2 \times 12.01 + 6 \times 1.008}$
$= \dfrac{5.0}{30.068}$
$= 0.17$ mol ✓
$n(O_2) = \dfrac{30.0}{2 \times 16.00} = 0.94$ mol ✓
Mole ratio:
$O_2 : C_2H_6 = 0.94 : 0.17 = 5.5 : 1$
Stoichiometry for balanced equation:
$O_2 : C_2H_6 = 7 : 2 = 3.5 : 1$ ✓
Therefore complete combustion can be achieved as there is sufficient oxygen present. ✓

10 **EM** This question needs students to determine that this is a synthesis reaction leading to the formation of an ionic compound. Students need to recall that chlorine gas is diatomic as well as the valencies of sodium and chlorine. A correctly balanced equation ensures the required stoichiometry for the calculation in (d).
a sodium chloride ✓
b synthesis reaction ✓
c $2Na(l) + Cl_2(g) \rightarrow 2NaCl(s)$ ✓
d $n(Na) = \dfrac{2.00}{22.99} = 0.08699$ mol ✓
Stoichiometry: Na : Cl_2 = 2 : 1
$n(Cl_2) = \dfrac{1}{2} \times n(Na)$
$= \dfrac{0.08699}{2}$
$= 0.04350$ mol ✓
$m(Cl_2) = n.M$
$= (0.04350)(2 \times 35.45)$
$= 3.08$ g ✓

How is the reactivity of various metals predicted?

Metals in Groups 1 and 2 of the periodic table are very reactive. The transition metals vary considerably in their reactivity. This chapter investigates the activity of a selection of common metals and uses various properties to explain differences in reactivity.

1 Metal reactivity

» Students conduct practical investigations to compare the reactivity of a variety of metals in water, dilute acid, oxygen and other metal ions in solution.
» Students construct a metal activity series using the data obtained from practical investigations and compare this series with that obtained from standard secondary-sourced information.

➔ Metals vary significantly in their reactivity with other substances. This can be shown by conducting some simple laboratory experiments in which a selection of metals is reacted with water, dilute acids, oxygen and solutions of other metal ions.

Reaction with water

➔ Water is slow to react with metals other than the very active metals, such as sodium and potassium. Magnesium will react slowly with hot water; zinc and iron will react with steam at high temperatures; and less reactive metals, such as lead and copper, show no reaction with water.

Summary: Reaction with water (H$_2$O)	
Very rapid reaction	K, Na, Ca
Slow reaction	Mg
Reacts only in steam	Al, Zn, Fe
No reaction	Sn, Pb, Cu, Ag, Au
Generally	**reactive metal + water → metal oxide (or hydroxide) + hydrogen**

Examples:

$$2Na(s) + 2H_2O(l) \rightarrow 2NaOH(aq) + H_2(g)$$
$$Zn(s) + H_2O(g) \rightarrow ZnO(s) + H_2(g)$$

Reaction with dilute acid

➔ Dilute hydrochloric acid and dilute sulfuric acid react with some metals and hydrogen gas is released. This type of reaction is a displacement reaction where hydrogen is displaced from solution as hydrogen gas and the metal forms metal ions in solution. For the reactive metals, bubbles of colourless hydrogen gas are observed on the metal's surface. The reactive metals will dissolve in the excess acid to form solutions of the metal salt. (Note that nitric acid should not be used because NO gas is released.)

Summary: Reaction with dilute hydrochloric acid (HCl)	
Very rapid reaction	K, Na
Rapid reaction	Ca, Mg
Slow to very slow reaction	Al, Zn, Fe, Sn, Pb
No reaction	Cu, Ag, Au
Generally	**reactive metal + acid → salt + hydrogen**

Examples:

$$Ca(s) + 2HCl(aq) \rightarrow CaCl_2(aq) + H_2(g)$$
$$Fe(s) + H_2SO_4(aq) \rightarrow FeSO_4(aq) + H_2(g)$$

➔ **KEY QUESTIONS**

1 Identify the gas produced when active metals are added to either dilute hydrochloric acid or dilute sulfuric acid.

2 Identify the formula of the salt formed when aluminium dissolves in warm, dilute sulfuric acid.

3 Apart from lead, name three metals that do not react with dilute hydrochloric acid.

Answers ➔ p. 114

Reaction with oxygen

→ Very active metals, such as sodium, burn readily in air or pure oxygen to produce peroxides (e.g. Na_2O_2) of the active metal. Reactive metals, such as magnesium and aluminium, burn brightly (especially when powdered) to form metallic oxides. Less active metals may only become coated in an oxide film on heating whereas noble metals, such as gold, do not react.

Summary: Reaction with air (O_2)	
Very rapid reaction	K, Na, Ca
Rapid to moderate reaction	Mg, Al, Zn, Fe
Slow reaction on surface	Sn, Pb, Cu
No reaction	Ag, Au
Generally	**reactive metal + oxygen → metallic oxide**

Examples:

$$2Mg(s) + O_2(g) \rightarrow 2MgO(s)$$
$$2Cu(s) + O_2(g) \rightarrow 2CuO(s)$$

Reaction with solutions of metal ions

→ Displacement reactions occur when a more reactive metal displaces another less reactive metal from a solution of its ions. The more reactive metal loses electrons and forms an ion whereas the ions of the less reactive metal gain electrons to form the metal.

Summary: Reaction with a solution of copper (II) sulfate (Cu^{2+})	
Very rapid reaction	K, Na
Rapid reaction	Ca, Mg, Al*
Moderate to slow reaction	Zn, Fe, Sn, Pb
No reaction	Cu, Ag, Au
Generally	**reactive metal (A) + metal ion (B) → metal ion (A) + metal (B)**

* The oxide coating on the aluminium has to be removed before a rapid reaction occurs; this is achieved by adding NaCl to the copper ion solution.

Examples:

$$Mg(s) + Cu^{2+}(aq) \rightarrow Mg^{2+}(aq) + Cu(s)$$
$$Sn(s) + Cu^{2+}(aq) \rightarrow Sn^{2+}(aq) + Cu(s)$$

→ The previous examples reveal that metals varied considerably in their reactivity when placed in different chemical environments. The following experiment investigates the relative reactivity of four metals.

 FIRSTHAND INVESTIGATION 1

Reactivity of metals

» Students conduct investigations to compare the reactivity of a variety of metals in water, dilute acid, oxygen and other metal ions in solution.

Aim

to investigate the reaction of selected metals (magnesium, zinc, iron, copper) with dilute acid, water, air (oxygen) and a solution of copper (II) ions and to use the collected data to rank these metals in order of reactivity

Method

- Dilute hydrochloric acid
  1 Place the four metals in separate test tubes and add 3 mL of dilute (1 mol/L) hydrochloric acid to each tube.
  2 Observe the metals over a 15- to 20-minute period.
  3 Repeat the experiment with the reaction tubes placed in a water bath at 80 °C.
- Water
  Repeat the method for dilute hydrochloric acid but substitute water for the acid.
- Air (oxygen)
  1 Heat strips of each metal in a hot, blue Bunsen flame using tongs to support the metal. (In the case of magnesium, avoid looking at the bright light produced on combustion.)
  2 Allow the hot metal to cool on a fibre mat and examine the surface of each sample.
- Copper (II) sulfate solution
  1 Place the four metals in separate test tubes and add 3 mL of 0.1 mol/L copper (II) sulfate to each tube.
  2 Observe the metals over a 15- to 20-minute period.

Sample results

Results are summarised in Figure 10.1 and Table 10.1.

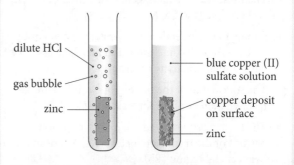

Figure 10.1 Zinc reacts with dilute hydrochloric acid and copper (II) sulfate solution

Table 10.1 Summary of reactivity results

Test	Magnesium	Zinc	Iron	Copper
dilute hydrochloric acid	rapid effervescence; metal dissolves quickly	bubbles slowly form on surface; rate increases on heating	some bubbles of gas form on surface	no observable change
water	bubbles of gas form on metal surface in hot water	no observable change	no observable change	no observable change
heating in air (oxygen)	burns brightly with a white flame; white ash remains	surface quickly becomes covered in a white coating	surface slowly becomes covered in a dark coating	surface slowly becomes covered in a dark coating
copper (II) sulfate solution	red-brown coating rapidly forms; magnesium dissolves; blue solution fades	red-brown coating slowly forms; some fading of blue colour	red-brown coating very slowly forms on the iron	no observable change

Conclusion

The result in Table 10.1 shows that magnesium is the most reactive of the four metals tested and that copper is the least reactive.

The decreasing order of reactivity is Mg, Zn, Fe, Cu.

The activity series of metals

→ The activity series of metals was established by comparing the reactivity of metals with many different chemicals. The order of activity for the common metals has been established by extensive experimentation. These results are shown in Table 10.2.

Table 10.2 Activity series

Most active										Least active
K	Na	Ca	Mg	Al	Zn	Fe	Sn	Pb	Cu	Ag	Au

→ The following generalisations can be made about metal reactivity and the periodic table:

- The most reactive metals are found in Group 1 (K, Na) and group 2 (Ba, Ca, Mg).

- Group 13 (Al) metals are less reactive than Groups 1 and 2, although some transition metals (e.g. Fe, Zn) have similar reactivity to Group 13.

- The soft metals at the bottom of Group 14 are less reactive than Group 13 metals.

- The least reactive metals are found in the lower periods of the transition metals (Ag, Au) or in the soft, heavy metal region (Pb).

These characteristics are illustrated in Figure 10.2.

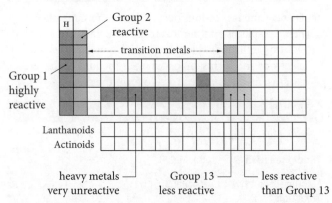

Figure 10.2 Comparison of metal reactivity in the periodic table

→ **KEY QUESTIONS**

4 Identify three metals that react with steam but not cold water.

5 Compare the reactions of magnesium and zinc in dilute hydrochloric acid.

6 The following list of metals are jumbled. Place the metals in order of decreasing activity:

Al, Sn, K, Ag, Pb

Answers ⊃ p. 114

2 Trends in properties of metals in the periodic table

» Students analyse patterns in metal activity on the periodic table and explain why they correlate with, for example, ionisation energy, atomic radius and electronegativity.

➜ Table 10.3 shows the trends in some selected physical properties of metals across a period and down a periodic table group.

There is some correlation between metal activity and first ionisation energy, as shown in Table 10.4.

Table 10.4 suggests that very active metals, such as potassium and sodium, have very low first ionisation energies whereas noble metals, such as gold, have high first ionisation energies. There is no simple relationship, however, between first ionisation and energy and activity series order. For example, zinc has a high first ionisation energy but is a moderately active metal.

➜ Within Periodic Groups 1 and 2, however, the reactivity of metals increases down a group as the first ionisation energy decreases. Thus, in Group 2, the order of decreasing reactivity and increasing first ionisation energy of the metals is (units = kJ/mol):

Ba(509) > Sr(556) > Ca(596) > Mg(744) > Be(906)

➜ However, in the transition metal subgroups, the least active metal is at the bottom of the group but there is not always a simple trend in the first ionisation energies.

Table 10.5 compares the electronegativities of metals in the activity series. In general the more active the metal, the lower its electronegativity. Copper and silver are exceptions to this correlation.

➜ Figure 10.3 shows the trends in atomic radii in Group 2 and across Period 2.

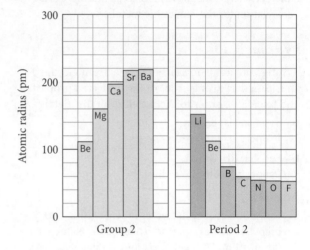

Figure 10.3 Atomic radius trends for Group 2 and Period 2

Table 10.3 Trends in physical properties in the main group

Property	Trend across a period (L to R)	Trend down a group	Explanation
Ionisation energy	increases	decreases	Ionisation energy refers to the energy required to remove an electron in the valence shell to form an ion. The ionisation energy increases across a period as the valence shell is closer to an increasingly positive nucleus. Thus more energy is required to remove a valence electron. Down a group it requires less energy to remove an electron as the valence shell is much further away from the nucleus.
Atomic radius	decreases	increases	The radius decreases across a period as the valence shell is attracted closer to the nucleus which has an increasing positive charge due to the presence of more protons. Down a group there are more protons but there are also more electron shells. The increasing number of shells dominates and the radius increases down a group.
Electronegativity	increases	decreases	Electronegativity is the tendency of an atom to attract electrons. Metals have low electronegativities compared with non-metals. Active metals have very low electronegativities.

Table 10.4 First ionisation energies for metals of the activity series

K	Na	Ca	Mg	Al	Zn	Fe	Sn	Pb	Cu	Ag	Au
425	502	596	744	584	913	766	715	722	752	737	896

Energies measured in kJ/mol.

Table 10.5 Electronegativities for metals of the activity series

K	Na	Ca	Mg	Al	Zn	Fe	Sn	Pb	Cu	Ag	Au
0.82	0.93	1.00	1.31	1.61	1.65	1.83	1.96	2.33	1.90	1.93	2.54

➔ The increase in atomic radius of metals in Group 2 is consistent with the increasing reactivity down the group. The further the valence shell is from the nucleus, the more reactive the metal. In Period 2, lithium is a more active metal than beryllium as lithium's valence electron is further from the nucleus than beryllium's valence electrons.

Table 10.6 shows the atomic radii of metals in the activity series. There is a correlation between and atomic radius and activity for metals from K to Fe but there is no correlation for the remaining metals.

EXAMPLE 1

Arrange the following sets of metals from Groups 1, 2 and 13 in decreasing order of the indicated property and relate this order to the activities of the metals.

a   Set: Na, Ca, K, Mg
    Property = Ionisation energy

b   Set: Ca, Rb, Ba, Al
    Property = Atomic radius

Recall the trends in properties across a period and down a group

Answer:

a   Ionisation energy decreases down a group and increases across a period. Thus for the elements of Groups 1 and 2 the highest ionisation energies are at the top of the group and further to the right in a period.

The decreasing order is Mg, Ca, Na, K.

This order is consistent with the measured activities of these metals.

b   Atomic radius increases down a group and decreases across a period. Thus for the elements of Groups 1, 2 and 13 the greatest atomic radii are at the bottom of the group and further to the left in a period.

The decreasing order is Rb, Ba, Ca, Al.

This order is consistent with the measured activities of these metals.

➔ KEY QUESTIONS

7   Explain why atomic radius decreases across a period.
....

8   Identify the element with the highest electronegativity.
....

9   Describe the trend in first ionisation energy for metals in Group 1.

Answers ➲ p. 114

3 Oxidation–reduction reactions

» Students apply the definitions of oxidation and reduction in terms of electron transfer and oxidation numbers to a range of reduction and oxidation (redox) reactions.
» Students construct relevant half-equations and balanced overall equations to represent a range of redox reactions.

Redox reactions

➔ An oxidation–reduction (or redox) reaction occurs between two substances when electrons are lost by one reacting species (reductant) and gained by another (oxidant).

➔ Chemical species (such as metals) that cause reduction are called reductants.

➔ Chemical species (such as metal ions) that cause oxidation are called oxidants.

➔ **Reduction** is the process in which electrons are gained.

➔ **Oxidation** is the process in which electrons are lost.

reduction: the gain of electrons
oxidation: the loss of electrons

➔ The reductant reduces the oxidant. The reductant transfers electrons to the oxidant, which causes the reduction of the oxidant.

➔ The oxidant oxidises the reductant. The oxidant removes electrons from the reductant, which causes oxidation of the reductant (Figure 10.4).

➔ The loss and gain of electrons can be shown in ion–electron half-equations.

Electron loss:

$$Zn(s) \rightarrow Zn^{2+}(aq) + 2e^-$$

Electron gain:

$$Br_2(aq) + 2e^- \rightarrow 2Br^-(aq)$$

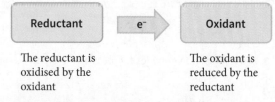

The reductant is oxidised by the oxidant

The oxidant is reduced by the reductant

Figure 10.4 Oxidation and reduction

Table 10.6 Atomic radius for metals of the activity series (radius measured in pm)

K	Na	Ca	Mg	Al	Zn	Fe	Sn	Pb	Cu	Ag	Au
227	186	197	160	143	133	124	151	175	128	144	144

Oxidation states

→ The term **oxidation state** (or **oxidation number**) can be used to explain oxidation and reduction.

> **oxidation state (oxidation number):** a number given to an atom to indicate (theoretically) the number of electrons it has lost or gained (i.e. its state of oxidation)

→ The oxidation state of a chemical species is a measure of its degree of oxidation. The processes of oxidation and reduction occur together.

→ The following rules are helpful in assigning oxidation states to elements:
- Oxygen (in most compounds) has an oxidation state of −2.
- Hydrogen (in most compounds) has an oxidation state of +1.
- Free elements have an oxidation state of 0.
- The oxidation state of simple ions equals the charge on the ion.
- In compounds the sum of the oxidation states of the elements must equal zero.

→ The halogens (F, Cl, Br and I) typically have an oxidation state of −1 in their ionic compounds. In molecular compounds their oxidation states are typically +1 and +7.

→ When naming ionic compounds in which variable oxidation states of metal ions are present, the oxidation state is shown using roman numerals.

Example:

$FeCl_2$—iron has an oxidation state of +2; name = iron (II) chloride

$FeCl_3$—iron has an oxidation state of +3; name = iron (III) chloride

→ When hydrogen burns in oxygen, water is formed.

$$2H_2(g) + O_2(g) \rightarrow 2H_2O(l)$$

- Both hydrogen and oxygen are free elements and their oxidation states are 0. The H atoms in water have an oxidation state of +1 and the oxygen atom has an oxidation state of −2. The sum of these oxidation states is 0 (i.e. 2 (+1) + (−2) = 0).

- The hydrogen atoms have increased their oxidation states from 0 to +1 during the reaction. Therefore hydrogen has been oxidised. Hydrogen is the reductant. The oxidation state of the oxygen atoms has decreased from 0 to −2. Thus the oxygen has been reduced. The oxygen is the oxidant.

Displacement reactions

→ **Displacement reactions** are oxidation–reduction (redox) reactions in which a more reactive metal displaces another less reactive metal from a solution of its ions. The more reactive metal loses electrons and forms an ion whereas the ions of the less reactive metal gain electrons to form the metal.

> **displacement reactions:** reactions in which a less active metal is displaced from solution by a more reactive metal

Example:

Magnesium (**reductant**) reacts with a solution of blue copper (II) ions (**oxidant**) to form magnesium ions and copper metal (Figure 10.5). Two electrons are lost from the magnesium and gained by the copper (II) ions. This reaction can be expressed in the form of two half-equations.

Oxidation half-equation:

$$Mg(s) \rightarrow Mg^{2+}(aq) + 2e^-$$

Reduction half-equation:

$$Cu^{2+}(aq) + 2e^- \rightarrow Cu(s)$$

Net redox reaction:

$$Mg(s) + Cu^{2+}(aq) \rightarrow Mg^{2+}(aq) + Cu(s)$$

> **reductant:** a substance that reduces an oxidant
> **oxidant:** a substance that oxidises a reductant

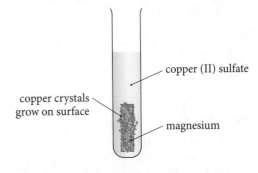

copper (II) sulfate

copper crystals grow on surface

magnesium

Figure 10.5 Displacement of copper

→ The movement of ions as well as electrons is an important feature of oxidation–reduction reactions.

→ Displacement reactions also apply to the reaction of active metals in dilute solutions of replacement acids, such as hydrochloric acid or sulfuric acid. In this case the metal displaces the hydrogen ions and hydrogen gas is formed.

EXAMPLE 2

Use half-equations to describe the displacement reaction between iron and dilute sulfuric acid.

Identify the element being displaced from solution

Answer:

The iron displaces the hydrogen from the solution. Bubbles of hydrogen gas form around the surface of the iron as the iron dissolves to form iron (II) ions. Iron is the reductant and hydrogen ions are the oxidants. Iron displaces hydrogen from solution because iron is a stronger reductant.

Oxidation:

$$Fe(s) \rightarrow Fe^{2+}(aq) + 2e^-$$

Reduction:

$$2H^+(aq) + 2e \rightarrow H_2(g)$$

Net redox reaction:

$$Fe(s) + 2H^+(aq) \rightarrow Fe^{2+}(aq) + H_2(g)$$

Redox reactions involving ions and molecules

→ Molecules and ions can behave as oxidants and reductants.

→ Halogen molecules are common oxidants. Fluorine is a very strong oxidant.

Examples:

- Chlorine as an oxidant

    Chlorine dissolved in water will oxidise iron (II) ions. Iron (III) ions are produced.

    Oxidation:

    $$Fe^{2+}(aq) \rightarrow Fe^{3+}(aq) + e^-$$

    Reduction:

    $$Cl_2(aq) + 2e^- \rightarrow 2Cl^-(aq)$$

    Net redox reaction:

    $$2Fe^{2+}(aq) + Cl_2(aq) \rightarrow 2Fe^{3+}(aq) + 2Cl^-(aq)$$

- Iodide ion as a reductant

    An aqueous solution of sodium iodide will reduce an orange, acidified solution of dichromate ions ($Cr_2O_7^{2-}$) to form green chromium (III) ions. The iodide ions are oxidised to form iodine.

    Oxidation:

    $$2I^-(aq) \rightarrow I_2(s) + 2e^-$$

    Reduction:

    $$Cr_2O_7^{2-}(aq) + 14H^+(aq) + 6e^- \\ \rightarrow 2Cr^{3+}(aq) + 7H_2O(l)$$

    Net redox reaction:

    $$6I^-(aq) + Cr_2O_7^{2-}(aq) + 14H^+(aq) \\ \rightarrow 3I_2(s) + 2Cr^{3+}(aq) + 7H_2O(l)$$

Corrosion

→ Corrosion is an oxidation–reduction process in which a metal becomes degraded or worn away such that it becomes unsuitable for its original purpose. Rusting is an example of the corrosion of iron.

→ The rusting of iron is a very common example of the chemical corrosion of an active metal. Other reactive metals also corrode when exposed to oxygen in the atmosphere. The surface of a reactive metal (e.g. magnesium, calcium) oxidises to form a metal oxide.

→ Metals such as gold and platinum are noble metals because they do not corrode.

→ Water usually accelerates the corrosion of reactive metals as the surface oxides can dissolve and diffuse away from the surface and expose a new metal surface to corrode. As oxides and other substances dissolve in the water an electrolyte forms that also promotes the redox processes.

→ In the case of iron the corrosion layer is permeable to oxygen and water and the corrosion process continues.

→ Oxygen and water are required for iron to rust.

→ Rust is a hydrated iron (III) oxide. Its formula is: $Fe_2O_3 \cdot xH_2O$ ($x = 1, 2$)

→ Rusting is a multi-step process. The relevant equations for the rusting process are:

- Oxidation of iron
    $$Fe(s) \rightarrow Fe^{2+}(aq) + 2e^-$$

- Reduction of dissolved oxygen
    $$O_2(aq) + 2H_2O(l) + 4e^- \rightarrow 4OH^-(aq)$$

- Precipitation of iron (II) hydroxide
    $$Fe^{2+}(aq) + 2OH^-(aq) \rightarrow Fe(OH)_2(s)$$

- Oxidation of iron (II) hydroxide to form rust
    $$4Fe(OH)_2(s) + O_2(aq) \rightarrow 2Fe_2O_3 \cdot H_2O(s) + 2H_2O(l)$$

→ Figure 10.6 shows the results of a rusting experiment using an iron alloy called mild steel. When the air is dried the mild steel does not rust. When dissolved air is removed from the water no rusting occurs. The experiment demonstrates that water and air are both required for rusting to occur.

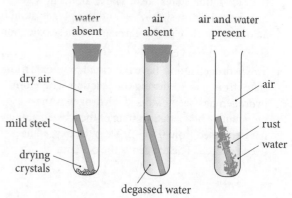

Figure 10.6 Rusting experiment

→ KEY QUESTIONS

10 Define the terms oxidation and reduction.

11 Identify the oxidation state of:
   a chromium metal   b chromium in CrCl₃.

12 Write an ionic equation for the reaction of zinc with dilute sulfuric acid. Identify the oxidant in this reaction.

13 Aqueous chlorine reacts with potassium bromide solution to form aqueous bromine. Write an ionic equation for this reaction and identify the reductant.

Answers ⊃ p. 114

4 Electrochemistry

» Students conduct investigations to measure and compare the reduction potential of galvanic half-cells.

Galvanic cells

→ Oxidation–reduction reactions can be investigated using electrochemical cells.

→ When oxidation–reductions are spontaneous, chemical potential energy is converted to electrical energy by the transfer of electrons between reductants and oxidants.

→ Electrochemical cells that generate electrical energy are called galvanic cells.

→ In galvanic cells the oxidation half-reaction and the reduction half-reaction occur in separate half-cells that are separated by a porous barrier (salt bridge or porous partition) and a conducting wire. The structure of a typical galvanic cell is shown in Figure 10.7.

galvanic cell: an electrochemical cell that generates electrical energy via redox reactions

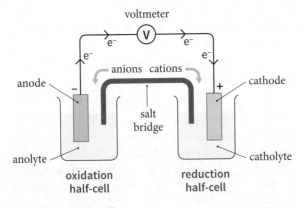

Figure 10.7 Galvanic cell

→ The galvanic cell is divided into two half-cells.

- The electrode where oxidation occurs is called the anode. The anode has a negative charge. The electrolyte in this half-cell is called the anolyte.

- The reduction electrode is called the cathode. The cathode has a positive charge. The electrolyte in this half-cell is called the catholyte.

- A salt bridge links the two half-cells. The salt bridge contains an electrolyte solution (such as saturated potassium nitrate) that internally completes the electrical circuit and allows ions to carry the current. Positive ions (cations) move towards the cathode and negative ions (anions) move towards the anode.

- A metallic conductor links the anode and cathode and completes the external circuit. A voltmeter in the external circuit can be used to measure the potential difference between the two half-cells.

- Electrons flow from the anode to the cathode through the external circuit in response to an electric potential difference between each half-cell.

→ Galvanic cells can be represented using a standard notation called the cell diagram. Consider the following example where zinc forms the anode and copper forms the cathode. The anolyte is an aqueous solution of zinc sulfate and the catholyte is an aqueous solution of copper (II) sulfate. The salt bridge that separates the two half-cells is represented by two vertical lines (||):

$$Zn(s) \mid ZnSO_4(aq) \parallel CuSO_4(aq) \mid Cu(s)$$

→ The anode is composed of a more active metal (i.e. a stronger reductant) than the cathode in a galvanic cell. The electron transfer then occurs from the anode to the cathode through the external conductor.

→ In the anode half-cell, oxidation can occur in two ways:

- the anode itself may oxidise; in this case the anode will gradually lose mass as the oxidation product (metal ions) dissolve into the anolyte

- ions, molecules or the water solvent in the anolyte may oxidise at the anode surface.

→ In the cathode half-cell, reduction of ions, molecules or water can occur at the surface of the cathode.

Example:

- Galvanic cell

   $$Mg(s) \mid MgSO_4(aq) \parallel CuSO_4(aq) \mid Cu(s)$$

   The magnesium anode oxidises:

   $$Mg(s) \rightarrow Mg^{2+}(aq) + 2e^-$$

   At the cathode, copper (II) ions are reduced. The copper that forms is deposited on the cathode surface:

   $$Cu^{2+}(aq) + 2e^- \rightarrow Cu(s)$$

   The net redox reaction is:

   $$Mg(s) + Cu^{2+}(aq) \rightarrow Mg^{2+}(aq) + Cu(s)$$

This is illustrated in Figure 10.8.

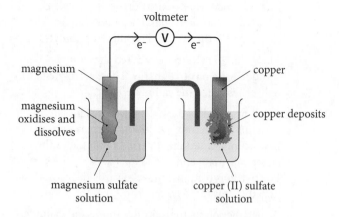

Figure 10.8 Magnesium and copper galvanic cell

Standard electrode potentials

→ The potential difference measured by the voltmeter in galvanic cells depends on a number of factors. These variables are:
- type of electrodes used
- type of electrolytes used
- concentration of the electrolytes
- temperature
- pressure (for cells in which gases are present).

→ Consequently in order to compare the potential differences in various galvanic cells standard conditions need to be used. These standard conditions are:
- temperature = 25 °C
- pressure = 100 kPa
- electrolyte concentration = 1.0 mol/L.

→ In addition to these standard conditions a standard half-cell has been developed. This is the standard hydrogen electrode which consists of a platinum foil electrode coated in fine platinum powder (called platinum black) immersed in a solution of 1.0 mol/L hydrogen ions. Hydrogen gas (at 100 kPa pressure) is bubbled over the surface of this electrode. The platinum is an inert conductor. This standard half-cell is represented as:

$Pt(s),H_2(g) \mid H^+(aq)$

The half-reaction associated with this electrode is:

$2H^+(aq) + 2e^- \rightleftharpoons H_2(g)$

→ Reversible arrows are used in redox half-equations as both the forward and reverse reactions can occur.

→ The standard electrode potential ($E^\ominus$) of the standard hydrogen electrode is 0.00 V.

→ Galvanic cells can now be formed using this standard hydrogen electrode linked to another half-cell. The digital voltmeter can record both positive and negative voltages.

For example, the voltage of a copper half-cell can be measured using the following galvanic cell:

$Pt(s),H_2(g) \mid H^+(aq) \parallel Cu^{2+}(aq) \mid Cu(s)$

In this example the platinum electrode is the negative anode and the copper is the positive cathode. Under standard conditions the cell voltage is +0.34 V.

The oxidation and reduction half-equations are as follows.

Oxidation:

$H_2(g) \rightarrow 2H^+(aq) + 2e^-$

Reduction:

$Cu^{2+}(aq) + 2e^- \rightarrow Cu(s)$

Net redox equation:

$H_2(g) + Cu^{2+}(aq) \rightarrow 2H^+(aq) + Cu(s)$

→ The cell potential (+0.34 V) is the difference in voltage across the two half-cells. By definition the electrode potential for the standard hydrogen cell is 0.00 V. In this example, this is the oxidation potential as the hydrogen electrode is the anode. Therefore the reduction potential for the copper half-cell is +0.34 V (Figure 10.9).

$E^\ominus_{reduction}(Cu^{2+}) = +0.34$ V

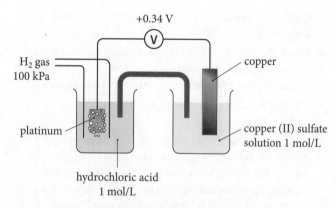

Figure 10.9 Hydrogen–copper galvanic cell

→ The sum of the oxidation and reduction potentials equals the cell potential.

$$E^\ominus_{cell} = E^\ominus_{reduction} + E^\ominus_{oxidation}$$

→ The cell potential is positive (>0) for a spontaneous galvanic process.

→ The voltage of a zinc half-cell can be measured using the following galvanic cell:

$Zn(s) \mid Zn^{2+}(aq) \parallel H^+(aq) \mid H_2(g),Pt(s)$

→ Under standard conditions the cell voltage is +0.76 V if the zinc is connected to the negative terminal and the platinum is connected to the positive terminal of the voltmeter. Therefore the zinc is the anode and the platinum is the cathode in this cell. Thus the oxidation and reduction half-equations are as follows.

Oxidation:

$$Zn(s) \rightarrow Zn^{2+}(aq) + 2e^-$$

Reduction:

$$2H^+(aq) + 2e^- \rightarrow H_2(g)$$

Net redox equation:

$$Zn(s) + 2H^+(aq) \rightarrow Zn^{2+}(aq) + H_2(g)$$

→ Using the formula for the cell potential, the oxidation potential for zinc can be calculated.

$$E^\ominus_{cell} = E^\ominus_{reduction} + E^\ominus_{oxidation}$$

$$0.76 = 0.00 + E^\ominus_{oxidation}(Zn)$$

$$E^\ominus_{oxidation}(Zn) = +0.76 \text{ V}$$

→ The reduction potential for Zn^{2+} can be obtained by reversing the sign of the electrode potential.

$$E^\ominus_{reduction}(Zn^{2+}) = -0.76 \text{ V}$$

→ KEY QUESTIONS

14 Identify the electrodes in a galvanic cell where oxidation and reduction occur.

15 Identify the direction in which electrons move in the galvanic cell circuit.

16 State the purpose of a salt bridge in a galvanic cell.

17 Identify the variables that can alter the cell potential in a galvanic cell.

Answers ⊃ p. 114

5 Standard electrode potentials

» Students predict the reaction of metals in solutions using the table of standard reduction potentials
» Students predict the spontaneity of redox reactions using the value of cell potentials

Table of standard reduction potentials

→ Tables of standard reduction potentials list the reduction half equations and potentials in increasing order of ease of reduction. A portion of this table is shown in Table 10.7.

Table 10.7 Standard reduction potentials

oxidant + electrons ⇌ reductant	$E^\ominus$ (V)
$K^+(aq) + e^- \rightleftharpoons K(s)$	−2.94
$Ba^{2+}(aq) + 2e^- \rightleftharpoons Ba(s)$	−2.91

oxidant + electrons ⇌ reductant	$E^\ominus$ (V)
$Ca^{2+}(aq) + 2e^- \rightleftharpoons Ca(s)$	−2.87
$Na^+(aq) + e^- \rightleftharpoons Na(s)$	−2.71
$Mg^{2+}(aq) + 2e^- \rightleftharpoons Mg(s)$	−2.36
$Al^{3+}(aq) + 3e^- \rightleftharpoons Al(s)$	−1.68
$Mn^{2+}(aq) + 2e^- \rightleftharpoons Mn(s)$	−1.18
$Zn^{2+}(aq) + 2e^- \rightleftharpoons Zn(s)$	−0.76
$Fe^{2+}(aq) + 2e^- \rightleftharpoons Fe(s)$	−0.44
$Ni^{2+}(aq) + 2e^- \rightleftharpoons Ni(s)$	−0.24
$Sn^{2+}(aq) + 2e^- \rightleftharpoons Sn(s)$	−0.14
$Pb^{2+}(aq) + 2e^- \rightleftharpoons Pb(s)$	−0.13
$2H^+(aq) + 2e^- \rightleftharpoons H_2(g)$	0.00
$Cu^{2+}(aq) + 2e^- \rightleftharpoons Cu(s)$	+0.34
$Ag^+(aq) + e^- \rightleftharpoons Ag(s)$	+0.80

Information about the table:
- All half-equations and potentials refer to reduction processes.
- The oxidation half-equations can be obtained by writing the reverse equations.
- The oxidation potentials can be determined by reversing the sign.
- The more positive the reduction potential, the more readily the species is reduced.
- The more positive the oxidation potential, the more readily the species is oxidised.

EXAMPLE 3

Use the table of standard reduction potentials to determine the cell reaction and standard cell potential for the following galvanic cell:

$$Mn(s) \mid Mn^{2+}(aq) \parallel Ag^+(aq) \mid Ag(s)$$

> Identify the more active metal: Mn or Ag?

Answer:

Oxidation half-reaction:

$$Mn(s) \rightarrow Mn^{2+}(aq) + 2e^-; \quad E^\ominus_{oxidation} = +1.18 \text{ V}$$

Reduction half-reaction:

$$Ag^+(aq) + e^- \rightarrow Ag(s); \quad E^\ominus_{reduction} = +0.80 \text{ V}$$

Cell reaction:

$$Mn(s) + 2Ag^+(aq) \rightarrow Mn^{2+}(aq) + 2Ag(s);$$
$$E^\ominus_{cell} = (+1.18) + (+0.80) = +1.98 \text{ V}$$

The positive potential shows that the redox reaction is spontaneous.

EXAMPLE 4

A piece of iron is placed in a solution of magnesium nitrate. Use the table of standard reduction potentials (Table 10.7) to predict whether a spontaneous reaction will occur.

> Reaction is spontaneous if the cell potential is positive

Answer:

Oxidation:

$$Fe(s) \rightarrow Fe^{2+}(aq) + 2e^-; \; E^{\ominus}_{oxidation} = +0.44 \text{ V}$$

Reduction:

$$Mg^{2+}(aq) + 2e^- \rightarrow Mg(s); \; E^{\ominus}_{reduction} = -2.36 \text{ V}$$

$$
\begin{aligned}
E^{\ominus}_{cell} &= E^{\ominus}_{reduction} + E^{\ominus}_{oxidation} \\
&= (-2.36) + (+0.44) \\
&= -1.92 \text{ V}
\end{aligned}
$$

Less than 0, therefore no spontaneous reaction can occur.

Reduction potentials involving molecules and ions

→ Tables of standard reduction potentials also include half-equations involving water, non-metals and their ions, as well as polyatomic ions. Some examples are shown in Table 10.8.

Table 10.8 Standard reduction potentials

Reduction half-equation	$E^{\ominus}$ (volts)
$2H_2O(l) + 2e^- \rightleftharpoons H_2(g) + 2OH^-(aq)$	−0.83
$O_2(g) + 2H_2O(l) + 4e^- \rightleftharpoons 4OH^-(aq)$	+0.40
$I_2(s) + 2e^- \rightleftharpoons 2I^-(aq)$	+0.54
$Fe^{3+}(aq) + e^- \rightleftharpoons Fe^{2+}(aq)$	+0.77
$Br_2(l) + 2e^- \rightleftharpoons 2Br^-(aq)$	+1.08
$O_2(g) + 4H^+(aq) + 4e^- \rightleftharpoons 2H_2O(l)$	+1.23
$Cr_2O_7{}^{2-}(aq) + 14H^+(aq) + 6e^- \rightleftharpoons 2Cr^{3+}(aq) + 7H_2O(l)$	+1.36
$Cl_2(g) + 2e^- \rightleftharpoons 2Cl^-(aq)$	+1.36
$MnO_4{}^-(aq) + 8H^+(aq) + 5e^- \rightleftharpoons Mn^{2+}(aq) + 4H_2O(l)$	+1.51
$F_2(g) + 2e^- \rightleftharpoons 2F^-(aq)$	+2.89

A complete table of reduction potentials is provided on the inside cover of this book.

EXAMPLE 5

Identify the strongest oxidant:

> Strong oxidants are more readily reduced

- acidified solution of potassium dichromate ($K_2Cr_2O_7$)
- iodine solid
- acidified solution of potassium permanganate ($KMnO_4$)
- oxygen bubbled through acidified water.

Answer:

The greater the reduction potential, the stronger the oxidant.

Thus the acidified solution of potassium permanganate is the strongest oxidant as its reduction potential is +1.51 V.

EXAMPLE 6

Consider the following standard galvanic cell:

$$Pt(s), Br_2(l) \mid Br^-(aq) \| Cl^-(aq) \mid Cl_2(g), Pt(s)$$

a Explain why 2 platinum electrodes are used in this cell.

b Write the cell reaction and calculate the standard potential of the cell using the electrode potential data in the previous table.

> Locate bromine and chlorine in the reduction potential table and determine the stronger oxidant

Answer:

a The cell reaction involves only non-metals and their ions and so inert metallic conductors, such as platinum, are used to transfer electrons.

b Oxidation half-reaction:

$$2Br^-(aq) \rightarrow Br_2(l) + 2e^-; \; E^{\ominus}_{oxidation} = -1.08 \text{ V}$$

Reduction half-reaction:

$$Cl_2(g) + 2e^- \rightarrow 2Cl^-(aq); \; E^{\ominus}_{reduction} = +1.36 \text{ V}$$

Cell reaction:

$$2Br^-(aq) + Cl_2(g) \rightarrow Br_2(l) + 2Cl^-(aq)$$

$$E^{\ominus}_{cell} = (-1.08) + (+1.36) = +0.28 \text{ V}$$

⚛ FIRSTHAND INVESTIGATION 2

Investigating cell potentials

» Students conduct investigations to measure and compare the reduction potential of galvanic half-cells.

Aim

to construct galvanic cells and measure cell potentials

Materials

- Electrodes: copper, magnesium, zinc, nickel
- Electrolytes: 0.1 mol/L solutions of copper (II) sulfate; magnesium sulfate; zinc sulfate; nickel sulfate

- Salt bridge: filter paper soaked in saturated potassium nitrate
- Beakers
- Voltmeter
- Electrical leads

Cells to investigate

1 Measure the cell potentials using a copper/copper (II) sulfate half-cell as a common reference half-cell.

2 Investigate the following cells:

   a $Mg(s) \mid Mg^{2+}(aq) \parallel Cu^{2+}(aq) \mid Cu(s)$

   b $Zn(s) \mid Zn^{2+}(aq) \parallel Cu^{2+}(aq) \mid Cu(s)$

   c $Ni(s) \mid Ni^{2+}(aq) \parallel Cu^{2+}(aq) \mid Cu(s)$

3 Tabulate your results and compare your voltage readings to those calculated using the table of standard potentials.

Reliability

Ensure that:

a all leads and connections are free of corrosion

b all electrodes are cleaned with emery paper

c all electrolytes have the same concentration (e.g. 0.1 mol/L)

d the temperature is constant.

Repeat each experiment five times.

Analysis

The experimental results should confirm the predictions made from the table of standard potentials. The cell potentials are unlikely to be equal to the predictions as the conditions of the experiment are not standard conditions.

→ KEY QUESTIONS

18 Use the table of standard reduction potentials to determine the voltage of a galvanic cell composed of a magnesium half-cell and a lead half-cell.

19 Use the table of standard reduction potentials to determine the voltage of a galvanic cell consisting of the following half-cells: a platinum electrode in a beaker of acidified dichromate ions ($Cr_2O_7^{2-}$) and a platinum electrode in a beaker of sodium iodide solution.

20 Use the table of standard reduction potentials to determine the voltage of a galvanic cell consisting of the following half-cells: a silver electrode in a beaker of silver nitrate solution and a platinum electrode in a beaker of iron (II) nitrate and iron (III) nitrate solution.

Answers ⊃ p. 114

Are you able to answer these questions from the syllabus for this chapter? Tick each question as you go through the checklist if you are able to answer it. If you cannot answer a question, turn to the relevant page in the study guide to find the answer. For NESA key word meanings, go to www.educationstandards.nsw.edu.au and search 'key words'.

	FOR A COMPLETE UNDERSTANDING OF THIS TOPIC:	PAGE NO.	✓
1	Can I describe the reactions of active metals in dilute hydrochloric and dilute sulfuric acid?	100	
2	Can I describe the reactions of metals with cold water, hot water and steam?	100	
3	Can I describe the reactions of metals when heated in air?	101	
4	Can I explain how the activity of metals can be determined experimentally?	101	
5	Can I use the activity series to predict reactions of metals with solutions of other metal ions?	102	
6	Can I recall where the most active metals are located in the periodic table?	102	
7	Can I recall where the most inactive metals are located in the periodic table?	102	
8	Can I recall the trends in atomic radius, ionisation energy and electronegativity across a period and down a group in the periodic table?	103	
9	Can I distinguish between oxidation and reduction?	104	
10	Can I explain oxidation–reduction reactions in terms of electron loss/gain as well as in terms of changes in oxidation state?	104–105	
11	Can I explain using half-equations why metal displacement reactions are examples of oxidation–reduction reactions?	105–106	
12	Can I explain the structure of a galvanic cell?	107	
13	Can I name the standard half-cell used to measure standard voltages in galvanic cells?	108	
14	Can I use the table of standard reduction potentials to write the net redox reaction in a galvanic cell and to determine the voltage generated?	109	
15	Can I predict the spontaneity of redox reactions using the table of standard reduction potentials?	110	

Objective-response questions

(1 mark each)

1 The most reactive metal in the presence of dilute hydrochloric acid is:

A gold B iron

C zinc D calcium

2 Identify the set of metals that are arranged in order of most reactive to least reactive.

A Mg, Pb, Fe, Ag B Mg, Pb, Ag, Fe

C Mg, Fe, Pb, Ag D Ag, Pb, Fe, Mg

3 The products of the reaction of magnesium and sulfuric acid are:

A $MgSO_3$ and H_2O B $MgSO_4$ and H_2

C MgO and H_2 D $MgSO_4$ and O_2

4 Use the table of standard reduction potentials to identify which combination of metals and metal ions will lead to a spontaneous displacement reaction on mixing.

A Cu and Pb^{2+} B Zn and Mg^{2+}

C Zn and Ag^+ D Sn and Al^{3+}

5 The following equation is the net reaction for a galvanic cell:

$$Ni(s) + Pb^{2+}(aq) \rightarrow Ni^{2+}(aq) + Pb(s)$$

Select the correct statement about this cell.

A Lead is the anode.

B Nickel is the cathode.

C Lead ions are reduced at the cathode.

D Nickel ions are oxidised at the anode.

Extended-response questions

6 Describe and explain the trends in first ionisation energy of the elements of Period 3 of the periodic table.

(2 marks)

7 Determine the oxidation state of the nominated element in each of the following compounds.

(4 marks)

a P in H_3PO_4

b Ti in $Na_2Ti_3O_7$

c W in K_2WO_4

d Au in $NaAuCl_4$

8 In order to determine the relative strengths of several metals as reductants, the following experiments were performed.

Pieces of each of four divalent metals (A, B, C and D) were placed in aqueous solutions of their sulfate salts.

The table shows the results. A tick (✓) indicates a reaction occurs; a cross (✗) indicates no reaction.

	A^{2+}	B^{2+}	C^{2+}	D^{2+}
A		✗	✓	✗
B	✓		✓	✗
C	✗	✗		✗
D	✓	✓	✓	

a Use the results in the table to arrange the metals in order of decreasing strength as reductants. (2 marks)

b Write a net ionic equation for the reaction of A with C^{2+}. (1 mark)

9 The following table shows the results of various tests performed on three metals (X, Y and Z).

Metal	X	Y	Z
Appearance	Silvery	Orange-pink	Silvery
metal heated in oxygen	burns rapidly when finely powdered forming a white solid	black coating slowly forms on the surface	burns rapidly and brilliantly to form a white powder
metal added to water	no reaction in hot or cold water; reacts with steam	no reaction	reacts vigorously with considerable heat production
metal added to dilute sulfuric acid	dissolves slowly with the evolution of a colourless gas	no reaction	reacts extremely vigorously; colourless gas evolved which ignites with a flame

a Determine the order of activity of the three metals from most active to least active. (1 mark)

b Identify from the following list the most likely identities of the three metals:

lead; sodium; gold; copper; zinc (1 mark)

10 Use the table of standard reduction potentials to determine which of the following experiments will lead to a spontaneous redox reaction.

a Tin metal is added to 1 mol/L silver nitrate solution. (2 marks)

b Nickel metal is added to 1 mol/L aluminium nitrate solution. (2 marks)

ANSWERS

Key questions ➲ p. 100

1 Hydrogen

2 $Al_2(SO_4)_3$

3 Copper, silver, gold

Key questions ➲ p. 102

4 Aluminium, zinc, iron

5 Magnesium reacts more rapidly than zinc. Effervescence occurs in both reactions as hydrogen gas is released.

6 K, Al, Sn, Pb, Ag

Key questions ➲ p. 104

7 The increasing nuclear charge across a period causes the valence shell to be attracted closer to the nucleus. Thus the atomic radius decreases.

8 Fluorine

9 First ionisation energy decreases down Group 1.

Key questions ➲ p. 107

10 Oxidation = loss of electrons; reduction = gain of electrons

11 a 0   b +3

12 $Zn(s) + 2H^+(aq) \rightarrow Zn^{2+}(aq) + H_2(g)$; oxidant = H^+

13 $Cl_2(aq) + 2Br^-(aq) \rightarrow 2Cl^-(aq) + Br_2(aq)$; reductant = bromide ion

Key questions ➲ p. 109

14 Oxidation occurs at the anode; reduction occurs at the cathode.

15 Electrons move from the anode to the cathode through the external circuit.

16 To complete the charge flow in the circuit

17 Temperature, gas pressure, electrolyte concentration, materials of the anode and cathode

Key questions ➲ p. 111

18 $E^{\ominus}_{cell} = E^{\ominus}_{reduction} + E^{\ominus}_{oxidation}$

$= E^{\ominus} Pb^{2+} | Pb + E^{\ominus} Mg | Mg^{2+}$

$= (-0.13) + (+2.36)$

$= +2.23$ V

19 $E^{\ominus}_{cell} = E^{\ominus}_{reduction} + E^{\ominus}_{oxidation}$

$= E^{\ominus} Cr_2O_7^{2-} | Cr^{3+} + E^{\ominus} I^- | I_2$

$= (+1.36) + (-0.54)$

$= +0.82$ V

20 $E^{\ominus}_{cell} = E^{\ominus}_{reduction} + E^{\ominus}_{oxidation}$

$= E^{\ominus} Ag^+ | Ag + E^{\ominus} Fe^{2+} | Fe^{3+}$

$= (+0.80) + (-0.77)$

$= +0.03$ V

Objective-response questions

1 **D.** Calcium is a member of Group 2. **A**, **B** and **C** are incorrect as transition metals are less reactive than Group 2 metals.

2 **C.** Magnesium is very reactive, silver is unreactive and iron is more reactive than lead. Thus **A**, **B** and **D** are incorrect.

3 **B.** Hydrogen gas is evolved when active metals react with dilute H_2SO_4, and sulfate salts form.

A is incorrect as sulfuric acid does not produce sulfite salts. **C** is incorrect as oxides are not formed when sulfuric acid attacks metals. **D** is incorrect as oxygen gas is not produced when acids react with metals.

4 **C.** Zinc is more active than silver. Cell potential is positive (+1.56 V) and therefore the reaction is spontaneous.

A, **B** and **D** are incorrect as the cell potentials are negative.

5 **C.** Lead ions are reduced at the cathode as the oxidation state decreases from +2 to 0.

A is incorrect as the lead ions are reduced. **B** is incorrect as the nickel is oxidised at the anode. **D** is incorrect as nickel ions have formed due to oxidation of the anode.

Extended-response questions

6 **EM** This question needs students to state that the nuclear charge increases across Period 3 and this causes the electron shells to be attracted to the nucleus. The valence electron is more strongly attracted and more energy is required to ionise the atom.

The ionisation energy increases from left to right across periods as the valence shell is closer to an increasingly positive nucleus. ✓
Thus more energy is required to remove a valence electron. ✓

7 **EM** In this question students should let x be the oxidation state of the nominated element. As all compounds are neutral the sum of the oxidation states is 0.

a Let the oxidation state of P be x.

The oxidation state of H = +1 and the oxidation state of O is −2.

Thus $3(+1) + x + 4(-2) = 0$

Solve for x.

$x = +5$

Oxidation state of P is +5. ✓

b Let the oxidation state of Ti be x. The oxidation state of Na = +1 and the oxidation state of O is −2.

Thus, $2(+1) + 3x + 7(-2) = 0$

$x = +4$

Oxidation state of Ti is +4. ✓

c Let the oxidation state of W be x. The oxidation state of K = +1 and the oxidation state of O is −2.

Thus $2(+1) + x + 4(-2) = 0$

$x = +6$

Oxidation state of W is +6. ✓

d Let the oxidation state of Au be x. The oxidation state of Na = +1 and the oxidation state of Cl is −1.

Thus $(+1) + x + 4(-1) = 0$

$x = +3$

Oxidation state of Au is +3. ✓

8 **EM** This question needs students to recall that when a displacement reaction occurs then the metal is more reactive than the metal that has been displaced from solution. In writing ionic equations, ensure both atoms and charges balance.

a D, B, ✓ A, C ✓

b $A(s) + C^{2+}(aq) \rightarrow A^{2+}(aq) + C(s)$ ✓

9 **EM** This question needs students to recall the experiments involving reactions of metals with air, water and acids. To determine the identity of the elements, recall the activity series and that gold is noble and lead is very slow to react with sulfuric acid. Lead does not react with steam.

a Z; X; Y ✓

b X = zinc; Y = copper; Z = sodium ✓

10 **EM** This question needs students to demonstrate that the cell potential is the sum of the oxidation potential and the reduction potential.

a $E^{\ominus}_{cell} = E^{\ominus}_{reduction} + E^{\ominus}_{oxidation}$

$= E^{\ominus}Ag^+ | Ag + E^{\ominus}Sn | Sn^{2+}$

$= (+0.80) + (+0.14)$

$= +0.94$ V ✓

Reaction is spontaneous as cell potential is positive. ✓

b **EM** The half-cell potential for the half-reaction at the anode must have its sign reversed. The total cell potential must be positive for a spontaneous reaction to occur.

$E^{\ominus}_{cell} = E^{\ominus}_{reduction} + E^{\ominus}_{oxidation}$

$= E^{\ominus}Al^{3+} | Al + E^{\ominus}Ni | Ni^{2+}$

$= (-1.68) + (+0.24)$

$= -1.44$ V ✓

Reaction is non-spontaneous as cell potential is negative. ✓

CHAPTER 11
RATES OF REACTIONS

What affects the rate of a chemical reaction?

In chemical industries it is important that chemical reactions that produce products for future sale occur as rapidly as possible. In this way chemical industries can ensure the highest monetary return. Chemical reactions in our body cells must occur at a high enough rate to ensure our bodies function properly. This chapter discusses how reaction rates are influenced by many variables.

1 Factors affecting reaction rates

» Students conduct a practical investigation using appropriate tools (including digital technologies) to collect data, analyse and report on how the rate of a chemical reaction can be affected by a range of factors, including but not limited to: temperature; surface area of reactant(s); concentration of reactant(s); and catalysts.

Chemical kinetics

→ Chemical kinetics is the study of the rates of chemical reactions. These studies have shown that various factors affect the rate of a chemical change.

Temperature

→ The rate of a chemical reaction increases as the temperature increases. When a cake is cooked in an oven it will cook faster if the temperature of the oven is increased. We keep food in a refrigerator to keep it fresher for longer. The low temperatures slow down the rate at which microbial action on the food occurs.

→ Figure 11.1 shows the effect of increasing the temperature on the rate of the reaction between zinc and 1 mol/L hydrochloric acid. At the higher temperature the rate

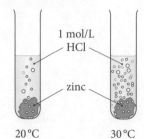

Figure 11.1 Effect of temperature on rate of a reaction

of hydrogen gas production is much greater than the rate at the lower temperature.

→ The measurement of the volume of hydrogen produced as a function of time allows a quantitative measure of **reaction rate** at different temperatures. Figure 11.2(a) shows a **quantitative experiment** to measure the rate of the reaction between zinc and hydrochloric acid. The rate of the reaction at any time can be determined by calculating the gradient of a tangent to the curve at that time. R_2 is the rate at 2 minutes and this rate is lower than the initial rate (R_0). The graphed data in (b) shows a much higher initial rate at 30 °C than at 20 °C.

(a)

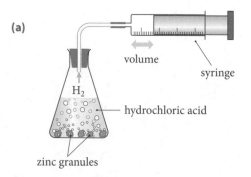

(b)

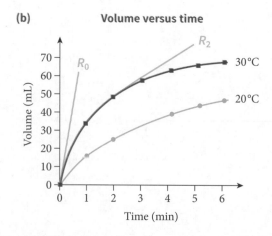

Figure 11.2 Quantitative measurement of reaction rate

reaction rate: the change in reactant or product concentration per unit of time

quantitative experiment: an experiment in which quantities of substances are measured

Concentration

➜ Reaction rates increase as the concentration of a reactant increases.

➜ Figure 11.3 shows the reaction between magnesium metal and sulfuric acid. The degree of **effervescence** in the second test tube is much greater in the more concentrated acid solution. The rate of dissolution of the magnesium and the production of hydrogen gas is much greater in 1 mol/L sulfuric acid than in 0.1 mol/L sulfuric acid.

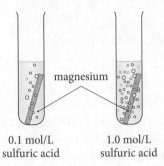

Figure 11.3 Effect of acid concentration on the rate of reaction of magnesium with sulfuric acid

effervescence: the froth of gas bubbles produced in a liquid by a chemical reaction

Gas pressure

➜ In reactions involving gases an increase in the gas pressure increases the rate of the reaction.

➜ At higher gas pressures the frequency of collisions between molecules increases. This is important in various chemical industries where reactions occur in the gaseous phase. For example, in the ammonia industry nitrogen gas and hydrogen gas are reacted at very high pressures such as 20 MPa. At low pressures the reaction is too slow to be economically viable.

Particle size and surface area

➜ In **heterogeneous reactions** between solids and liquids or gases, the size of the solid particle affects the rate of the reaction.

heterogeneous reactions: reactions involving different states of matter

➜ Large pieces of solid have a smaller surface area than smaller solid pieces of the same mass. An increase in the surface area of the solid creates more sites in which the liquid or gaseous particles can react with the solid.

➜ Nanoparticles have extremely small diameters (1–100 nm) and therefore a powdered solid composed of nanoparticles has a very high surface area and reaction rates are very high.

Example 1:

Caster sugar is finely ground sugar. It is used in recipes in place of crystalline sugar to increase the rate at which the sugar dissolves in the other ingredients.

Example 2:

Sawdust burns more rapidly in air than larger pieces of solid wood.

Example 3:

Marble chips react more slowly with dilute hydrochloric acid than pieces of marble that have been ground into a powder.

➜ Figure 11.4 shows a model of the reaction between a metallic solid, such as magnesium, and an acid solution, such as hydrochloric acid. The rate of the reaction increases on powdering the metal as more surface is exposed to the hydrogen ions in the acid.

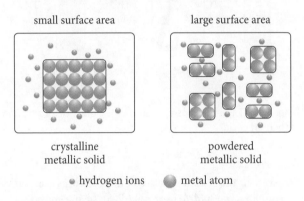

Figure 11.4 Powdering a solid increases its surface area

➜ **KEY QUESTIONS**

1 Identify changes in reaction conditions that will increase the rate of the reaction between magnesium and 2.0 mol/L sulfuric acid.

2 Identify a laboratory procedure to increase the rate of combustion of a candle.

3 Explain why caster sugar dissolves more readily than granular sugar in whipped egg white during the preparation of a cake.

Answers ⊃ p. 126

Catalysts

➜ A catalyst is a substance that increases the rate of a chemical reaction.

➜ Catalysts alter one or more of the stages of the **reaction pathway** to make the process faster.

➜ An important characteristic of catalysts is that they are not consumed in the chemical reaction.

→ Figure 11.5 shows the effect of a copper catalyst on the reaction between zinc metal and dilute hydrochloric acid. Copper is too weak a reductant to react with the acid. Hydrogen gas bubbles form slowly on the zinc surface as it reacts with the acid. When the copper makes contact with the zinc the hydrogen bubbles form more rapidly. The mass of the copper does not change.

reaction pathway: the stages in a reaction in which intermediate substances form and then react

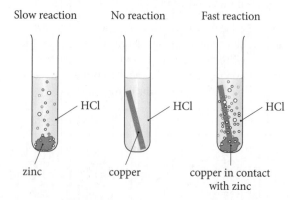

Figure 11.5 Copper acts as a catalyst in the reaction of zinc and hydrochloric acid

EXAMPLE 1

The rate of the reaction between marble chips (calcium carbonate) and hydrochloric acid can be measured in the apparatus shown in Figure 11.6.

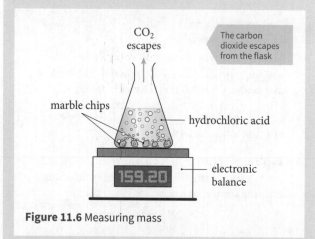

Figure 11.6 Measuring mass

Sketch a graph of mass versus time and explain how the graph could be used to compare the reaction rate during the course of the reaction.

Answer:

The rate of carbon dioxide evolution decreases with time and therefore the rate of mass loss decreases with time. By drawing tangents to the graph at different times the decreasing rate can be quantified (Figure 11.7).

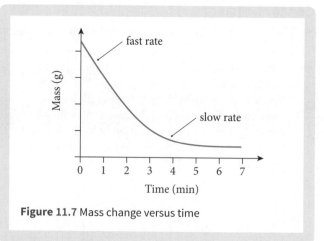

Figure 11.7 Mass change versus time

EXAMPLE 2

Ethanol (C_2H_5OH) can be oxidised to form acetic acid in an acidified solution of potassium dichromate. The dichromate ion ($Cr_2O_7^{2-}$) is a yellow-orange colour and in the reaction it is converted into green chromium ions (Cr^{3+}):

$$3C_2H_5OH(aq) + 16H^+(aq) + 2Cr_2O_7^{2-}(aq)$$
$$\rightarrow 3CH_3COOH(aq) + 4Cr^{3+}(aq) + 11H_2O(l)$$

A colourimeter is a device used to measure the amount of light that passes through a coloured solution. The colourimeter uses an orange filter to create a beam of orange light that passes through the glass tube containing the reaction mixture. As the orange solution turns slowly green there is a decrease in the percentage of light transmitted. Figure 11.8 shows a typical result. A student drew a tangent to the curve at 3 minutes. Explain how the rate of reaction at 3 minutes could be determined.

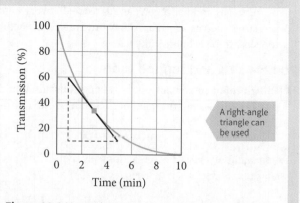

A right-angle triangle can be used

Figure 11.8 Measuring rate using a change in colour of a solution

Answer:

The slope of the tangent is a measure of the rate. The slope is calculated by measuring the rise and run of the right-angle triangle constructed with the tangent as the hypotenuse: rate = rise/run.

Rate of an acid–carbonate reaction

» Students conduct a practical investigation, using appropriate tools (including digital technologies), to collect data, analyse and report on how the rate of a chemical reaction can be affected by a range of factors, including but not limited to: surface area of reactant(s).

Aim

to undertake a firsthand investigation to determine the effect of particle size on the rate of the reaction between hydrochloric acid and calcium carbonate

Materials

- calcium carbonate chips (marble chips)
- powdered calcium carbonate
- 1 mol/L hydrochloric acid
- 150 mL beakers
- stopwatch

Method

1 Use a beaker and an electronic balance to weigh out marble chips (e.g. 3.0 g) into the beaker.
2 Add 100 mL of 1 mol/L hydrochloric acid to a second beaker and place both beakers on an electronic balance. Record the total mass.
3 Pour the acid into the beaker of marble chips and place the empty acid beaker back on the balance.
4 Record the total mass each 30 seconds until reaction ceases.
5 Repeat the experiment with the same mass of powdered calcium carbonate.

Results

1 Use a computer spreadsheet program or a sheet of graph paper to plot a line graph of mass versus time for each experiment.
2 Compare the initial gradients of each graph. This gradient is a measure of the initial reaction rate.

Conclusion

Write an appropriate conclusion that compares the initial rates of the reactions in each beaker.

→ **KEY QUESTIONS**

4 Describe a quantitative method that can be used in a laboratory to demonstrate that zinc granules in 1.0 mol/L hydrochloric acid produce hydrogen at a faster rate when the acid is hot.

5 Explain why the surface area of a heterogeneous solid catalyst is important.

Answers ⊃ p. 126

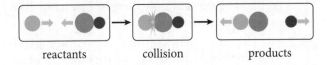

2 Collision theory, activation energy and catalysis

» Students investigate the role of activation energy, collisions and molecular orientation in collision theory.
» Students explain a change in reaction rate using collision theory.

Collisions and kinetic energy

→ In order for chemicals to react their atoms or molecules must collide with sufficient kinetic energy in order that bonds can be broken. Figure 11.9 shows the collision of reactants and the formation of products.

reactants   collision   products

Figure 11.9 Molecular collision

→ At low temperatures the reactant atoms or molecules have low kinetic energies. As the temperature is raised the particles move faster and faster. Eventually they have sufficient kinetic energy to react.

→ A good illustration of this concept is the reaction between hydrogen gas and oxygen gas to form water. If these gases are mixed together at room temperature they do not react. If the temperature is raised by using a flame or a spark then an explosion occurs. This is the 'pop' test for hydrogen.

→ In a mixture of reacting gas molecules at a fixed temperature, there is a distribution of molecular velocities (speeds). Some molecules are moving more rapidly than others. Figure 11.10 shows the distribution of molecular velocities for oxygen gas at two different temperatures. At the temperature increases there is an increasing proportion of molecules with higher molecular velocities.

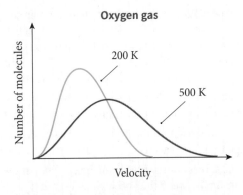

Figure 11.10 Distribution of velocities in oxygen gas

Activation energy

→ Svante Arrhenius (1859–1927) formulated a model to explain why increasing temperatures lead to the increase in reaction rate. He proposed that few collisions between reactant molecules are successful in producing reaction products. He reasoned that a reaction will only occur if reactants have sufficient kinetic energy to react. He introduced the concept of activation energy (E_A).

activation energy: the minimum energy required by the reactants in order to react to form products

→ As a mixture of reactants is heated their kinetic energies increase and when the total kinetic energy exceeds the activation energy the reaction occurs. The activation energy is like a barrier that separates the reactants from their potential products.

→ Figure 11.11 shows how the proportion of reactants that will successfully react to form products increases when the temperature is raised. At the higher temperature ($T2$) the number of molecules having an energy greater than E_A has increased compared with the lower temperature ($T1$).

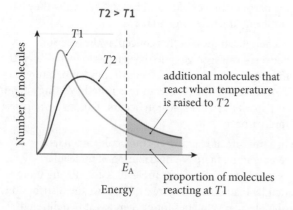

Figure 11.11 Activation energy

Energy profile diagrams

→ Energy profile diagrams can be drawn to demonstrate the connection between the activation energy for a reaction and the energy released or absorbed during the reaction. Chemical reactions can be classified as exothermic if heat was liberated and endothermic if heat was absorbed.

→ In an endothermic reaction the products have a higher energy or enthalpy than the reactants.

→ In an exothermic reaction the products have less energy or enthalpy than the reactants.

→ Figure 11.12 shows energy profile diagrams. They show the relationship between the enthalpy change and activation energy for an endothermic and an exothermic reaction.

enthalpy (H): the heat content of a substance under standard conditions (25 °C; 100 kPa)

enthalpy change (ΔH): the change in heat content as the result of a chemical or physical change

→ In a reaction the reactants have to absorb sufficient energy to reach the top of the activation energy 'hill'. At this point the bonds of the reactants start to break and the new bonds of the product start to form. This structure is called the activated complex. Energy is released as the products form from the breakdown of the activated complex. The energy released is much less for an endothermic reaction compared with an exothermic reaction.

→ The enthalpy change (ΔH) for each reaction is equal to the difference between the enthalpy of the products and the enthalpy of the reactants.

Endothermic:

$$\Delta H = H_P - H_R > 0$$

Exothermic:

$$\Delta H = H_P - H_R < 0$$

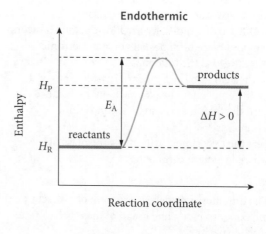

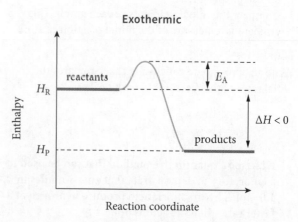

Figure 11.12 Energy profile diagrams

EXAMPLE 3

Figure 11.13 shows a molecular collision between X_2 and Y_2 leading to the formation of a new compound XY. Explain what is happening when the activated complex is formed during the collision.

> Consider the processes of bond breaking and bond forming

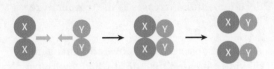

Figure 11.13 Collision between X_2 and Y_2

Answer:

The covalent bonds of the X_2 and Y_2 molecules start to break and new covalent bonds start to from between X and Y atoms. The activated complex is a transition state.

➡ When reactions occur between molecules the orientation of the molecules during collision is important. Electron rearrangement occurs during the collision and this will only occur in a specific orientation of colliding reactants. The final rate of the reaction is determined by the proportion of collisions in which the orientation is correct. Figure 11.14 illustrates this idea for the reaction of ethylene (C_2H_4) and hydrogen chloride (HCl) molecules.

$$C_2H_4(g) + HCl(g) \rightarrow CH_3CH_2Cl(g)$$

If collisions occur in other orientations there is no reaction.

Correct orientation of molecules on collision   Product formed

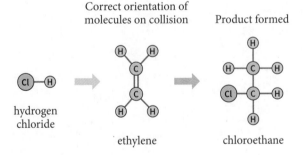

Figure 11.14 Orientation of molecules during collision

Catalysis

➡ A catalyst is a substance that increases the rate of a chemical reaction. Catalysts alter one or more of the stages of the reaction pathway to make the process faster. These stages are called the *reaction mechanism*.

➡ Catalysed reactions have a lower activation energy (E_A) than for a similar uncatalysed reaction. The **activated complex** is a short-lived transition state that exists at the top of the activation energy hill. As the activated complex forms, the bonds that held the reactants together are partially broken and new bonds to produce the products are partially formed. The activated complex starts to break up. At this point there are two possible ways in which the reaction could proceed:

- the activated complex breaks up and the reactants re-form; no reaction occurs
- the activated complex separates and product molecules are formed; a reaction occurs.

activated complex: a transition state in a reaction where reactant bonds are breaking and new bonds are forming

➡ Figure 11.15 shows the reaction profile for a catalysed and uncatalysed reaction. Note that the enthalpy change of the reaction has not changed. More reactant molecules can be converted into products when the energy barrier is lower. Although the reaction occurs faster, the amount of products formed does not change.

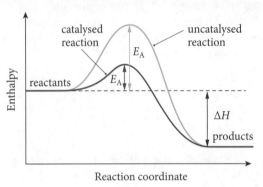

Figure 11.15 Reaction profile for catalysed and uncatalysed reactions

➡ In some reactions the catalyst is a solid and the reactants are gases or ions in solution. This type of catalysis is called heterogeneous catalysis. In one or more stages of the reaction reactant molecules adsorb onto the surface of the solid catalyst. On the catalyst surface the bonds of the adsorbed molecules break and a reaction occurs that ultimately produces the products. These products now leave or desorb from the surface.

➡ An example of this process occurs in the industrial manufacture of ammonia. The industrial production of ammonia is called the Haber Process. In this process nitrogen gas and hydrogen gas are combined over a porous iron-based catalyst at high pressures (20–25 MPa) and moderately high temperatures (400–550 °C).

$$N_2(g) + 3H_2(g) \rightleftharpoons 2NH_3(g)$$

The iron catalyst lowers the activation energy of the reaction. Under these conditions the reaction is fast enough to make it economic. The stages of the catalytic process are as follows:

1 Hydrogen gas and nitrogen gas adsorb onto the catalyst surface and the H–H bond and N≡N bond break.

$$H_2(g) \rightleftharpoons 2H(ad)$$

$$N_2(g) \rightleftharpoons 2N(ad)$$

(ad = adsorbed)

2 Hydrogen atoms combine sequentially with the adsorbed nitrogen atoms to form adsorbed ammonia.

$$N(ad) + H(ad) \rightleftharpoons NH(ad)$$

$$NH(ad) + H(ad) \rightleftharpoons NH_2(ad)$$

$$NH_2(ad) + H(ad) \rightleftharpoons NH_3(ad)$$

3 The adsorbed ammonia molecules desorb from the surface of the catalyst.

$$NH_3(ad) \rightleftharpoons NH_3(g)$$

→ **Nanoparticle** catalysts are very useful in speeding up the catalytic process. Such materials have very high surface areas on which the heterogeneous reaction can occur. One common use of heterogeneous catalysts is in a galvanic cell such as the hydrogen–oxygen fuel cells, which are used to generate electricity. Typically platinum is used as the catalyst but the cost of platinum is high. Energy production rates can be increased with the use of zirconium/yttrium nanoparticle catalysts, which are much cheaper than platinum.

nanoparticle: a particle in the size range 1–100 nm

EXAMPLE 4

Figure 11.16 shows a graph of the rate of production of nitric oxide gas in the presence or absence of a platinum–rhodium catalyst when ammonia gas is oxidised by oxygen gas. State the conclusions that can be made from the graph.

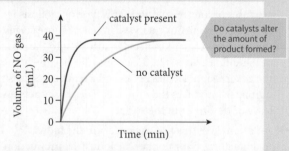

Figure 11.16 Rate of NO production

Answer:

The initial slope of the catalyst graph is greater than the graph without the catalyst. Thus the initial rate has increased with the catalyst present. The same volume of NO gas is produced whether the catalyst is present or absent.

→ KEY QUESTIONS

6 Describe the contribution that Svante Arrhenius made to the theory of reaction kinetics.

7 Hydrogen peroxide molecules slowly decompose into water and oxygen gas at room temperature. Use kinetic theory to explain why the rate of decomposition increases as the temperature is increased.

8 A student observed that powdered manganese dioxide increased the rate at which hydrogen peroxide decomposed into water and oxygen gas. What must the student do to confirm the hypothesis that the MnO_2 is acting as a catalyst?

Answers ⊃ p. 126

CHAPTER SYLLABUS CHECKLIST

Are you able to answer these questions from the syllabus for this chapter? Tick each question as you go through the checklist if you are able to answer it. If you cannot answer a question, turn to the relevant page in the study guide to find the answer. For NESA key word meanings, go to www.educationstandards.nsw.edu.au and search 'key words'.

	FOR A COMPLETE UNDERSTANDING OF THIS TOPIC:	PAGE NO.	✓
1	Can I explain why an increase in temperature increases the rate of a reaction?	116	
2	Can I explain why an increase in concentration of one reactant increases the rate of a reaction?	117	
3	Can I explain why an increase in gas pressure in reactions involving gases increases the rate of a reaction?	117	
4	Can I explain why an increase in surface area increases the rate of a heterogeneous reaction?	117	
5	Can I explain how catalysts increase the rate of a reaction?	117–118	
6	Can I use collision theory to explain the variation in reaction rates under different conditions?	119	
7	Can I draw energy profile diagrams to distinguish between endothermic and exothermic reactions?	120	
8	Can I explain why molecule orientation is important in the progress of a chemical reaction?	121	
9	Can I explain the concept of the activated complex?	121	

Objective-response questions
(1 mark each)

1 Identify which change will result in a faster reaction rate.

   A adding water to a 4 mol/L HCl solution in contact with a strip of magnesium

   B increasing the air pressure during a reaction between solid zinc oxide and dilute sulfuric acid

   C heating a solid mixture of zinc powder and iodine crystals

   D reducing the voltage during the electrolysis of salt water

2 Select the statement that is true of catalysts.

   A Catalysts lower the activation energy for a reaction.

   B Catalysts are consumed during the reaction.

   C Catalysts are always solids.

   D Catalysts reduce the heat liberated or consumed in a reaction.

3 Svante Arrhenius proposed a model to explain why increasing temperatures lead to the increase in reaction rate. In his model he proposed that, as the temperature increased:

   A the enthalpy change of the reaction increased.

   B a greater proportion of molecules had sufficient kinetic energy to overcome the activation energy barrier.

   C all reactant molecules had sufficient kinetic energy to overcome the activation energy barrier.

   D the rates of the forward and reverse reactions increased equally.

4. Select the correct statement about catalysts, reaction rates and energy.

   A The presence of a catalyst leads to a decrease in the enthalpy change for a reaction.

   B The catalysis of the reaction of hydrogen gas with nitrogen gas to form ammonia using porous iron is an example of homogeneous catalysis.

   C Catalysts prevent the reverse reaction from occurring.

   D When a suitable catalyst is added the activation energy decreases.

5 Figure 11.17 shows graphs of the distribution of molecular velocities of a diatomic gas at three different temperatures (W, X and Y).

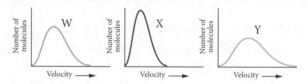

Figure 11.17 Molecular velocity distribution at three temperatures

The set showing the distribution of molecular velocities as a function of increasing temperatures is:

A X, Y, W   B Y, W, X   C W, X, Y   D X, W, Y

Extended-response questions

6 The initial rate of a chemical reaction was determined as a function of temperature. The average results of the experiment are tabulated below.

Temperature (°C)	20	30	40	50	60
Rate (mmol/s)	0.200	0.395	0.810	1.555	3.100

   a At each temperature, how many times should the experiment be repeated to improve reliability? (1 mark)

   b Plot a line graph of the experimental data.   (4 marks)

   c What conclusion can be made about the effect of increasing temperature on reaction rate?   (1 mark)

   d Use your graph to determine the reaction rate at 55 °C.   (1 mark)

7 Nitrogen dioxide (NO_2) is a brown gas and nitric oxide (NO) is a colourless gas. Nitrogen dioxide gas reacts with carbon monoxide gas to form nitric oxide and carbon dioxide.

   a Write a balanced equation for this reaction.   (1 mark)

   b How will the colour of the reaction mixture change with time.   (1 mark)

   c The reaction was performed at a fixed temperature in a 5 L glass vessel. The amount of nitrogen dioxide present in the flask was measured over 3 minutes. The results are shown in the table.

Time (s)	0	30	60	90	120	150	180
$n(NO_2)$ (mol)	2.60	2.10	1.82	1.60	1.40	1.24	1.10

   i Plot a line graph of the data.   (4 marks)

   ii When is the greatest reaction rate observed? Justify your answer.   (2 marks)

8 In the presence of a catalyst the activation energy for the reaction graphed below (Figure 11.18) drops by 5 kJ. Copy the graph and draw the energy profile of the catalysed reaction. (2 marks)

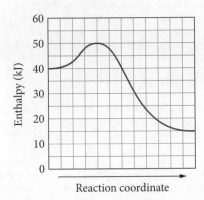

Figure 11.18 Energy profile diagram

9 The rate of a reaction between sodium hydrogen carbonate and a solution of acetic acid (CH_3COOH) was investigated. Carbon dioxide gas is produced and the rate of the effervescence was estimated on a 6-point star rating scale. In each experiment 5 g of sodium hydrogen carbonate is used and 50 mL of acid solution at 25 °C. The variables investigated were:
- particle size—crystals of sodium hydrogen carbonate and powdered sodium hydrogen carbonate
- concentration of the acetic acid solution
- stirring or not stirring the reactants.

The results of the experiments are tabulated below. The greater the number of stars, the greater the rate of effervescence.

	$NaHCO_3$ crystals without stirring	$NaHCO_3$ crystals with stirring	$NaHCO_3$ powder without stirring	$NaHCO_3$ powder with stirring
1.0 mol/L acetic acid	**	***	*****	******
0.1 mol/L acetic acid	*	**	***	****

a Identify the controlled variables in this investigation. (3 marks)

b Explain the results of the investigation. (3 marks)

10 Catalysts can be used to increase the rate of oxidation of the pollutant carbon monoxide to form carbon dioxide. Gold nanoparticles have been identified as excellent catalysts in this process.

a Write a balanced equation for the oxidation of carbon monoxide. (1 mark)

b Define the term *nanoparticle*. (1 mark)

c The following data on the rate of carbon monoxide oxidation at 273 K versus the size of gold nanoparticles was collected.

Diameter of gold nanoparticle (nm)	1	2	3	4	5
Rate of oxidation (mmol/g/s)	0.60	0.18	0.05	0.02	0.01

i Plot this data as a line graph. (4 marks)

ii What conclusion can be made about the rate of carbon monoxide oxidation and catalyst particle size? (1 mark)

d Explain why such research is important for the environment. (2 marks)

ANSWERS

Key questions ⊃ p. 117

1 Heating the acid; using more concentrated acid; increasing the surface area of the magnesium

2 Burn the candle in a gas jar of pure oxygen.

3 Caster sugar is finely ground sugar. It has a much higher surface area than granulated sugar and dissolves faster.

Key questions ⊃ p. 119

4 Use a flask connected to a gas syringe. In the first experiment place 50 mL of 2 mol/L HCl in the flask at room temperature. Add 5.0 g of zinc granules and collect the gas evolved in the gas syringe. Measure the volume of gas each 15 seconds. Repeat the experiment with hot acid at 50 °C. Gas will be released at a faster rate in the first minute than at room temperature.

5 The larger the surface area the greater the rate increase as more reactants can adsorb at one time.

Key questions ⊃ p. 122

6 Arrhenius proposed that a reaction will only occur if the reactants have sufficient kinetic energy to overcome an energy barrier called the activation energy.

7 As molecules are heated the proportion of molecules with higher molecular velocities increases. On collision more molecules will have sufficient energy to overcome the activation energy barrier and therefore the reaction rate increases.

8 The rate of the reaction is faster with the addition of MnO_2. To confirm that the MnO_2 acts catalytically the MnO_2 must be recovered and dried. Its mass should be the same as it was initially.

YEAR 11 EXAM-TYPE QUESTIONS

Objective-response questions

1 **C.** The kinetic energy of the reactants increases and the rate increases. **A** is incorrect as water will reduce the frequency of collisions between the magnesium and the acid. **B** is incorrect as the reaction has no gaseous reactants. **D** is incorrect as the higher the voltage, the faster the electrolysis proceeds.

2 **A.** Catalysts change the reaction pathway so less energy is required for the reaction to occur. **B** is incorrect as catalysts reform after the reaction. **C** is incorrect as catalysts can also be in the dissolved state. **D** is incorrect as catalysts do not alter the enthalpy change.

3 **B.** At a fixed temperature molecules have a distribution of velocities. At a higher temperature this velocity distribution changes so that more molecules have higher kinetic energies. **A** is incorrect as no change in enthalpy occurs. **C** is incorrect as only a portion of the reactants have sufficient energy to react. **D** is incorrect as the forward rate increased more than the reverse rate.

4 **D.** Catalysts do not change the enthalpy change but do reduce the activation energy. **A** is incorrect as catalysts have no effect on the enthalpy change. **B** is incorrect as this reaction is heterogeneous. **C** is incorrect as catalysts also change the rate of the reverse reaction but do not stop it.

5 **D.** In X the maximum is at a lower velocity than W, whereas in Y the maximum is at a higher energy than W. **A** is incorrect as the maxima of Y is less than the maxima in W. **B** is incorrect as this is the reverse order. **C** is incorrect as W and X are in the reverse order.

Extended-response questions

6 **EM** This question needs students to recall that when conducting chemistry experiments the more repeats that are performed, the more reliable the results. Assuming no outliers, a minimum of five repeats is sufficient. In graphing the line of best fit should pass as close as possible to the data points. In this case the smooth curve passes through each point. The scale on the axes should ensure that the graph occupies at least 80% of the grid. Ensure that the units of each quantity are recorded and that the graph has a title.

a Minimum of five repeats. ✓

b Figure A11.1 shows rate versus temperature.

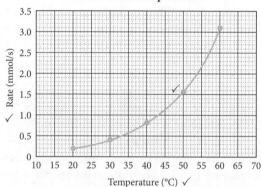

Figure A11.1 Rate versus temperature

c As temperature increases the reaction rate increases. The rate approximately doubles for each ten degree rise in temperature. ✓

d Rate = 2.20 mmol/s ✓

7 **EM** This question needs students to ensure states of matter are shown in the equation. Gas pressure does not change in this reaction as 2 moles of reactants produce 2 moles of products. As the colour changes, change in light intensity for light of a suitable wavelength is a suitable way to follow the rate of reaction. The gradient of tangents drawn to selected points on the graph is a simple way to measure rate.

a $NO_2(g) + CO(g) \rightarrow NO(g) + CO_2(g)$ ✓

b The intensity of the brown colour will decrease over time as nitrogen dioxide reacts. ✓

c i Figure A11.2 shows nitrogen dioxide versus time.

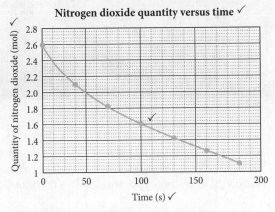

Figure A11.2 Nitrogen dioxide quantity versus time

ii The rate is greatest initially ✓ as shown by the greatest slope to a tangent drawn to the curve in the first 10 seconds. ✓

8 **EM** In this question students should show that the catalyst curve starts and ends at the same enthalpies but the activation energy is reduced by 5 kJ.

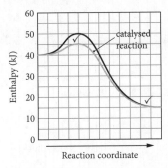

Figure A11.3 Catalysed reaction showing the reduced activation energy but the same change in enthalpy

9 **EM** This question needs students to recall that controlled variables are factors that must not change during the experiment. Only one variable can be investigated in any one investigation. The independent variables being tested are acid concentration, stirring rate and particle size.

a The temperature, ✓ mass of sodium hydrogen carbonate ✓ and the volume of acid ✓ were controlled.

b Powdering the solid sodium hydrogen carbonate increased the rate of effervescence as the powder has a greater surface area than the crystals. This provides a greater number of sites for the hydrogen ions in the acid to attack. ✓

The higher the acid concentration, the greater the rate as there are more collisions between the hydrogen ions and the surface of the sodium hydrogen carbonate. ✓

Stirring increases the rate of reaction as the products are removed from the surface of the solid and hydrogen ions can gain access to the surface to react. Without stirring, the rate is affected by the diffusion of ions only. The effervescenece also helps to stir the mixture. ✓

10 **EM** In this question students should recall that carbon monoxide is a poisonous pollutant released in the incomplete combustion of fossil fuels. By reducing these emissions the quality of the atmosphere is improved. The line of best fit is a curve that passes through all data points. The title of a graph is the title of the vertical axis versus the title of the horizontal axis.

a $2CO(g) + O_2(g) \rightarrow 2CO_2(g)$ ✓
b 1–100 nm diameter particles ✓
c i Figure A11.4 shows rate of CO oxidation versus nanoparticle size.

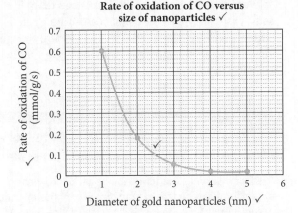

Figure A11.4 Rate of oxidation of CO versus size of nanoparticles

ii The smaller the diameter of the gold nanoparticles, the greater is their catalytic ability in the oxidation of carbon monoxide. Gold nanoparticles of 1 nm diameter are excellent heterogeneous catalysts at 273 K. ✓

d As the gold nanoparticles are excellent catalysts at such low temperatures (273 K = 0 °C), this would be very useful in industry ✓ as CO pollutants could be rapidly oxidised before gaseous emissions are released into the atmosphere from factories or motor vehicles. ✓

CHAPTER 12 ENERGY CHANGES IN CHEMICAL REACTIONS

What energy changes occur in chemical reactions?

When magnesium burns in air a bright white light and considerable heat energy are produced. When some salts are dissolved in water the water cools down in some cases and heats up in other cases. Energy changes occur in chemical reactions as well as physical changes. This chapter investigates energy changes in a variety of chemical reactions.

1 Investigating endothermic and exothermic reactions

» Students conduct practical investigations to measure temperature changes in examples of endothermic and exothermic reactions, including dissociation of ionic substances in aqueous solution, and combustion.

» Students investigate enthalpy changes in reactions using calorimetry and $q = mC\Delta T$ (heat capacity formula) to calculate, analyse and compare experimental results with reliable secondary-sourced data, and to explain any differences.

Calorimetry

→ When heat is absorbed into a system from the surroundings during a physical or chemical change the process is **endothermic**. The melting of ice and the evaporation of liquid water are endothermic processes. The temperature of the surroundings decreases as a result of heat transfer to the system. In nature green plants absorb solar energy to power photosynthesis.

→ When heat is liberated from a system into the surroundings during a physical or chemical change the process is **exothermic**. When acids neutralise bases or when fuels undergo combustion, heat is released. The temperature of the surroundings increases as a result.

→ The amount of heat liberated or absorbed in a chemical reaction or physical change can be measured using a **calorimeter**. In a school laboratory a calorimeter can be constructed from a polystyrene foam cup, which is an excellent heat insulator (Figure 12.1). Known amounts of the reactants are mixed inside the calorimeter and the change in temperature recorded with a thermometer.

endothermic: a process in which heat is absorbed from the surroundings

exothermic: a process in which heat is liberated to the surroundings

calorimeter: apparatus used to measure heat changes in a chemical reaction or physical change

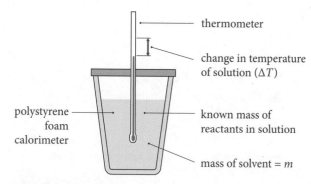

thermometer

change in temperature of solution (ΔT)

polystyrene foam calorimeter

known mass of reactants in solution

mass of solvent = m

Figure 12.1 Calorimetry

→ The quantity of heat (q) (measured in joules) absorbed or liberated by the solvent of mass (m) (measured in kilograms or grams) is given by the calorimetry equation.

Calorimetry equation

$$q = m.c.\Delta T$$

where ΔT = change in temperature of the solution
c = specific heat capacity of the solution

→ The temperature change is measured in Celsius degrees. This change in temperature is the same using the absolute or Kelvin temperature scale (K) as 1 Celsius degree is equal to 1 Kelvin temperature unit. Using the Kelvin or absolute temperature scale, the melting point of ice (0 °C) is 273 K, and the boiling point of water (100 °C) is 373 K. The lowest temperature in the universe is −273 °C (or 0 Kelvin).

→ The specific heat capacity (c) is a constant that depends on the nature of the material absorbing the heat.

For dilute solutions in water the typical value of the specific heat capacity is close to (or slightly less than) the specific heat capacity of pure water.

$$c_{water} = 4.18 \times 10^3 \text{ J/kg/K or } 4.18 \text{ J/g/K}$$

→ If it is assumed that no heat is lost from the calorimeter and that negligible heat is absorbed by the polystyrene, then the heat liberated by the reaction will equal the heat absorbed (q) by the solution.

Heats of dissolution

→ When various ionic crystals dissolve in water, the ions in the crystal dissociate to produce independent aquated ions. This process is an example of **dissolution** where a solute dissolves in a solvent to produce a solution.

$$NaCl(s) \rightarrow Na^+(aq) + Cl^-(aq)$$

dissolution: the process in which a solute dissolves in a solvent to form a solution

→ The temperature of the water may increase or decrease. The heat liberated or absorbed is called the heat of dissolution (or heat of solution).

→ The molar heat of dissolution can be calculated by dividing the quantity of heat (q), which is absorbed or liberated by the number of moles (n) of solute undergoing dissolution.

Key equation

$$\text{Heat of dissolution} = q/n$$

EXAMPLE 1

Consider the following experiment to measure the heat of dissolution of ammonium nitrate.

50.0 mL (50.0 g) of water was transferred to a polystyrene calorimeter. The initial temperature was measured. 1.0 g of ammonium nitrate was weighed and transferred to the calorimeter. The mixture was stirred and the change in temperature was measured. The results are tabulated below. Use this data to calculate the heat of dissolution of ammonium nitrate in kJ/mol.

initial temperature (°C)	21.6
final temperature (°C)	20.2

 Calculate the change in temperature

Answer:

Calculate the absolute decrease in temperature of the water as some heat is lost from the water to dissolve the ammonium nitrate.

$\Delta T = 1.4\,°C$ (endothermic process)

$$q = m.c.\Delta T = (0.0500)(4.18 \times 10^3)(1.4)$$
$$= 292.6 \text{ J}$$

$$n(NH_4NO_3) = m/M = \frac{1.0}{2 \times 14.01 + 4 \times 1.008 + 3 \times 16.00}$$

$$= \frac{1.0}{80.052}$$

$$= 0.0125 \text{ mol}$$

$$\text{Heat of dissolution} = q/n = \frac{292.6}{0.0125}$$

$$= 23\,408 \text{ J/mol}$$

$$= 23.4 \text{ kJ/mol}$$

⚛ FIRSTHAND INVESTIGATION 1

Heat of dissolution of sodium hydroxide

» Students conduct practical investigations to measure temperature changes in examples of endothermic and exothermic reactions, including dissociation of ionic substances in aqueous solution.

Aim

to use calorimetry to measure the molar heat of dissolution of sodium hydroxide

Safety

NaOH is highly caustic. Do not touch this solid and ensure safety glasses are worn.

Method

1 Measure 50.0 mL (= 50.0 g) of water into the calorimeter.

2 Measure the initial temperature of the water.

3 Weigh out 2.00 g of NaOH crystals from a freshly opened bottle onto a watch glass.

4 Add the NaOH to the water in the calorimeter and stir gently with the thermometer to ensure complete dissolution.

5 Record the maximum temperature.

6 Repeat the experiment or collect results from other groups to improve reliability.

Calculations

1 Calculate the change in temperature (ΔT).

2 Calculate the heat liberated using $q = m.c.\Delta T$ (assume $c = 4.18 \times 10^3$ J/kg/K).

3 Calculate number of moles (n) of NaOH.

4 Calculate the molar heat of dissolution, which equals q/n.

Conclusion

State the average value of the molar heat of dissolution of NaOH by averaging your results. Compare your experimental result to the standard heat of solution (= 44.5 kJ/mol) and give reasons for any differences.

Use secondary sources (e.g. Internet searches) to compare the molar heat of dissolution of NaOH to other alkalis such as KOH and $Ba(OH)_2$.

Heat of combustion

→ Combustion reactions are exothermic. Fuels such as coal or petrol undergo combustion to provide heat which can be used for the generation of electricity or to power motor vehicles.

→ Combustion reactions of hydrocarbons or other carbonaceous fuels can be classified as complete or incomplete. For complete combustion the products are carbon dioxide and water. For incomplete combustion a mixture of carbon dioxide, carbon monoxide, soot and water forms. Less heat energy is generated by incomplete combustion reactions.

Complete combustion of ethane:

$$2C_2H_6(g) + 7O_2(g) \rightarrow 4CO_2(g) + 6H_2O(l)$$

Incomplete combustion of heptane:

$$C_7H_{16}(l) + 8O_2(g) \rightarrow 2CO_2(g) + 4CO(g) + C(s) + 8H_2O(l)$$

EXAMPLE 2

Decane ($C_{10}H_{22}$) was burnt in a restricted oxygen supply to produce water, carbon dioxide, carbon monoxide and carbon. The mole ratio of $CO_2 : CO : C$ was $3 : 1 : 1$. Write a balanced equation for this incomplete combustion reaction.

> Balance the elements in the order C, H, O

Answer:

1. Balance the C atoms first then the H atoms.

$$C_{10}H_{22}(l) + O_2(g) \rightarrow 6CO_2(g) + 2CO(g) + 2C(s) + 11H_2O(l)$$

The $CO_2 : CO : C$ ratio is $6 : 2 : 2 = 3 : 1 : 1$ as required.

2. The O atoms can be initially balanced using a fraction as a coefficient for O_2:

$$\text{coefficient} = \frac{25}{2}O_2$$

$$C_{10}H_{22}(l) + \frac{25}{2}O_2(g) \rightarrow 6CO_2(g) + 2CO(g) + 2C(s) + 11H_2O(l)$$

3. Multiply the whole equation by 2 to remove the fraction. The equation is now balanced.

$$2C_{10}H_{22}(l) + 25O_2(g) \rightarrow 12CO_2(g) + 4CO(g) + 4C(s) + 22H_2O(l)$$

→ The combustion of alcohols can be investigated in the school laboratory using the principles of calorimetry. **Alcohols** include molecules such as methanol (CH_3OH) and ethanol (C_2H_5OH). The combustion of alcohols is an exothermic process. In a plentiful supply of oxygen the alcohol burns completely to produce carbon dioxide and water. In air or a restricted oxygen supply the combustion is incomplete and carbon monoxide and carbon (soot) are also produced.

alcohol: organic compounds containing the hydroxyl (OH) functional group

→ The appearance of the flame is an indication of the completeness of combustion. A blue flame without any yellow in it is indicative of complete combustion. The more yellow the flame, the more incomplete is the combustion as carbon particles cause the flame to become yellow. The following equation shows the complete combustion of ethanol.

Complete combustion:

$$C_2H_5OH(l) + 3O_2(g) \rightarrow 2CO_2(g) + 3H_2O(l)$$

 FIRSTHAND INVESTIGATION 2

Heat of combustion of ethanol

» Students conduct practical investigations to measure temperature changes in examples of endothermic and exothermic reactions, including combustion.

Aim

to measure the molar heat of combustion of ethanol

Method

1. Clamp a 250 mL conical flask to a retort stand (Figure 12.2).
2. Add 200 g (200 mL) of water to the flask and measure the initial temperature.
3. Fill the spirit burner with ethanol and weigh the burner.
4. Place the burner just below the flask and light the wick. Allow the heat from the flame to heat the water until the temperature of the water has increased by about 10 °C.

5 Extinguish the burner and stir the water and measure the final temperature.

6 Reweigh the burner.

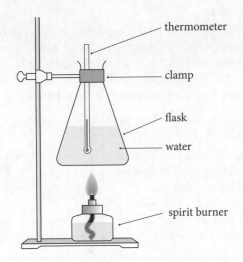

Figure 12.2 Heat of combustion

Sample results

Mass of water in calorimeter = 200 g = 0.200 kg

Initial temperature of water = 23.5 °C

Final temperature of water = 33.5 °C

Initial mass of spirit burner = 225.00 g

Final mass of spirit burner = 224.50 g

Sample calculations

1 Heat (q) absorbed by the water:

$q = mc\Delta T = (0.200)(4.18 \times 10^3)(33.5 - 23.5)$
     $= 8360$ J

2 Mass of ethanol burnt = 225.00 − 224.50 = 0.50 g

3 $n(C_2H_5OH) = m/M = \dfrac{0.50}{2 \times 12.01 + 6 \times 1.008 + 16.00}$

$= \dfrac{0.50}{46.068}$

$= 0.0109$ mol

Assuming heat gained by water = heat produced by the flame

Molar heat of combustion $= q/n = \dfrac{8360}{0.0109}$

$= 766\,972$ J/mol

$= 767$ kJ/mol (3 sig. fig.)

4 Use secondary sources (e.g. Internet searches) to compare the molar heat of combustion of ethanol to other alcohols such as methanol and propan-1-ol.

Accuracy and reliability

- Considerable heat is lost to the surroundings. In addition the flame colour is not blue and thus incomplete combustion has occurred. The heat of combustion obtained (767 kJ/mol) is much less than the accepted value of the molar heat of complete combustion, which is 1367 kJ/mol.

- The reliability of the results can be improved by performing at least five repetitions and then averaging the results. The water should be constantly stirred so as to uniformly distribute the heat. The apparatus should be surrounded by draught guards so as to minimise heat loss. A 0–50° thermometer will be more accurate than a 0–100° thermometer as the scale divisions are smaller.

- The only accurate and valid method to measure the heat of complete combustion is to use a device called a *bomb calorimeter*. This device is made of stainless steel and has a screw-down lid. It uses an atmosphere of pure high-pressure oxygen. The fuel in the calorimeter is sparked electrically and the fuel vapour combusts explosively. The calorimeter is submerged in a large insulated outer vessel containing a known mass of well-stirred water. The heat released by the combustion is absorbed by the stainless steel and the water. Using the known specific heat capacities of the stainless steel and the water, the heat of combustion can be calculated.

→ KEY QUESTIONS

1 Classify the following reactions as endothermic or exothermic:

a condensation of water vapour

b neutralisation of an acid and a base

c photosynthesis

2 The calorimetry equation is $q = m.c.\Delta T$.

State the meaning of each term in the equation.

3 Acetylene (C_2H_2) can undergo complete or incomplete combustion.

Explain the differences in the products produced.

4 Explain why measuring the heat of complete combustion of an alcohol using a spirit burner and calorimeter produces very inaccurate results.

Answers ⊃ p. 139

2 Enthalpy changes and activation energy

» Students construct energy profile diagrams to represent and analyse the enthalpy changes and activation energy associated with a chemical reaction.

Heat and enthalpy

→ The heat energy changes that are measured using calorimetry occur due to changes in the kinetic and chemical potential energies of the components of the system. Heat energy changes can be measured under many different conditions.

→ Chemists use the term **enthalpy** (H) to specify the heat content of a substance. The enthalpy change (ΔH) is related to the experimentally measured heat changes that occur when the reaction is performed in a calorimeter. The calorimetry equation is modified (for n moles of material) to allow the enthalpy change to be measured in kJ/mol.

Key equation

$$\Delta H = \pm q/n = \pm mc\Delta T/n$$

> **enthalpy:** the heat content of a system

→ Positive and negative signs for enthalpy changes are used for endothermic and exothermic processes (illustrated in Figure 12.3):

- *Endothermic*—physical or chemical changes in which heat is absorbed and the temperature of the system decreases: $\Delta H = +q/n$
- *Exothermic*—physical or chemical changes in which heat is released and the temperature of the system increases: $\Delta H = -q/n$

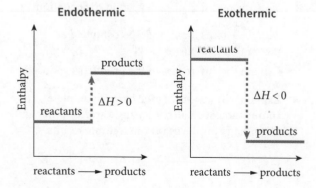

Figure 12.3 Enthalpy profile

→ In an endothermic reaction the products have a greater enthalpy than the reactants. In an exothermic reaction the products have a lower energy than the reactants. Calorimetry does not measure the enthalpy value for the reactants and products; it measures the change in enthalpy.

→ The dissolution of ionic compounds in water can be measured using calorimetry. In the dissolution process the solid salts dissolve in water to form electrolyte solutions. The following example shows how the enthalpy changes for such a process can be calculated.

EXAMPLE 3

4.00 g of potassium chloride was weighed out and dissolved in 100.0 g of water in a calorimeter. The temperature of the mixture decreased from 22.0 °C to 19.8 °C during the dissolution process. Calculate the molar enthalpy of dissolution of potassium chloride. Assume the specific heat capacity is 4.18 J/g/K.

> Calculate the number of moles of KCl; enthalpy changes for endothermic dissolutions have a positive sign

Answer:

$m = 0.100$ kg

$\Delta T = 22.0 - 19.8 = 2.2\,°C = 2.2K$

$q = m.c.\Delta T = (0.100)(4.18 \times 10^3)(2.2)$
$\qquad = 920$ J
$\qquad = 0.920$ kJ

The number of moles of potassium chloride in the 4.00 g undergoing dissolution can be calculated:

$$n(KCl) = m/M = \frac{4.00}{39.10 + 35.45}$$
$$= 0.0537 \text{ mol}$$

Molar enthalpy of dissolution (KCl) $= \Delta H$
$$= +q/n$$
$$= \frac{0.920}{0.0537}$$
$$\Delta H = +16.8 \text{ kJ/mol}$$

→ The molar enthalpy change for a reaction can be incorporated into the balanced equation. Such equations are called thermochemical equations. The thermochemical equation for the dissolution of potassium chloride in water is:

$$KCl(s) \rightarrow K^+(aq) + Cl^-(aq); \Delta H = +16.8 \text{ kJ/mol.}$$

→ The following examples show that some dissolution processes are endothermic and some are exothermic:

$$NH_4NO_3(s) \rightarrow NH_4^+(aq) + NO_3^-(aq);$$
$$\Delta H = +25.8 \text{ kJ/mol}$$

$$NaOH(s) \rightarrow Na^+(aq) + OH^-(aq); \Delta H = -44.5 \text{ kJ/mol}$$

Activation energy

→ The concept of activation energy was discussed in Chapter 11. Review that section now. Activation energy is the minimum energy required by the reactants in order to react to form products.

→ Energy profile diagrams show the relationship between activation energy (E_A) and the enthalpy change (ΔH) for a reaction. Figure 12.4 shows the energy profile diagram for the combustion of a gaseous molecule (X_2) to form a gaseous oxide of X:

$$X_2(g) + 2O_2(g) \rightarrow 2XO_2(g)$$

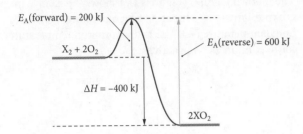

Figure 12.4 Energy profile diagram

→ The forward reaction has an activation energy of 200 kJ and the reverse reaction has a very high activation energy (600 kJ). In the forward reaction the product has a lower enthalpy than the reactants. Therefore the reaction is exothermic ($\Delta H = -400$ kJ). Higher temperatures increase the proportion of reactant molecules with sufficient energy to overcome the activation energy barrier and this in turn increases the rate of the forward reaction. The reverse reaction rate is not increased to the same extent when the temperature increased due to the very high activation energy.

→ KEY QUESTIONS

5 The enthalpy change for a reaction is −54 kJ/mol. What is the significance of the negative sign?

6 5.0 g of sodium carbonate was dissolved in 80.0 g of water in a calorimeter. Determine the change in temperature due to the dissolution of the salt. ($c = 4.18 \times 10^3$ J/kg/K; $\Delta H = -24$ kJ/mol)

7 One mole of water vapour was decomposed to form gaseous atoms of hydrogen and oxygen.

Write a balanced equation for the reaction and explain why this reaction will only occur at elevated temperatures.

8 The heat released on the combustion of dry black coal is typically 33 MJ/kg. Calculate the mass of dry black coal that will produce 250 kJ of energy on combustion.

Answers ⊃ p. 139

3 Modelling catalytic behaviour

» Students model and analyse the role of catalysts in reactions.

Catalysts

→ In Chapter 11, catalysts were defined as substances that increased the rate of a chemical reaction. These catalysts created alternative reaction pathways involving the formation and breaking of different chemical bonds compared with the uncatalysed pathway. The new catalytic pathways have lower activation energies.

→ Some catalytic reactions are **heterogeneous**. In these reactions the catalyst is in a different phase than the reactants. An example of a heterogeneous catalytic reaction is the production of ammonia gas using a porous iron catalyst. Figure 12.5 shows the stages of the process. Nitrogen and hydrogen molecules adsorb onto the catalyst surface and their covalent bonds break and new bonds form with the catalyst. The atoms migrate on the surface and then atoms combine to form ammonia molecules, which then desorb off the surface.

$$N_2(g) + 3H_2(g) \rightleftharpoons 2NH_3(g)$$

heterogeneous reaction: a reaction in which one or more reactants and products are in different phases

1 Molecules adsorb onto catalyst surface

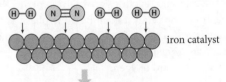

2 Bonds break and atoms bond to catalyst

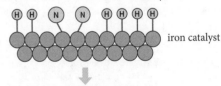

3 Atoms migrate on catalyst surface

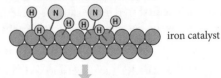

4 Atoms combine to form molecules and desorb

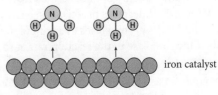

Figure 12.5 Manufacture of ammonia using a porous iron catalyst

→ The activation energy (E_A) for the ammonia synthesis process is significantly reduced in the presence of the catalyst.

→ Uncatalysed reaction:

E_A = 325 kJ/mol

Catalysed reaction:

E_A = 105 kJ/mol

→ Figure 12.6 shows the energy profile of the catalysed reaction. Two activation energy hills are present. The first activation energy hill refers to steps 1 and 2 in Figure 12.5. This is an exothermic stage. This stage is the one that controls the net rate of the overall reaction as the activation energy is high. The second activation energy hill refers to the remaining steps, which are endothermic.

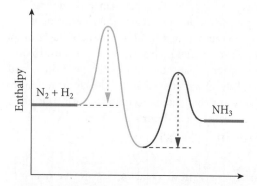

Figure 12.6 Energy profile for the catalysed ammonia synthesis

→ Some catalytic reactions are **homogeneous**. In these reactions the catalyst is in the same phase as the reactants. An example of a homogeneous catalysed reaction is the decomposition of hydrogen peroxide to form water and oxygen:

$$2H_2O_2(aq) \rightarrow 2H_2O(l) + O_2(g)$$

The activation for the uncatalysed reaction is 75 kJ/mol.

homogeneous reaction: a reaction in which all reactants and products are in the same phase

→ Iodide ions catalyse the decomposition in a two-step reaction. The first step in the catalysed reaction is the one that controls the net rate of the overall reaction:

1 $H_2O_2(aq) + I^-(aq) \rightarrow H_2O(l) + IO^-(aq)$

2 $H_2O_2(aq) + IO^-(aq) \rightarrow H_2O(l) + I^-(aq) + O_2(g)$

→ The activation energy of the catalysed reaction is 57 kJ/mol. This decrease in activation energy from 75 kJ/mol to 57 kJ /mol leads to an approximate 1900 times increase in the reaction rate at room temperature.

→ Enzymes act as biological catalysts in the body. Like other catalysts, enzymes lower the activation energy for a reaction by creating an alternative mechanism for the reaction. Enzymes bind to a particular substrate (reactant molecule) and promote the conversion of that substrate into the products of the specific reaction. For example, the enzyme maltase binds to the maltose substrate and catalyses its hydrolysis to form glucose. Amylase is an enzyme in saliva that catalyses the breakdown of the starch substrate into glucose. Enzymes are highly specific to a particular substrate and their activity is temperature dependent and pH dependent. For amylase that pH is 6.8. Enzymes sustain life as they speed up the rate of biochemical reactions.

→ The following graph (Figure 12.7) shows the change in enzyme activity as a function of temperature. Normal body temperature (~37 °C) is the optimum temperature for maximum enzyme activity.

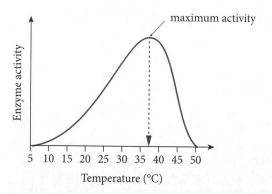

Figure 12.7 Enzyme activity versus temperature

Catalysis modelling

→ Catalysis can be modelled using atomic model kits.

→ Consider the decomposition of ozone gas (O_3) to form diatomic oxygen gas (O_2). In the upper atmosphere this reaction is activated by ultraviolet light, which is absorbed by the ozone molecules:

→ $2O_3(g) \rightarrow 3O_2(g)$

→ Nitric oxide (nitrogen monoxide) acts as a homogeneous catalyst in this decomposition reaction. The steps of this catalysed reaction are:

• Step 1: $O_3(g) + UV \rightarrow O_2(g) + O\bullet(g)$

• Step 2: $O_3(g) + NO(g) \rightarrow O_2(g) + NO_2(g)$

• Step 3: $NO_2(g) + O\bullet(g) \rightarrow NO(g) + O_2(g)$

→ In these reaction steps a reactive oxygen atom called an oxygen **free radical** is formed. This reactive atom has unpaired electrons in its valence shell and the O• symbol is used.

free radical: a reactive atom or molecule with an unpaired electron in an excited energy state

→ The addition of the three steps in the reaction eliminates the intermediates (NO_2 and O•). The NO catalyst reacts in step 2 and is reformed in step 3 and it can then continue to catalyse the decomposition of other ozone molecules.

→ Figure 12.8 demonstrates the modelling process that students can use to demonstrate the steps of the reaction. Select two different coloured balls to represent the oxygen and nitrogen atoms. Use connectors to join atoms together.

- For step 1, construct an ozone molecule and then break it into an oxygen molecule and an oxygen free radical.
- For step 2, construct an NO molecule and an ozone molecule. Demonstrate this reaction by removing an O atom from the ozone and add it to NO to form NO_2. O_2 also forms.
- For step 3, use the NO_2 from step 2 and the O free radical from step 1 to model the reaction. NO and O_2 are formed.

→ KEY QUESTIONS

9 Distinguish between homogeneous and heterogeneous catalysis.
....
10 Hydrogen peroxide solutions slowly decompose to produce oxygen gas and water at 25 °C. A rapid evolution of oxygen gas resulted when powdered manganese dioxide catalyst was added. Is this a heterogeneous or homogeneous catalytic reaction?
....
11 A platinum/rhodium gauze is used as a catalyst in the production of nitric oxide (nitrogen monoxide) when ammonia is oxidised with oxygen gas. During this reaction the gauze glows brightly. Explain why a gauze catalyst is used and identify the observation that this reaction is exothermic.

Answers ⊃ p. 139

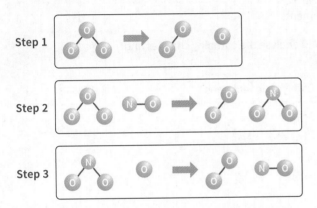

Step 1

Step 2

Step 3

Figure 12.8 Modelling the catalytic decomposition of ozone

CHAPTER SYLLABUS CHECKLIST

Are you able to answer these questions from the syllabus for this chapter? Tick each question as you go through the checklist if you are able to answer it. If you cannot answer a question, turn to the relevant page in the study guide to find the answer. For NESA key word meanings, go to www.educationstandards.nsw.edu.au and search 'key words'.

	FOR A COMPLETE UNDERSTANDING OF THIS TOPIC:	PAGE NO.	✓
1	Can I explain the principle of calorimetry?	128	
2	Can I use the calorimetry equation to calculate heat absorbed or released in calorimetry experiments?	128	
3	Can I describe experiments to measure heats of reaction?	129	
4	Can I distinguish between complete and incomplete combustion?	130	
5	Can I define the term *enthalpy*?	132	
6	Can I calculate enthalpy changes in calorimetry experiments?	132	
7	Can I construct energy profile diagrams to represent and analyse the enthalpy changes and activation energy associated with a chemical reaction?	133	
8	Can I model catalytic reactions and explain the role of catalysts in reactions?	133–134	

Objective-response questions

(1 mark each)

1 An electrical immersion heater is placed in 500 g of water. It heats the water from 25 °C to 90 °C. Calculate the amount of heat (in kilojoules) supplied to the water from the electrical heater assuming no loss in heat. (c.(H_2O) = 4.18×10^3 J/kg/K)

A 271.7 kJ   B 188.1 kJ

C 135 850 kJ   D 136 kJ

2 Identify which of the following is an endothermic process?

A melting a sample of solid wax

B respiration of glucose

C neutralisation of an acid with a base

D conversion of water to ice

3 1.0 g of a salt was dissolved in 110 g of water in a polystyrene calorimeter. The temperature of the solution rose from 25.0 °C to 35.0 °C during the dissolution of the salt. Calculate the quantity of heat released in the dissolution process given that the heat capacity of the solution is 4.18×10^3 J/kg/K.

A 4620 J   B 4200 J   C 4180 J   D 4.62 J

4 An 8.0 g sample of ammonium nitrate was dissolved in water. The equation for the dissolution reaction is:

$$NH_4NO_3(s) \rightarrow NH_4^+(aq) + NO_3^-(aq);$$
$$\Delta H = +25.8 \text{ kJ/mol}$$

Select the correct response.

A The dissolution is endothermic and 2.6 kJ of heat is released to the water.

B The dissolution is exothermic and 25.8 kJ of heat is released to the water.

C The dissolution is endothermic and 2.6 kJ of heat is absorbed from the water.

D The dissolution is exothermic and 25.8 kJ of heat is absorbed from the water.

5 A firsthand investigation using spirit burners and a calorimeter was performed to determine the heat of combustion of methanol (CH_3OH). Select the statement that correctly identifies an issue associated with this experiment.

A The procedure is inaccurate and invalid as considerable heat is lost to the surroundings.

B Heat loss can be considerably reduced by using polystyrene foam calorimeters.

C Accuracy can be improved by using spirit burners with new wicks for each run.

D Methanol and other alcohols are too volatile to be safely used in spirit burners.

Extended-response questions

6 The following equation shows the incomplete combustion of methane to form carbon monoxide and water:

$$CH_4(g) + \tfrac{3}{2}O_2(g) \rightarrow CO(g) + 2H_2O(l);$$
$$\Delta H = -609 \text{ kJ/mol}$$

Calculate the heat released on the incomplete combustion of 5.0 g of methane. (3 marks)

7 400 kJ of heat is released when ethanol undergoes complete combustion. Calculate the mass of ethanol that has been burnt. (2 marks)

$$C_2H_5OH(l) + 3O_2(g) \rightarrow 2CO_2(g) + 3H_2O(l);$$
$$\Delta H = -1367 \text{ kJ/mol}$$

8 A student investigated the heat released when an almond nut was burnt in air. The almond was weighed and it had a mass of 1.2 g. It was held on a thin needle and a beaker containing 300 g of water was supported above the burning nut (Figure 12.9). The temperature of the water was measured before the combustion began and the highest temperature of the water was recorded after the nut ceased burning. In one experiment the temperature of the water rose from 20 °C to 25 °C.

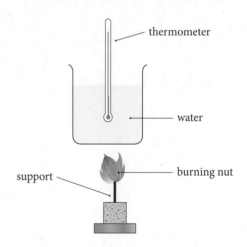

Figure 12.9 Combustion of a nut

a Use the calorimetry equation to calculate the heat absorbed by the water from the burning almond. (C = 4.18×10^3 J/kg/K) (1 mark)

b In nutritional terms the energy content of an almond is 24 kJ/g. Determine the energy content of the almond used and discuss whether all this energy has been transferred to the calorimeter during the combustion of the almond. (2 marks)

9 Hexan-1-ol is a flammable organic liquid. Its structural formula is shown in Figure 12.10.

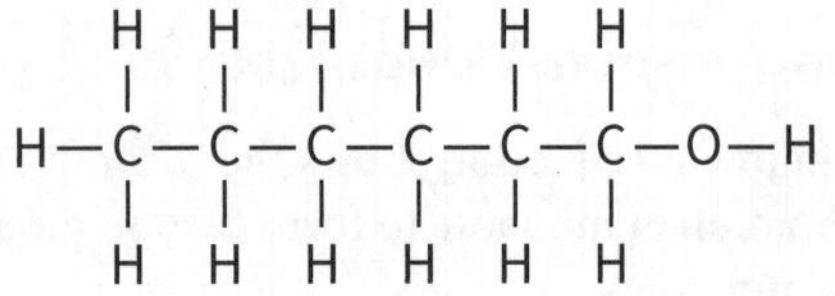

$$
\begin{array}{ccccccc}
& H & H & H & H & H & H \\
& | & | & | & | & | & | \\
H- & C- & C- & C- & C- & C- & C-O-H \\
& | & | & | & | & | & | \\
& H & H & H & H & H & H
\end{array}
$$

Figure 12.10 Hexan-1-ol

a Determine the molecular formula of hexan-1-ol.
(1 mark)

b Calculate the molar mass of hexan-1-ol. (1 mark)

c 2.044 g of hexan-1-ol undergoes complete combustion in excess oxygen to form carbon dioxide and water.

  i Write a balanced equation for the combustion. (1 mark)

  ii 7968 J of heat is produced in the combustion. Calculate the molar heat of combustion of hexan-1-ol. (2 marks)

10 Figure 12.11 shows the enthalpy profile for an uncatalysed reaction and the same reaction using a homogeneous catalyst.

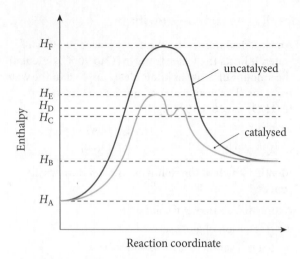

Figure 12.11 Enthalpy profiles

The following symbols can be used to answer some of the following questions: $H_A, H_B, H_C, H_D, H_E, H_F$

a Identify the enthalpy change for the reaction. (1 mark)

b Classify the reaction as endothermic or exothermic. (1 mark)

c Identify the activation energy for the uncatalysed reaction. (1 mark)

d The catalysed reaction occurs in two steps.

  i Identify the activation energy for the first step in the catalysed reaction. (1 mark)

  ii Identify the activation energy for the second step in the catalysed reaction. (1 mark)

  iii Explain which of the two steps of the catalysed reaction is the slower (1 mark)

ANSWERS

KEY QUESTIONS

Key questions ⊃ p. 131

1 a exothermic   b exothermic
   c endothermic

2 q = heat energy; c = specific heat capacity; m = mass of material absorbing or losing the heat; ΔT = change in temperature

3 Complete combustion: carbon dioxide and water.
   Incomplete combustion: carbon dioxide, carbon monoxide, carbon and water.

4 Considerable amounts of heat are lost to the surroundings. The combustion will be incomplete due to a limited oxygen supply.

Key questions ⊃ p. 133

5 The negative sign indicates that the reaction is exothermic.

6 $n(Na_2CO_3) = m/M$
   $$= \frac{5.0}{2 \times 22.99 + 12.01 + 3 \times 16.00}$$
   $$= \frac{5.0}{105.99}$$
   $$= 0.0472 \text{ mol}$$
   $q = n\Delta H = (0.0472)(24) = 1.133 \text{ kJ} = 1133 \text{ J}$
   $q = m.c.\Delta T$
   $1133 = (0.080)(4.18 \times 10^3)\Delta T$
   $\Delta T = 3.4 \, ^\circ C$

7 $H_2O(g) \rightarrow 2H(g) + O(g)$
   The reaction has a high activation energy and higher temperatures are required to break the covalent bonds in the water molecule.

8 250 kJ = 0.250 MJ
   One kilogram of black coal produces 33 MJ.
   Therefore the mass of black coal that produces 0.250 MJ = $\frac{0.250}{33}$
   $$= 7.58 \times 10^{-3} \text{ kg}$$
   $$= 7.58 \text{ g}$$

Key questions ⊃ p. 135

9 Homogeneous catalysis: catalyst is in the same phase as the reactants.
   Heterogeneous catalysis: catalyst is in a different phase to the reactants.

10 Heterogeneous, as the manganese dioxide is a solid and the hydrogen peroxide is in an aqueous solution.

11 The gauze has a high surface area, which increases the reaction rate. The gauze glows, indicating that energy is released as heat and light.

YEAR 11 EXAM-TYPE QUESTIONS

Objective-response questions

1 **D.** $q = m.c.\Delta T = 0.500 \times 4.18 \times 10^3 \times (90 - 25)$
   $= 135\,850 \text{ J} = 136 \text{ kJ}$
   Therefore **A**, **B** and **C** must be incorrect. In C the units are incorrect.

2 **A.** Heat energy has to be added to melt the wax. **B**, **C** and **D** are incorrect as they are all exothermic.

3 **A.** $q = m.c.\Delta T = 0.110 \times 4.18 \times 10^3 \times 10.0 = 4620$ J. Thus **B**, **C** and **D** are incorrect.

4 **C.** Reaction is endothermic; heat is absorbed from the water and the solution decreases in temperature.
   $M(NH_4NO_3) = 80.052$ g/mol
   $n(NH_4NO_3) = m/M = \dfrac{8.0}{80.052}$
   $= 0.09994$ mol
   Heat absorbed from the water
   $= n\Delta H = (0.09994)(25.8)$
   $= 2.58$ kJ
   $= 2.6$ kJ (2 s.f.)
   A and **B** are incorrect as the positive enthalpy change indicates an endothermic process. **D** is incorrect as this amount of heat is involved with one mole instead of 0.09994 moles.

5 **A.** Heat escapes away from the flame into the surrounding air and only some heat is absorbed by the water in the calorimeter. **B** is incorrect as foam calorimeters cannot be used as they would burn. **C** is incorrect as new wicks do not improve accuracy because they do not ensure that more heat is absorbed by the calorimeters. **D** is incorrect as these spirit burners are safe to use, assuming normal safety practices.

Extended-response questions

6 **EM** Students need to recall that an improper fraction in the equation is allowed. The enthalpy change records the heat liberated per mole of methane. Therefore the number of moles in 5.0 g must be calculated. Remember that enthalpy change has a negative sign whereas the quantity of heat (q) does not have a sign.
   $M(CH_4) = 12.01 + 4(1.008)$
   $= 16.042$ g/mol ✓
   $n(CH_4) = m/M = \dfrac{5.0}{16.042} = 0.312$ mol ✓
   Change in enthalpy = $n\Delta H = (0.312)(-609)$
   $= -190$ kJ
   q = heat released = 190 kJ
   $= 1.9 \times 10^2$ kJ (2 s.f.) ✓

7 **EM** Students need to demonstrate that the amount of ethanol burnt is obtained by calculating the ratio of heat released to enthalpy change. From the moles of ethanol the mass of ethanol is calculated.
   n = moles of ethanol burnt = $\dfrac{400}{1367}$
   $= 0.293$ mol ✓
   $m(\text{ethanol}) = n.M$
   $= (0.293)(2 \times 12.01 + 6 \times 1.008 + 16.00)$
   $= (0.293)(46.068) = 13.5$ g ✓

8 **EM** Students apply the calorimetry equation and ensure units cancel to produce joules. The energy content of the almond is obtained by multiplying 24 kJ/g by the mass of the almond used.
   a $q = m.c.\Delta T = 0.300 \times 4.18 \times 10^3 \times 5$
   $= 6270$ J = 6.27 kJ ✓
   b The 1.2 g almond has an energy content of $1.2 \times 24 = 29$ kJ (2 s.f.) ✓
   Thus the heat absorbed by the calorimeter is only a small fraction of the energy content of the nut. The combustion of the nut is incomplete as only the more volatile compounds have burnt under these conditions. Considerable heat has also been lost to the surroundings. ✓

9 **EM** Students need to recall that the molecular formula is obtained by adding up the number of C, H and O atoms in the structural formula. Check atom balance in the equation to ensure the mark is awarded. The molar heat of combustion relies on a correct calculation of the number of moles.
   a $C_6H_{14}O$ ✓
   b $M = 6 \times 12.01 + 14 \times 1.008 + 16.00$
   $= 102.172$ g/mol ✓
   c i $C_6H_{14}O(l) + 9O_2(g)$
   $\rightarrow 6CO_2(g) + 7H_2O(l)$ ✓
   ii $n(\text{hexan-1-ol}) = m/M$
   $= \dfrac{2.044}{102.172}$
   $= 0.0200$ mol ✓
   Thus 0.0200 mol of hexan-1-ol produces 7968 J of heat.
   Thus 1 mol of hexan-1-ol produces $\dfrac{7968}{0.0200}$ J = 398 400 J
   $= 3984$ kJ
   Molar heat of combustion
   $= 3984$ kJ/mol ✓

10 **EM** Students should first revise the section of this chapter on activation energy and reaction profiles. Reactions are slower when their activation energies are higher.
   a $H_B - H_A$ ✓   b endothermic ✓
   c $H_F - H_A$ ✓
   d i $H_E - H_A$ ✓   ii $H_D - H_C$ ✓
   iii Step 1 as it has a much greater activation energy than step 2. ✓

CHAPTER 13
ENTHALPY AND HESS'S LAW

How much energy does it take to break bonds and how much is released when bonds are formed?

When physical changes or chemical reactions occur, heat energy is either liberated or absorbed. The liberation of energy helps to drive the reaction forward. Calculations of changes in energy can determine whether reactions are endothermic or exothermic.

1 Energy conservation and enthalpy

» Students explain the enthalpy changes in a reaction in terms of breaking and reforming bonds, and relate this to the law of conservation of energy.

Enthalpy changes and chemical bonds

→ In a chemical reaction the chemical bonds of the reactants break and the atoms recombine to form the products. Thus new bonds have formed.

→ The bond-breaking process is endothermic and the bond-forming process is exothermic.

→ The bond energy is a measure of the strength of a chemical bond. It is the energy required to break 1 mole of bonds (in the gaseous state) and is therefore an endothermic process.

bond energy: the energy required to break 1 mole of covalent bonds

→ The bond energy is typically measured in the units of kJ/mol. For example, the bond energy for single C–H covalent bonds is 414 kJ/mol. This means that 414 kJ of energy must be supplied to break 1 mole of these bonds in the gaseous state. Double and triple covalent bonds typically have greater bond energies than single bonds. Table 13.1 shows some examples of bond energies for common covalent bonds.

Table 13.1 Bond energies

Bond	Bond energy (BE) (kJ/mol)
C–C	346
C–H	414
H–H	436
O–H	463
C=C	614
O=O	498
N≡N	945

→ Bond energies can be used to calculate the enthalpy change for a reaction. Consider the following example.

EXAMPLE 1

Hydrogen gas burns in oxygen gas to form water vapour. Use bond energy data to calculate the enthalpy change for the following gaseous reaction:

$$2(H–H) + O=O \rightarrow 2(H–O–H)$$

Answer:

Energy is required to break the bonds of the reactants.

Count the number of bonds being broken and forming

Total energy absorbed = $2 \times BE(H–H) + BE(O=O)$
= $2(436) + (498)$
= 1370 kJ

Energy is released when product bonds are formed.

Total energy released = $4 \times BE(O–H)$
= $4(463)$
= 1852 kJ

ΔH = energy absorbed − energy released
= $(1370) − (1852)$
= $−482$ kJ

This is an exothermic reaction as more energy is released than was absorbed by the reactants.

→ The first law of thermodynamics is the law of energy conservation. It is a fundamental law of science.

Law of energy conservation

> **Energy can neither be created nor destroyed.**

→ Thus the total energy of an isolated system remains constant. Energy can be transformed from one form to another but the total energy is conserved. In an exothermic chemical reaction some chemical energy is transformed into heat energy.

→ Compounds are formed from elements that chemically combine in fixed ratios. In order to specify the enthalpy change for such compound formation reactions, we must start with elements in their standard states. The standard states refer to the normal state of the element at 25 °C and 100 kPa. Thus the standard state of iron is a solid and the standard state of oxygen is a gas.

> **standard state:** the state of elements or compounds at 25 °C and 100 kPa; in the case of the concentration of solutions, the standard state is 1.0 mol/L

→ Elements in their standard states have zero enthalpy of formation. $H°$ is the symbol for enthalpy under standard state conditions:

$$H°_{element} = 0$$

→ When elements combine to form 1 mole of a compound then the change in enthalpy is called the standard enthalpy of formation ($\Delta_f H°$):

$$\Delta_f H° = H°_{compound} - H°_{element} = H°_{compound} - 0 = H°_{compound}$$

Examples:

- Formation of ethane gas

  $2C(s) + 3H_2(g) \rightarrow C_2H_6(g); \Delta_f H° = -85 \text{ kJ/mol}$

  Therefore when 1 mole of ethane forms from its elements (all in their standard states) 85 kJ of heat is released. The standard state of carbon is its graphite allotropic form. The reaction is exothermic.

> **allotrope:** different structural forms of an element

- Formation of hydrogen selenide gas

  $H_2(g) + Se(s) \rightarrow H_2Se(g); \Delta_f H° = +30 \text{ kJ/mol}$

  In this case the enthalpy of formation refers to an endothermic reaction.

- Formation of sodium chloride solution

  $Na(s) + \frac{1}{2}Cl_2(g) \rightarrow Na^+(aq) + Cl^-(aq);$
  $\Delta_f H° = -407 \text{ kJ/mol}$

  In this example the standard state for a salt in solution is a 1 mol/L solution at 25 °C.

EXAMPLE 2

Ethylene (C_2H_4) gas burns completely in excess oxygen to form carbon dioxide and water vapour.

a Write the equation for this reaction using structural formulae.

b Use the following bond energy data to determine the molar enthalpy of combustion ($\Delta_c H$) of ethylene.

> Bond breakage is endothermic and bond forming is exothermic

Bond	C=C	C–H	O–H	O=O	C=O
Bond energy (kJ/mol)	614	414	463	498	804

Answer:

a Figure 13.1 illustrates the structural equation for the combustion of ethylene.

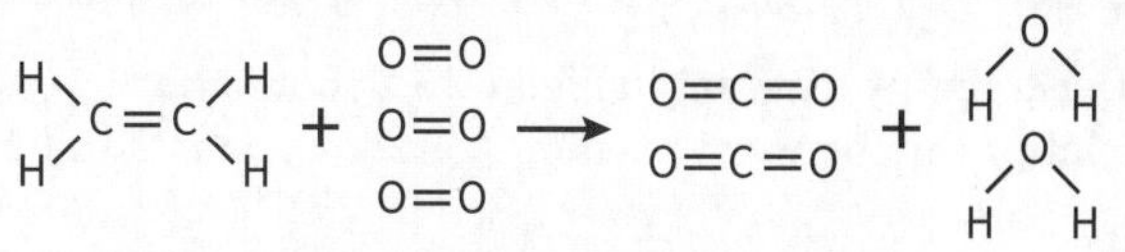

Figure 13.1 Structural equation

b Total energy to break reactant bonds
= 614 + 4(414) + 3(498)
= 3764 kJ

Total energy released on forming product bonds
= 4(804) + 4(463)
= 5068 kJ

$\Delta_c H$ = energy absorbed – energy released
= (3764) – (5068)
= –1304 kJ/mol

2 Hess's Law

» Students investigate Hess's law in quantifying the enthalpy change for a stepped reaction using standard enthalpy change data and bond energy data; for example, carbon reacting with oxygen to form carbon dioxide via carbon monoxide.

→ In 1840 GH Hess discovered a generalisation concerning the conservation of enthalpy. This has subsequently become known as Hess's law of heat summation.

Hess's law

> **The enthalpy change for a reaction is independent of the reaction pathway.**

→ If a reaction is carried out in a series of steps, the overall change in enthalpy is the same as the sum of the enthalpy changes of the separate steps.

→ Standard enthalpies of formation can be used in conjunction with Hess's law to determine the enthalpy change for various chemical reactions.

EXAMPLE 3

Calculate the enthalpy change of the following reaction A using the enthalpy of formation data supplied in 1 and 2.

> Determine how the two data equations can be combined to form the equation for reaction A in Figure 13.2

Reaction A:

$CuCl(s) + \frac{1}{2}Cl_2(g) \rightarrow CuCl_2(s)$

Data:

1 $Cu(s) + Cl_2(g) \rightarrow CuCl_2(s); \Delta_f H^\circ = -220$ kJ/mol

2 $Cu(s) + \frac{1}{2}Cl_2(g) \rightarrow CuCl(s); \Delta_f H^\circ = -137$ kJ/mol

The enthalpy diagram in Figure 13.2 shows the relationship between reaction A and reactions 1 and 2.

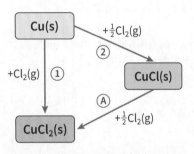

Figure 13.2 Alternative paths to convert copper to copper (II) chloride

Answer:

Reaction A is obtained by subtracting equation 2 from equation 1. When an equation is subtracted, reverse the equation and then add it. Eliminate like terms to obtain the final equation.

Equation 1:

$Cu(s) + Cl_2(g) \rightarrow CuCl_2(s)$

Reverse equation 2:

$CuCl(s) \rightarrow Cu(s) + \frac{1}{2}Cl_2(g)$

Equation 1 plus reverse equation 2:

$CuCl(s) + \frac{1}{2}Cl_2(g) \rightarrow CuCl_2(s)$

Using Hess's law:

$\Delta H(A) = \Delta_f H(1) - \Delta_f H(2)$
$= (-220) - (-137)$
$= -83$ kJ/mol

EXAMPLE 4

Figure 13.3 shows three linked reaction paths.

> Write equations for each of the three paths

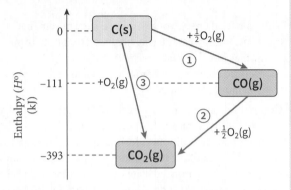

Figure 13.3 Hess's law diagram (not to scale)

Use the data provided in Figure 13.3 to verify Hess's law.

Answer:

The equations for each path are:

Path 1: $C(s) + \frac{1}{2}O_2(g) \rightarrow CO(g); \Delta H_1 = -111$ kJ/mol

Path 2: $CO(g) + \frac{1}{2}O_2(g) \rightarrow CO_2(g); \Delta H_2 = -282$ kJ/mol

Path 3: $C(s) + O_2(g) \rightarrow CO_2(g); \Delta H_3 = -393$ kJ/mol

Using Hess's law, path 1 + path 2 = path 3.

Thus the sum of the enthalpy changes for path 1 and path 2 should equal the enthalpy change for path 3:

$(-111) + (-282) = (-393)$.

Therefore Hess's law has been verified.

EXAMPLE 5

Examine the enthalpy diagram in Figure 13.4 and answer the questions.

> Match reactions A, B and C to the numbered paths in the Hess's law diagram

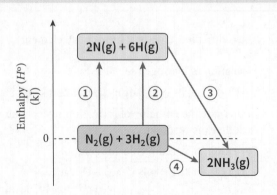

Figure 13.4 Enthalpy diagram for ammonia

Example 5 continued

a Use the following data to assign enthalpy values for three of the four steps 1, 2, 3 and 4 in Figure 13.4:

   A $H(g) \rightarrow \frac{1}{2}H_2(g)$; $\Delta H = -218$ kJ

   B $\frac{1}{2}N_2(g) + \frac{3}{2}H_2(g) \rightarrow NH_3(g)$; $\Delta H = -46$ kJ

   C $NH_3(g) \rightarrow N(g) + 3H(g)$; $\Delta H = +1173$ kJ

b Determine the enthalpy change for the remaining step.

Answer:

a Reaction 2 = 6 × (–equation A)

$3H_2(g) \rightarrow 6H(g)$; $\Delta H(2) = 6(+218)$
$= +1308$ kJ

Reaction 3 = 2 × (–equation C)

$2N(g) + 6H(g) \rightarrow 2NH_3(g)$; $\Delta H(3) = -2(1173)$
$= -2346$ kJ

Reaction 4 = 2 × (equation B)

$N_2(g) + 3H_2(g) \rightarrow 2NH_3(g)$; $\Delta H(4) = 2(-46)$
$= -92$ kJ

b Using Hess's law:

Reaction (1) + reaction (2) + reaction (3) = reaction (4)

$\Delta H(1) + \Delta H(2) + \Delta H(3) = \Delta H(4)$
$\Delta H(1) + (+1308) + (-2346) = (-92)$
$\Delta H(1) = +946$ kJ

→ **KEY QUESTIONS**

1 Define the conditions in which elements exist in their standard states.

2 State the enthalpy of formation of copper in its standard state.

3 Write an equation for the formation of aluminium chloride in its standard state.

Answers ⊃ p. 149

3 Energy cycles and Hess's law

» Students apply Hess's law to simple energy cycles and solve problems to quantify enthalpy changes within reactions, including but not limited to heat of combustion; enthalpy changes involved in photosynthesis; and enthalpy changes involved in respiration.

Hess's law and enthalpy of combustion

→ The following examples shows how Hess's law can be applied to combustion reactions.

EXAMPLE 6

Use the following data in these equations to calculate the enthalpy of complete combustion of acetylene gas (C_2H_2):

> Balance the elements in the combustion equation in the order C, H, O

1 $C(s) + O_2(g) \rightarrow CO_2(g)$; $\Delta H_1 = -393$ kJ/mol

2 $H_2(g) + \frac{1}{2}O_2(g) \rightarrow H_2O(l)$; $\Delta H_2 = -285$ kJ/mol

3 $2C(s) + H_2(g) \rightarrow C_2H_2(g)$; $\Delta H_3 = +227$ kJ/mol

Answer:

Write the equation for the complete combustion of *1 mole* of acetylene:

4 $C_2H_2(g) + \frac{5}{2}O_2(g) \rightarrow 2CO_2(g) + H_2O(l)$;
$\Delta H_4 = $ unknown

Examine the data equations and determine how they can be combined to give equation (4):

Equation (4) = 2 × equation (1) + equation (2) – equation (3)

$\Delta H_4 = 2\Delta H_1 + \Delta H_2 - \Delta H_3$
$= 2(-393) + (-285) - (+227)$
$= -1298$ kJ/mol

Thus the enthalpy of complete combustion of acetylene is –1298 kJ/mol.

EXAMPLE 7

Diamond and graphite are allotropes of carbon. Both allotropes can undergo combustion to form carbon dioxide. Figure 13.5 shows that the combustion of diamond to carbon dioxide can occur directly (step 3) or via two steps (1 and 2).

Use Hess's law to calculate the enthalpy change for the conversion of diamond to graphite.

> Determine the relationship between the three steps

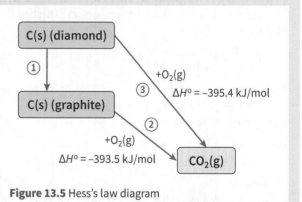

Figure 13.5 Hess's law diagram

Answer:

According to Hess's law:

$\Delta H^\circ(3) = \Delta H^\circ(1) + \Delta H^\circ(2)$

Example 7 continued

The standard enthalpies of steps 2 and 3 have been measured accurately to four significant figures.

$$\Delta H^\circ(2) = -393.5 \text{ kJ/mol}$$
$$\Delta H^\circ(3) = -395.4 \text{ kJ/mol}$$

Therefore $(-395.4) = \Delta H^\circ(1) + (-393.5)$
$$\Delta H^\circ(1) = (-395.4) + (393.5)$$
$$= -1.9 \text{ kJ/mol}$$

$$C(s)(\text{diamond}) \rightarrow C(s)(\text{graphite}); \Delta H^\circ = -1.9 \text{ kJ/mol}$$

Therefore the conversion of 1 mole of diamond to 1 mole of graphite is an exothermic process. Thus graphite is the more stable allotropic form of carbon.

EXAMPLE 8

The reaction of magnesium with oxygen is classified as a combustion reaction. The enthalpy change for this reaction is a measure of the enthalpy of formation of magnesium oxide. The enthalpy of formation of magnesium oxide is to be determined from the following supplied data obtained from firsthand investigations and second-hand data.

> Use the calorimetry formula to determine the heat released in Part A and B

Required reaction:

$$Mg(s) + \tfrac{1}{2}O_2(g) \rightarrow MgO(s); \Delta_f H(MgO) = \text{unknown}$$

Data: Part A
Measurement of heat of reaction: magnesium and hydrochloric acid

Reaction A:

$$Mg(s) + 2HCl(aq) \rightarrow MgCl_2(aq) + H_2(g); \Delta H_A$$

Method:

1 Measure 50.0 mL (0.0500 kg) of 2.0 mol/L HCl into a foam calorimeter. Measure the initial temperature.
2 Add 0.10 g of magnesium ribbon to the acid and after mixing measure the highest temperature reached.

Results:

Initial temperature = 20.6 °C
Final temperature = 29.7 °C

Data: Part B
Measurement of heat of reaction: magnesium oxide and hydrochloric acid

Reaction B:

$$MgO(s) + 2HCl(aq) \rightarrow MgCl_2(aq) + H_2O(l); \Delta H_B$$

Method:

1 Measure 50.0 mL (50.0 g) of 2.0 mol/L HCl into a foam calorimeter. Measure the initial temperature.
2 Add 0.50 g of magnesium oxide to the acid and after mixing measure the highest temperature reached.

Results:

Initial temperature = 21.1 °C
Final temperature = 29.8 °C

Data: Part C
Second-hand data collection: enthalpy of formation of water

Reaction C:

$$H_2(g) + \tfrac{1}{2}O_2(g) \rightarrow H_2O(l); \Delta_f H = \Delta H_C$$

Results:

$$\Delta_f H(H_2O) = -285 \text{ kJ/mol}$$

Use all the data from Parts A, B and C to calculate the heat of formation of magnesium oxide.

Answer:

Calculate the enthalpy change of the reactions for Parts A and B.

Part A

1 Mass of water = $m = 0.0500$ kg
2 $q = m.c.\Delta T = (0.0500)(4.18 \times 10^3)(29.7 - 20.6) = 1902$ J
3 $n(Mg) = \dfrac{0.10}{24.31} = 0.00411$ mol

4 $\Delta H_A = -q/n = \dfrac{-1902}{0.00411}$
$$= -46\,277 \text{ J/mol}$$
$$= -463 \text{ kJ/mol}$$

Part B

1 Mass of solution = $m = 0.0500$ kg
2 $q = m.c.\Delta T = (0.0500)(4.18 \times 10^3)((29.8 - 21.1) = 1818$ J

3 $n(MgO) = \dfrac{0.50}{24.31 + 16.00} = 0.0124$ mol

4 $\Delta H_B = -q/n = \dfrac{-1818}{0.0124}$
$$= -146\,613 \text{ J/mol}$$
$$= -147 \text{ kJ/mol}$$

Part C

Second-hand data:

$$\Delta H_C = \Delta_f H(H_2O) = -285 \text{ kJ/mol}$$

The enthalpy change for reaction D can now be calculated using Hess's law.

Reaction D:

$$Mg(s) + \tfrac{1}{2}O_2(g) \rightarrow MgO(s); \Delta_f H(MgO) = \text{unknown}$$

Reaction D = reaction A – reaction B + reaction C

$$Mg(s) + 2HCl(aq) + H_2O(l) + MgCl_2(aq) + H_2(g) + \tfrac{1}{2}O_2(g)$$
$$\rightarrow MgCl_2(aq) + H_2(g) + MgO(s) + 2HCl(aq) + H_2O(l)$$

Cancel out like terms.

Reaction A – reaction B + reaction C
$$= Mg(s) + \tfrac{1}{2}O_2(g) \rightarrow MgO(s)$$

Therefore $\Delta_f H(MgO) = \Delta H_A - \Delta H_B + \Delta H_C$
$$= (-463) - (-147) + (-285)$$
$$= -601 \text{ kJ/mol}$$

Enthalpy changes in photosynthesis and respiration

→ Living organisms make compounds that are important sources of energy. Photosynthetic organisms utilise solar radiation to power biochemical processes that lead to the production of simple molecules, including sugars. Chemical compounds are then a source of chemical energy for other organisms.

Photosynthesis

→ Photosynthesis is a photochemical process in which carbon dioxide and water are converted into simple carbohydrates (such as glucose) and oxygen (Figure 13.6). The process is powered by solar energy that is absorbed by **chlorophyll** molecules present in the cells of phytoplankton, green plants and algae. For each mole of glucose formed, 2807 kJ of energy must be supplied. Photosynthesis is therefore an endothermic process.

carbon dioxide + water → glucose + oxygen

$$6CO_2(g) + 6H_2O(l) \rightarrow C_6H_{12}O_6(s) + 6O_2(g);$$
$$\Delta H^\circ = +2807 \text{ kJ/mol}$$

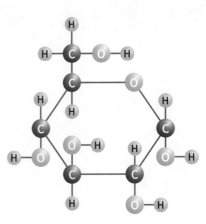

Figure 13.6 Glucose molecular structure

chlorophyll: a green molecule found in green plants that absorbs solar energy to power the photosynthetic process

→ Chlorophyll molecules are located in structures called chloroplasts in green plant cells. These molecules weakly absorb green light but strongly absorb the red and violet ends of the electromagnetic spectrum. The energy that is absorbed is used to oxidise water molecules to form oxygen gas. The electrons released from the breakdown of the water molecules are then used to convert carbon dioxide to simple carbohydrate molecules such as glucose. The whole process is a complex, multi-step reaction sequence.

EXAMPLE 9

Use the following enthalpy of formation data to determine the enthalpy change for the photosynthesis reaction.

Heat from the formation of oxygen is zero

$$6CO_2(g) + 6H_2O(l) \rightarrow C_6H_{12}O_6(s) + 6O_2(g)$$

Data:

$\Delta_f H^\circ$: $CO_2(g) = -394 \text{ kJ/mol}$;

$H_2O(l) = -286 \text{ kJ/mol}$;

$C_6H_{12}O_6(s) = -1273 \text{ kJ/mol}$

Answer:

$\Delta H^\circ = \Delta_f H^\circ(\text{glucose}) - 6 \times \Delta_f H^\circ(CO_2) - 6 \times \Delta_f H^\circ(H_2O)$
$= (-1273) - 6(-394) - 6(-286)$
$= +2807 \text{ kJ/mol}$

Respiration

→ The carbohydrates that are formed in photosynthesis are classified as high-energy compounds. They store chemical potential energy in their bonds. We can think of high-energy carbohydrates as an important step in the stabilisation of the Sun's energy. Life on Earth is dependent on this stabilised energy.

→ Very little (~4%) of the solar energy striking a leaf surface is ultimately converted to chemical potential energy. Much is lost in the form of heat energy. Producers such as green plants use some of this chemical potential energy for their cellular biochemical processes including respiration. **Cellular respiration** is an exothermic process.

Cellular respiration:

$$C_6H_{12}O_6(s) + 6O_2(g) \rightarrow 6CO_2(g) + 6H_2O(l);$$
$$\Delta H = -2807 \text{ kJ/mol}$$

cellular respiration: a chemical reaction occurring in living cells that generates energy to power chemical reactions and warm the organism

→ **Herbivores** (first-order consumers) eat plant material and utilise some of the stored chemical potential energy to power biochemical processes within their own cells. Some energy is used to make fat and protein, which are also forms of stored chemical potential energy. Much of the energy (~75%) is lost as heat.

→ Second-order consumers (**carnivores**) eat the herbivores and utilise some of the stored chemical potential energy.

→ **Decomposers** ultimately use some of the remaining energy to break down the dead remains of plants and animals to provide the raw materials to be recycled.

→ At all stages along the food chain much of the available energy is dissipated as heat. Some of this heat warms the environment and the rest is radiated back into space.

herbivores: living things that eat producers such as green plants and algae

carnivores: living things that eat herbivores or other carnivores

decomposers: living things such as bacteria and mould that break down the remains of dead organisms

→ KEY QUESTIONS

4   Use the standard enthalpies of formation data to calculate the standard enthalpy of complete combustion of liquid ethanol.
($\Delta_f H^\circ$: $C_2H_5OH(l)$ = –278 kJ/mol;
$CO_2(g)$ = –393 kJ/mol; $H_2O(l)$ = – 285 kJ/mol)

5   Write an equation for photosynthesis. Given that the enthalpy change for photosynthesis is +2807 kJ/mol, calculate the amount of energy required by plant cells to produce 50.0 g of glucose.

6   Identify the importance of cellular respiration in living things.

Answers ⊃ p. 149

CHAPTER SYLLABUS CHECKLIST

Are you able to answer these questions from the syllabus for this chapter? Tick each question as you go through the checklist if you are able to answer it. If you cannot answer a question, turn to the relevant page in the study guide to find the answer. For NESA key word meanings, go to www.educationstandards.nsw.edu.au and search 'key words'.

	FOR A COMPLETE UNDERSTANDING OF THIS TOPIC:	PAGE NO.	✓
1	Can I state the law of energy conservation?	140–141	
2	Can I define the enthalpy of formation of a compound?	141	
3	Can I state Hess's law?	141	
4	Can I solve numerical problems using Hess's law?	142–143	
5	Can I apply Hess's law to determine the enthalpy of combustion?	143	
6	Can I write equations for photosynthesis and respiration, and compare the enthalpy changes for these reactions?	145	

Objective-response questions

(1 mark each)

1 Identify which statement is true about the following reaction:

$$2HI(g) \rightarrow H_2(g) + I_2(s); \Delta H^\circ = -52kJ$$

   A The reaction is endothermic.

   B In a closed vessel the temperature will decrease as the reaction occurs.

   C The standard enthalpy of formation of hydrogen iodide is +26 kJ/mol.

   D The reverse reaction is exothermic.

2 Calculate the enthalpy change for the following reaction:

$$2NO(g) + O_2(g) \rightarrow 2NO_2(g)$$

   Data:

   Standard enthalpies of formation: NO (90 kJ/mol); NO_2 (33 kJ/mol)

   A −57 kJ   B +57 kJ   C +114 kJ   D −114 kJ

3 Calculate the enthalpy change for the formation of gaseous sulfur trioxide using the supplied data:

   1 $S(s) + O_2(g) \rightarrow SO_2(g); \Delta_f H^\circ = -297$ kJ/mol

   2 $SO_3(g) \rightarrow SO_2(g) + \frac{1}{2}O_2(g); \Delta H^\circ = +99$ kJ/mol

   A +198 kJ   B +396 kJ   C −198 kJ   D −396 kJ

4 Calculate the enthalpy change for the formation of gaseous phosphorus trichloride from one mole of white phosphorus (P_4) and chlorine gas.

   Data:

   1 $PCl_3(g) + Cl_2(g) \rightarrow PCl_5(g); \Delta H_1 = -137kJ$

   2 $P_4(s) + 10Cl_2(g) \rightarrow 4PCl_5(g); \Delta H_2 = +716kJ$

   A −1264 kJ   B +1264 kJ

   C +579 kJ   D −579 kJ

5 Identify the equation which shows the formation of potassium hydroxide in its standard state.

   A $K(s) + \frac{1}{2}O_2(g) + \frac{1}{2}H_2(g) \rightarrow KOH(aq)$

   B $K(s) + \frac{1}{2}O_2(g) + \frac{1}{2}H_2(g) \rightarrow KOH(s)$

   C $K(l) + \frac{1}{2}O_2(g) + \frac{1}{2}H_2(g) \rightarrow KOH(aq)$

   D $K(s) + O_2(g) + H_2(g) \rightarrow K(OH)_2(s)$

Extended-response questions

6 Iron can form iron (II) chloride and iron (III) chloride when it reacts directly with chlorine. Iron (II) chloride can also be converted to iron (III) chloride by reaction with chlorine. Use Figure 13.7 to verify Hess's law.

(5 marks)

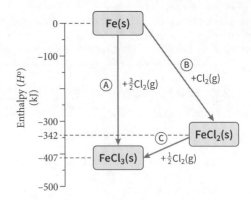

Figure 13.7 Hess's law diagram

7 Powdered aluminium reacts with iron (III) oxide powder to form solid iron and solid aluminium oxide.

   a Write an equation for this reaction.   (1 mark)

   b Calculate the enthalpy change for this reaction using the following data:

   $\Delta_f H(Fe_2O_3(s)) = -821$ kJ/mol;
   $\Delta_f H(Al_2O_3(s)) = -1670$ kJ/mol   (2 marks)

   c Determine whether the heat released in (b) for 1 mole of Fe_2O_3 is sufficient to melt the iron in a closed vessel, given the following data:

   $Fe(s) \rightarrow Fe(l); \Delta H = +14$ kJ/mol   (2 marks)

8 Dodecane ($C_{12}H_{26}$) liquid undergoes incomplete combustion to produce equimolar amounts of soot (carbon graphite) and carbon monoxide.

   a Write a balanced equation for the incomplete combustion of one mole of dodecane.   (1 mark)

   b Use the following data to calculate the enthalpy of combustion. Data:

   $\Delta_f H^\circ$ values: $C_{12}H_{26}(l) = -256$ kJ/mol;
   $H_2O(l) = -285$ kJ/mol;
   $CO(g) = -111$ kJ/mol   (2 marks)

9 The standard enthalpy of formation of solid silver chloride is −127 kJ/mol.

   a Write the formation equation for silver chloride.   (1 mark)

   b How much heat is released when 10 g of silver chloride is formed from its elements in their standard states?   (3 marks)

10 a Write the equation for the standard enthalpy of combustion of liquid propan-1-ol (C_3H_7OH). (1 mark)

   b Use the standard enthalpy of formation data to calculate the molar enthalpy of complete combustion. Data:

   $\Delta_f H^\circ$: $C_3H_7OH(l) = -305$ kJ/mol;
   $CO_2(g) = -393$ kJ/mol;
   $H_2O(l) = -285kJ/mol$ (2 marks)

ANSWERS

KEY QUESTIONS

Key questions ⊃ p. 143

1 25 °C and 100 kPa   2 0 (zero)

3 $Al(s) + \frac{3}{2}Cl_2(g) \rightarrow AlCl_3(s)$

Key questions ⊃ p. 146

4 $C_2H_5OH(l) + 3O_2(g) \rightarrow 2CO_2(g) + 3H_2O(l)$

$\Delta_c H = 2\Delta_f H°(CO_2) + 3\Delta_f H°(H_2O) - \Delta_f H°(C_2H_5OH)$
$= 2(-393) + 3(-285) - (-278)$
$= -786 - 855 + 278$
$= -1363$ kJ/mol

5 $6CO_2(g) + 6H_2O(l) \rightarrow C_6H_{12}O_6(s) + 6O_2(g)$

$M(C_6H_{12}O_6) = 6 \times 12.01 + 12 \times 1.008 + 6 \times 16.00$
$= 180.156$ g/mol

$n(C_6H_{12}O_6) = m/M = \dfrac{50.0}{180.156}$
$= 0.2775$ mol

Energy required $= (0.2775)(2807)$
$= 779$ kJ

6 In cellular respiration the chemical potential energy in foods such as carbohydrates is converted to heat energy and other usable forms of energy that are used to power chemical reactions in cells.

YEAR 11 EXAM-TYPE QUESTIONS

Objective-response questions

1 **C.** The reverse reaction describes the formation of 2 moles of HI. The reverse reaction is endothermic as the enthalpy change is positive. Thus the enthalpy change per mole will be $\dfrac{+52.2}{2} = +26$ kJ/mol. **A** is incorrect as the negative enthalpy change shows the reaction is exothermic. **B** is incorrect as the temperature will rise in the surroundings. **D** is incorrect as the reverse reaction is endothermic.

2 **D.** $\Delta H = \Delta_f H_{(products)} - \Delta_f H_{(reactants)}$
$= (2 \times 33 - 2 \times 90)$
$= -114$ kJ

Thus **A**, **B** and **C** are incorrect. The enthalpy change calculation must involve the reaction stoichiometry.

3 **D.** Required is (3): $S(s) + \frac{3}{2}O_2(g) \rightarrow SO_3(g)$; $\Delta_f H° =$ unknown
Reaction (3) = reaction (1) − reaction (2)
$\Delta H°(3) = \Delta H°(1) - \Delta H°(2)$
$= (-297) - (+99)$
$= -396$ kJ

Thus **A**, **B** and **C** are incorrect.

4 **B.** Required is (3): $P_4(s) + 6Cl_2(g) \rightarrow 4PCl_3(g)$
Reaction (3) = reaction (2) − 4 × reaction (1)
$\Delta H°(3) = \Delta H°(2) - 4 \times \Delta H°(1)$
$= (+716) - 4(-137)$
$= +1264$ kJ

Thus **A**, **C** and **D** are incorrect.

5 **B.** The standard states of K and KOH are solids. Thus **A** and **C** are incorrect as KOH is not aqueous in its standard state. **D** is wrong as the incorrect formula of potassium hydroxide is used.

Extended-response questions

6 **EM** Students must show that the enthalpy change of a reaction is independent of the path taken. The enthalpy scale can be used to determine the enthalpy change for each step.

Reactions:

A $Fe(s) + \frac{3}{2}Cl_2(g) \rightarrow FeCl_3(s)$; $\Delta H_A = (-407) - 0$
$= -407$ kJ ✓

B $Fe(s) + Cl_2(g) \rightarrow FeCl_2(s)$; $\Delta H_B = (-342) - 0$
$= -342$ kJ ✓

C $FeCl_2(s) + \frac{1}{2}Cl_2(g) \rightarrow FeCl_3(s)$; $\Delta H_A = (-407) - (-342)$
$= -65$ kJ ✓

Reaction A = reaction B + reaction C

$\Delta H_A = -407$ kJ ✓

$\Delta H_B + \Delta H_C = (-342) + (-65)$
$= -407$ kJ ✓

Therefore Hess's law is verified.

7 **EM** Students need to show that the reaction is exothermic in order to determine whether the iron formed will melt.

a $Fe_2O_3(s) + 2Al \rightarrow 2Fe(s) + Al_2O_3(s)$ ✓

b $\Delta H = \Delta_f H(Al_2O_3(s)) - \Delta_f H(Fe_2O_3(s))$ ✓
$= (-1670) - (-821)$
$= -849$ kJ ✓

c The iron will melt as 849 kJ ✓ of heat is released and only 14 kJ is required to melt each mole of iron. ✓

8 **EM** Students need to realise that carbon in its standard state has a zero enthalpy. Water will exist as a liquid at 298 K. Combustion reactions are exothermic and the calculation should show that the enthalpy change is negative.

a $C_{12}H_{26}(l) + \frac{19}{2}O_2(g) \rightarrow 6C(s) + 6CO(g) + 13H_2O(l)$ ✓

b $\Delta H = \Delta_f H°_{(products)} - \Delta_f H°_{(reactants)}$
$= 6(-111) + 13(-285) - (-256)$ ✓
$= -4115$ kJ/mol ✓

9 **EM** Students need to recall that the standard states of silver and chlorine are solid and gas respectively. Formation equations should show the formation of one mole of product.

a $Ag(s) + \frac{1}{2}Cl_2(g) \rightarrow AgCl(s)$ ✓

b $M(AgCl) = 107.9 + 35.45 = 143.35$ g/mol

$n(AgCl) = m/M = \dfrac{10}{143.35} = 0.0698$ mol ✓

Heat released $= (0.0698)(127) = 8.9$ kJ ✓

10 **EM** Students need to recall that in complete combustion carbon dioxide and liquid water are formed. The combustion equation can be balanced using a fraction.

a $C_3H_7OH(l) + \frac{9}{2}O_2(g) \rightarrow 3CO_2(g) + 4H_2O(l)$ ✓

b $\Delta_c H° = 3\Delta_f H°(CO_2) + 4\Delta_f H°(H_2O) - \Delta_f H°(C_3H_7OH)$ ✓
$= 3(-393) + 4(-285) - (-305)$
$= -2014$ kJ/mol ✓

CHAPTER 14
ENTROPY AND GIBBS FREE ENERGY

INQUIRY QUESTION:

How can enthalpy and entropy be used to explain reaction spontaneity?

Another factor that drives a reaction is the change in entropy, which is a measure of disorder. Crystals are highly ordered whereas gases are disordered because the particles are able to move about randomly. The spontaneity of a reaction therefore depends on both energy and entropy changes.

1 Entropy as a driving force

» Students analyse the differences between entropy and enthalpy. They use modelling to illustrate entropy changes in reactions and predict entropy changes from balanced chemical reactions to classify as increasing or decreasing entropy.

Entropy and disorder

➜ This module examines energy changes in chemical processes. Energy is released in exothermic processes as the products have lower energy contents than the reactants. This tendency in nature to seek states of lower potential energy is a driving force for reactions.

➜ Another driving force is the tendency to move from ordered states to states of disorder in isolated systems. This driving force is called entropy.

entropy (S): a measure of the disorder of a system

➜ Figure 14.1 shows an example of increasing entropy of a system when ice melts to form water and then vapourises to form water vapour.

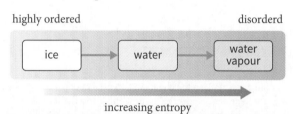

Figure 14.1 Entropy and disorder

➜ The higher the entropy of an isolated system, the greater is its disorder. The system in chemistry is defined as the *reacting particles*. The surroundings are the rest of the universe, which includes the walls of the reaction vessel and the solvent in which the reacting chemicals are dissolved.

➜ In everyday life we can think of a student tidying up a messy bedroom as an example of negative entropy (Figure 14.2). Energy has to be used to tidy up the bedroom and put things in their proper places.

Figure 14.2 Tidying a room and changes in entropy

Image courtesy G Thickett, 2017

The bedroom is the system becoming more ordered. The energy to do the tidying is coming from the food eaten by the student to power his muscles. However, the cellular respiration of the food produces a lot of wasted heat, which is lost to the surroundings. The entropy of the surroundings increases to a greater extent than the decrease in entropy when the room is tidy. Thus the total entropy of the universe has increased. This idea is explored in the next section.

→ Entropy changes occur when ice blocks melt. The water molecules are very ordered in their crystal lattice. When the ice melts the molecules move apart and randomly move throughout the liquid. The water molecules are then in a more random state. Therefore the entropy of the system (i.e. water molecules) has increased.

$$H_2O(s) \rightarrow H_2O(l)$$

→ Entropy changes occur during chemical reactions. When hydrochloric acid is added to a marble chip, carbon dioxide gas is produced and it escapes out of the solution. The solid dissolves and produces free ions in solution. The final state of the system has higher entropy as the gas molecules and dissolved ions are in a much more disordered state than the reactants.

$$CaCO_3(s) + 2H^+(aq) \rightarrow Ca^{2+}(aq) + H_2O(l) + CO_2(g)$$

→ The following examples involve changes in entropy.

Example:

- **Food dye added to water**

  If a beaker is filled with water and one drop of food dye is added to the water, we observe that the dye molecules spread out over time into the surrounding water (Figure 14.3). Eventually the dye becomes evenly dispersed throughout the water. This happens because of the motion of water molecules and the random collisions that occur between them and the dye molecules. Initially the dye molecules were contained in the drop but later they are spread out and more randomly arranged. Chemists describe this change as *an increase in entropy of the system*.

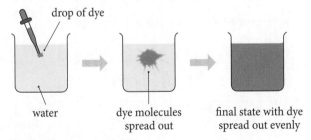

Figure 14.3 Dye diffuses into water

Example:

- **Gas expands into a vacuum**

  Figure 14.4 shows a vessel in which two equal volume chambers are separated by a tap. Initially the molecules are confined in the left chamber and a

vacuum exists in the right chamber. When the tap is opened the gas molecules move into the right chamber until the gas fills both chambers. The gas pressure is halved in the final state. The process is dynamic and molecules continue to move randomly back and forth between the chambers.

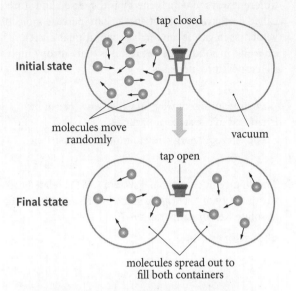

Figure 14.4 Gas expands into a larger space

There is an increase in entropy in this isolated system as the molecules have a greater degree of freedom in terms of their molecular motions.

Example:

- **Precipitation reaction**

  When sodium chloride solution and silver nitrate solution are mixed a white precipitate of silver chloride forms (Figure 14.5). The reaction is exothermic:

  $$AgNO_3(aq) + NaCl(aq) \rightarrow AgCl(s) + NaNO_3(aq)$$

  The net ionic equation is:

  $$Ag^+(aq) + Cl^-(aq) \rightarrow AgCl(s)$$

  In this reaction the entropy of the system has decreased as the silver ions and chloride ions have become more ordered in the crystalline silver chloride precipitate.

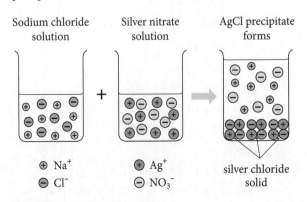

Figure 14.5 Precipitation reaction

Entropy and temperature

→ Temperature is a factor that alters the entropy of a system. High temperature systems have more heat content (or thermal energy). This energy can be distributed in many different ways. Each of these different ways in which energy is dispersed and stored is called a microstate. Heat energy can increase molecular velocities in gas. It can increase vibrational kinetic energies in solids. The net result is that entropy increases as temperature increases.

> **microstate:** different ways in which energy can be distributed in a system of particles
>
> **kinetic energy:** energy due to motion of a particle

→ The change in entropy of a system (ΔS) is related to the quantity of heat (q) produced or absorbed and the absolute Kelvin temperature (T).

Change in entropy

$$\Delta S = q/T$$

→ Standard entropy values are measured under standard conditions. The symbol for the standard entropy is S^o. The symbol for the standard entropy change is ΔS^o:

$$\Delta S^o = \Sigma S^o_{products} - \Sigma S^o_{reactants}$$

Example:

- **Vapourisation of liquid water**

  The vapourisation of liquid water at 25 °C is an endothermic process:

  $$H_2O(l) \rightarrow H_2O(g); \Delta H^o = +44 \text{ kJ/mol}$$

  The heat required for this vapourisation comes from the surroundings. The surroundings lose heat and their entropy decreases. The system increases in entropy as it absorbs heat and the gaseous water has a higher disordered state. The following standard molar entropy data is provided for the liquid water and water vapour:

  $$H_2O(l) \rightarrow H_2O(g)$$
  $$S^o(H_2O(l)) = 70 \text{ J/K/mol}$$
  $$S^o(H_2O(g)) = 189 \text{ J/K/mol}$$
  $$\Delta S^o = (189) - (70)$$
  $$= +119 \text{ J/K/mol}$$

  Thus the entropy of the system increases as heat flows in and causes the change in state.

Example:

- **Combustion of methane gas**

  Methane gas burns in oxygen releasing carbon dioxide and water. Heat is released into the surroundings.

The system will decrease in entropy due to the heat escaping. As the system cools down the water vapour will turn back to a liquid and become more ordered:

$$CH_4(g) + 2O_2(g) \rightarrow CO_2(g) + 2H_2O(l);$$
$$\Delta H^o = -891 \text{ kJ/mol}$$

The standard molar entropies (S^o) of reactants and products are:

$$CH_4(g) = 186 \text{ J/K/mol}; O_2(g) = 205 \text{ J/K/mol}$$
$$CO_2(g) = 214 \text{ J/K/mol}; H_2O(l) = 70 \text{ J/K/mol}$$
$$\Delta S^o = (214) + 2(70) - (186) - 2(205)$$
$$= -242 \text{ J/K/mol}.$$

Thus the entropy of the system decreased as heat flowed out and liquid water formed.

> ### EXAMPLE 1
>
> Butane (C_4H_{10}) gas undergoes complete combustion in excess oxygen to form carbon dioxide gas and water.
>
> > Ensure the combustion equation is balanced because the answer to the calculation depends on the reaction stoichiometry
>
> a Write an equation for the combustion of 1 mole of butane.
>
> b The graph in Figure 14.6 shows the molar standard entropies of reactants and products for this reaction. Calculate the molar entropy change for the combustion of 1 mole of butane.
>
>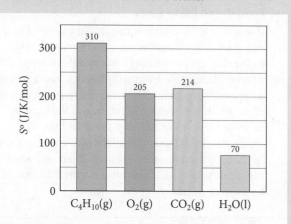
>
> **Figure 14.6** Molar entropy column graph
>
> **Answer:**
>
> a $C_4H_{10}(g) + \frac{13}{2}O_2(g) \rightarrow 4CO_2(g) + 5H_2O(l)$
>
> b $\Delta S^o = 4S^o(CO_2(g)) + 5S^o(H_2O(l)) - S^o(C_4H_{10}(g))$
> $$- \frac{13}{2}S^o(O_2(g))$$
> $$= 4(+214) + 5(+70) - (+310) - \frac{13}{2}(+205)$$
> $$= (+856) + (+350) - (+310) - (+1332.5)$$
> $$= -436.5 \text{ J/K/mol}$$

Thus the entropy of the system has decreased. There has been a decrease in the number of moles of gas and the water exists in the more ordered liquid state.

1   Solid copper (II) sulfide dissolves in hydrochloric acid to produce aqueous copper (II) chloride and hydrogen sulfide gas which bubbles out into the air. Write an ionic equation for the reaction and explain whether the final state has a higher or lower entropy than the initial state.

2   State the two quantities on which the entropy change of a system depends.

3   Explain why entropy increases in the dissolution of an ionic solid in water.

Answers ⊃ p. 159

2 Reaction spontaneity

» Students explain reaction spontaneity using terminology including Gibbs free energy, enthalpy and entropy.
» Students solve problems using standard references and $\Delta G° = \Delta H° - T\Delta S°$ (Gibbs free energy formula) to classify reactions as spontaneous or non-spontaneous.
» Students predict the effect of temperature changes on spontaneity.

Spontaneity

→ Everyday observations reveal that liquid water spontaneously runs downhill rather than uphill, unless an opposing force is supplied. The second law of thermodynamics states that a **spontaneous** process involves an increase in the entropy of the universe.

The universe is the system plus its surroundings. Thus the second law requires:

$$\Delta S_{universe} = \Delta S_{system} + \Delta S_{surroundings}$$
$$\Delta S_{universe} > 0$$

spontaneous reaction: a reaction that occurs without being driven by some outside force

As the entropy change of the surroundings is opposite to the system, then:

$$\Delta S_{surroundings} = - q_{system}/T = - \Delta H_{system}/T$$

$$\Delta S_{universe} = \Delta S_{system} - \Delta H_{system}/T > 0$$

Or, $T\Delta S - \Delta H > 0$

Or, $\Delta H - T\Delta S < 0$

→ Therefore if the quantity ($\Delta H - T\Delta S$) decreases for a system, then the change is spontaneous.

→ This quantity is called the Gibbs energy (or Gibbs free energy) (ΔG).

Gibbs free energy

$$\Delta G = \Delta H - T\Delta S$$

For a spontaneous change, $\Delta G < 0$.

Under standard state conditions, the equation is written:

$$\Delta G° = \Delta H° - T\Delta S°$$

Classifying reactions as spontaneous or non-spontaneous

→ When liquid water is placed in a freezer it turns to ice. The temperature inside the freezer is less than 0 °C:

$$H_2O(l) \rightarrow H_2O(s)$$

→ Experimental observations show that this reaction is spontaneous below 0 °C. At 0 °C both ice and liquid water coexist in **equilibrium**. Because the entropy of the system has decreased as the system has become more ordered, then ΔG will only be < 0 if the entropy of the surroundings increases to a greater extent. This occurs because heat is lost to the surroundings and this compensates for the decrease in entropy of the system.

equilibrium: a state of dynamic balance in which the forward and reverse processes occur at the same rate

→ ΔG can be calculated as follows from the Gibbs free energies of formation data:

$$\Delta_f G°(H_2O(l)) = -237 \text{ kJ/mol};$$
$$\Delta_f G°(H_2O(s)) = -240 \text{ kJ/mol}$$

$$\Delta G° = (-240) - (-237)$$
$$= -3 \text{ kJ/mol} < 0$$

Thus the process is spontaneous.

→ Because ΔH and ΔS can both be positive or negative, there are four possibilities that determine whether or not a process is spontaneous, as described below.

• $\Delta H < 0$ and $\Delta S > 0$
  In this case the process is exothermic and there is an increase in entropy.

  Consequently, $\Delta G < 0$ under all temperature conditions. Such reactions are always spontaneous.

• $\Delta H < 0$ and $\Delta S < 0$
  In this case the process is exothermic and there is a decrease in entropy.

Consequently, ΔG will only be negative (< 0) if ΔH is more negative than the positive value of $(-T\Delta S)$. For these systems the temperature of the system will be critical in determining spontaneity. Figure 14.7 illustrates this idea.

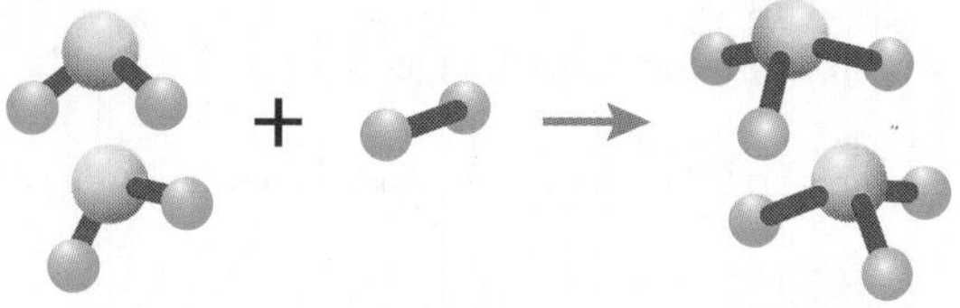

$$2SO_2(g) + O_2(g) \longrightarrow 2SO_3(g) \quad \boxed{\begin{array}{l} \Delta H < 0 \\ \Delta S < 0 \end{array}}$$

$\Delta G < 0$, only if $T < 1059$ K

Figure 14.7 The oxidation of sulfur dioxide is exothermic and the entropy change is negative as 3 moles of gas react to form 2 moles of gas. To ensure a spontaneous reaction the temperature of the system has to be kept low (< 1059 K).

- $\Delta H > 0$ and $\Delta S > 0$

In this case the process is endothermic and there is an increase in entropy.

Consequently ΔG will only be negative (< 0) if the $(-T\Delta S)$ term is more negative than the positive value of ΔH. For each physical or chemical process the temperature of the system will be critical in determining spontaneity.

- $\Delta H > 0$ and $\Delta S < 0$

In this case the process is endothermic and there is a decrease in entropy.

Consequently ΔG will never be negative and so such processes are never spontaneous.

EXAMPLE 2

Hydrogen gas is oxidised by oxygen to form water. Use the supplied data to determine whether or not the process is spontaneous at 298 K.

Equation	$\Delta_f H^\circ$ (kJ/mol)	S° (J/K/mol)
$H_2(g) + \frac{1}{2}O_2(g) \rightarrow H_2O(l)$	$H_2O(l) = -286$	$H_2(g) = +131$
		$O_2(g) = +205$
		$H_2O(l) = +70$

Answer:

Calculate the changes in enthalpy and entropy

$\Delta H^\circ = \Delta H_{products} - \Delta H_{reactants}$
$= (-286) - 0 - 0$
$= -286$ kJ/mol

$\Delta S^\circ = \Delta S_{products} - \Delta S_{reactants}$
$= (+70) - (+131) - (\frac{1}{2} \times (+205))$
$= -163.5$ J/K/mol
$= -0.1635$ kJ/K/mol

$T = 298$ K

$\Delta G^\circ = \Delta H^\circ - T\Delta S^\circ$
$= (-286) - (298)(-0.1635)$
$= -237$ kJ/mol < 0

Thus the combustion of hydrogen in oxygen at 298 K is spontaneous.

EXAMPLE 3

Silver carbonate solid thermally decomposes to form silver metal, oxygen gas and carbon dioxide gas.

Ensure that joules are converted to kilojoules in the entropy calculation

a Write a balanced equation for the decomposition.

b Calculate the change in Gibbs free energy and determine whether the reaction is spontaneous under standard conditions.

Data:

	$Ag_2CO_3(s)$	$Ag(s)$	$O_2(g)$	$CO_2(g)$
$\Delta_f H^\circ$ (kJ/mol)	−506	0	0	−394
S° (J/K/mol)	+167	+43	+205	+214

Answer:

a $Ag_2CO_3(s) \rightarrow 2Ag(s) + \frac{1}{2}O_2(g) + CO_2(g)$

b The standard enthalpy change can be calculated:

$\Delta H^\circ = \Delta_f H^\circ(\text{products}) - \Delta_f H^\circ(\text{reactants})$
$= 0 + 0 + (-394) - (-506)$
$= +112$ kJ/mol

The standard entropy change can be calculated:

$\Delta S^\circ = \Delta S^\circ(\text{products}) - \Delta S^\circ(\text{reactants})$
$= 2(+43) + \frac{1}{2}(+205) + (+214) - (+167)$
$= +154.5$ J/K/mol
$= +0.1545$ kJ/K/mol

The standard Gibbs free energy change can be calculated:

$\Delta G^\circ = \Delta H^\circ - T\Delta S^\circ$
$= (+112) - (298)(+0.1545)$
$= +66$ kJ/mol > 0

Thus the reaction is not spontaneous at 298 K as the Gibbs free energy change is positive (> 0).

EXAMPLE 4

White phosphorus (P_4) vapour can be chlorinated using chlorine gas to form solid phosphorus pentachloride.

a Write a balanced equation for the synthesis of 1 mole of product.

> Use fractions to balance the equation

b Use the supplied Gibbs free energy data to determine whether this reaction is spontaneous.

Data:

	$P_4(g)$	$Cl_2(g)$	$PCl_5(s)$
ΔG° (kJ/mol)	+59	0	−305

Answer:

a $\frac{1}{4}P_4(g) + \frac{5}{2}Cl_2(g) \rightarrow PCl_5(s)$

b $\Delta G^\circ = \Delta G^\circ_{products} - \Delta G^\circ_{reactants}$
   $= (-305) - \frac{1}{4}(+59) - \frac{5}{2}(0)$
   $= -319.75$ kJ/mol < 0

Thus the reaction is spontaneous.

→ KEY QUESTIONS

4 Determine whether the following reaction is spontaneous or non-spontaneous:

$Zn(s) + 2Ag^+(aq) \rightarrow Zn^{2+}(aq) + 2Ag(s)$

Data:

ΔG°: $Zn(s) = 0$;
    $Zn^{2+}(aq) = -147$ kJ/mol;
    $Ag(s) = 0$;
    $Ag^+(aq) = +77$ kJ/mol

5 One mole of gaseous X undergoes a phase change and is converted to solid X. Determine whether this change is spontaneous under standard conditions.

Data: $\Delta H^\circ = -50$ kJ/mol;
    $\Delta S^\circ = -20$ J/K/mol

6 A chemical change is endothermic and there is a decrease in entropy in this reaction. Determine whether such a change can be spontaneous under standard conditions.

Answers ⊃ p. 159

CHAPTER SYLLABUS CHECKLIST

Are you able to answer these questions from the syllabus for this chapter? Tick each question as you go through the checklist if you are able to answer it. If you cannot answer a question, turn to the relevant page in the study guide to find the answer. For NESA key word meanings, go to www.educationstandards.nsw.edu.au and search 'key words'.

	FOR A COMPLETE UNDERSTANDING OF THIS TOPIC:	PAGE NO.	✓
1	Can I relate entropy changes to changes in disorder of a system?	150	
2	Can I describe examples of processes that lead to increases or decreases in entropy?	151	
3	Can I calculate changes in entropy using standard entropy data for reactants and products?	152	
4	Can I relate enthalpy and entropy changes to the Gibbs free energy change in a system?	153	
5	Can I calculate ΔG given ΔH, ΔS and the temperature?	154	
6	Can I use information on changes in Gibbs free energy to determine the spontaneity of a reaction?	154–155	

Objective-response questions
(1 mark each)

1   Identify which of the following reactions involves a decrease in entropy.

   A $CO_2(g) \rightarrow CO_2(s)$

   B $H_2O(l) \rightarrow H_2O(g)$

   C $2SO_3(g) \rightarrow 2SO_2(g) + O_2(g)$

   D $I_2(s) \rightarrow I_2(g)$

2   In which of the following examples is there an increase in entropy?

   A   During distillation of an alcohol/water mixture the alcohol vapour condenses back to form a liquid in the condenser.

   B   Compressed air in a tyre escapes into the atmosphere when the valve is opened.

   C   Blue copper (II) sulfate crystals form as its saturated solution evaporates.

   D   Clouds of water droplets form in the upper atmosphere as water vapour cools.

3   Calculate the standard entropy change for the complete combustion of ethane.

   $$C_2H_6(g) + 7/2O_2(g) \rightarrow 2CO_2(g) + 3H_2O(l)$$

   Data (standard entropies):

   $C_2H_6(g) = 230$ J/K/mol; $O_2(g) = 205$ J/K/mol;

   $CO_2(g) = 214$ J/K/mol; $H_2O(l) = 70$ J/K/mol

   A -151 J/K/mol   B -309.5 J/K/mol

   C $+151$ J/K/mol   D $+309.5$ J/K/mol

4   Below 0 °C liquid water spontaneously turns into ice. Select the true statement about this process.

   A   There is an entropy increase in the system and the process is endothermic.

   B   The Gibbs free energy change in the system is positive.

   C   The water molecule become more disordered as the ice forms.

   D   The loss of heat energy to the surroundings compensates for the entropy decrease of the system.

5   Sulfur dioxide gas can be oxidised to form sulfur trioxide gas.

   $$2SO_2(g) + O_2(g) \rightarrow 2SO_3(g)$$

   Determine the temperature below which the reaction is spontaneous using the following data for this reaction.

   Data: ΔH(reaction) $= -198$ kJ/mol;
   ΔS (reaction) $= -187$ J/K/mol

   A   1.1 K   B   2118 K   C   1059 K   D   529.5 K

Extended-response questions

6   Use the supplied data to determine whether or not the following reaction is spontaneous at 298K.   (4 marks)

   $$NH_3(g) + HCl(g) \rightarrow NH_4Cl(s)$$

   Data:

$\Delta_f H^\circ$ (kJ/mol)	S° (J/K/mol)
$NH_3(g) = -46$	$NH_3(g) = +193$
$HCl(g) = -92$	$HCl(g) = +187$
$NH_4Cl(s) = -314$	$NH_4Cl(s) = +95$

7   a   Write a synthesis equation for the formation of 1 mole of hexane (C_6H_{14}) liquid from its elements in their standard states.   (1 mark)

   b   Use the supplied entropy data to calculate the standard entropy of formation of hexane.   (1 mark)

   c   One mole of hexane undergoes complete combustion to form carbon dioxide and liquid water. Write an equation for this reaction and use the supplied data to determine the enthalpy of combustion.   (2 marks)

   Data:

   S°: $C(s) = 0$; $H_2(g) = 0$;
   $C_6H_{14}(l) = +388$ J/K/mol

   $\Delta_f H^\circ$: $CO_2(g) = -393$ kJ/mol;
   $H_2O(l) = -285$kJ/mol;
   $C_6H_{14}(l) = -167$ kJ/mol

8   Figure 14.8 shows water undergoing changes of state.

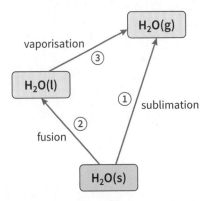

Figure 14.8 Changes of state of water

The enthalpy of fusion of water is +6 kJ/mol and the enthalpy of vaporisation is +41 kJ/mol.

   a   Calculate the enthalpy of sublimation for water.

   (1 mark)

b Use the following data to determine the change in entropy for the sublimation process. Has the entropy of the system increased or decreased? Explain why. (2 marks)

Data:

$S^o(H_2O(s) = +41$ J/K/mol;
$S^o(H_2O(g) = 189$ J/K/mol

9 The equation for photosynthesis is:

$$6CO_2(g) + 6H_2O(l) \rightarrow C_6H_{12}O_6(s) + 6O_2(g);$$
$$\Delta H = +2807 \text{ kJ/mol}$$

a The process is endothermic. Identify the source of the required energy. (1 mark)

b Use the following entropy data to determine whether the reaction leads to an increase or a decrease in entropy under standard state conditions.

Data: (2 marks)

S^o: $C_6H_{12}O_6(s) = +212$ J/K/mol;
$O_2(g) = +205$ J/K/mol;
$H_2O(l) = +70$ J/K/mol;
$CO_2(g) = +214$ J/K/mol

10 The complete combustion of methane gas is a spontaneous process.

The entropy change is −242 J/K/mol.

a Write a balanced equation for the combustion of one mole of methane. (1 mark)

b Use the following data to determine the standard entropy of methane. (2 marks)

Data:

S^o: $O_2(g) = 205$ J/K/mol;
$CO_2(g) = 214$ J/K/mol;
$H_2O(l) = 70$ J/K/mol

ANSWERS

KEY QUESTIONS

Key questions ⊃ p. 153

1. $CuS(s) + 2H^+(aq) \rightarrow Cu^{2+}(aq) + H_2S(g)$

   The final state has a higher entropy as the gas is more disordered than the solid reactant.

2. Heat (q); temperature (T)

3. In the crystal the ions are highly ordered whereas in the dissociated state in water the ions are in a more random and disordered state. Thus entropy has increased.

Key questions ⊃ p. 155

4. $\Delta G^\circ = (-147) - 2(+77)$
   $= -301$ kJ/mol < 0

   Therefore the reaction is spontaneous.

5. $\Delta H^\circ = -50$ kJ/mol; $\Delta S^\circ = -20$ J/K/mol $= -0.020$ kJ/K/mol; $T = 298$ K
   $\Delta G^\circ = (-50) - (298)(-0.020)$
   $= -44.04$ kJ/mol < 0

   Thus the change is spontaneous.

6. As $\Delta H^\circ > 0$ and $\Delta S^\circ < 0$, then $\Delta G^\circ > 0$ and therefore the reaction is not spontaneous.

YEAR 11 EXAM-TYPE QUESTIONS

Objective-response questions

1. **A.** Gas molecules become more ordered as they turn into a solid. **B** is incorrect as the water molecules in the gaseous state are more disordered. **C** is incorrect as 3 molecules form from 2 molecules. **D** is incorrect as the gaseous iodine molecules are in a more disordered state.

2. **B.** In the tyre the air molecules have less freedom of movement whereas in the atmosphere they become more disordered. **A** is incorrect as alcohol vapour is more disordered than liquid alcohol. **C** is incorrect as the ions become highly ordered in the crystal. **D** is incorrect as the water vapour molecules have greater disorder than the water in the liquid drops.

3. **B.** $\Delta S^\circ = 2(214) + 3(70) - (230) - \left(\frac{7}{2}\right)(205) = -309.5$ J/K/mol

   A is incorrect as the molar stoichiometry has not been used. **C** and **D** are incorrect as the entropy does not increase as liquid water forms.

4. **D.** ΔG is negative as ΔH is negative and this compensates for the entropy decrease. **A** is incorrect as the entropy decreases and the reaction is exothermic. **B** is incorrect as the Gibbs free energy is negative. **C** is incorrect as the water molecules become more ordered in ice.

5. **C.** $\Delta G = \Delta H - T\Delta S$; $0 = (-198) - T(-0.187)$,
   T(maximum) = 1059 K. **A** is incorrect as the entropy change has to be converted to the units of kJ/K/mol. **B** and **D** are incorrect as the supplied data already takes into account the stoichiometry.

Extended-response questions

6. **EM** Students need to recall that the enthalpy change is calculated by subtracting the total enthalpies of formation of the reacts from the enthalpy of formation of the product. In similar fashion the entropy change can be calculated but the unit conversion is required.

   $\Delta H^\circ = \Sigma\Delta H^\circ_{products} - \Sigma\Delta H^\circ_{reactants}$
   $= (-314) - (-46) - (-92) = -176$ kJ/mol ✓

   $\Delta S^\circ = \Sigma\Delta S^\circ_{products} - \Sigma\Delta S^\circ_{reactants}$
   $= (+95) - (+193) - (+187)$
   $= -285$ J/K/mol
   $= -0.285$ kJ/K/mol ✓

   $T = 298$ K
   $\Delta G^\circ = \Delta H^\circ - T\Delta S^\circ$
   $= (-176) - (298)(-0.285)$
   $= -91.07$ kJ/mol < 0 ✓

   Therefore the reaction is spontaneous. ✓

7. **EM** Students need to show that the balanced equation should show that 1 mole of hexane forms. For (c) the equation should be balanced using a fraction in order to show the combustion of 1 mole of hexane.
   a $6C(s) + 7H_2(g) \rightarrow C_6H_{14}(l)$ ✓
   b $\Delta S^\circ = (+388) - 0 - 0 = +388$ J/K/mol ✓
   c $C_6H_{14}(l) + \frac{19}{2}O_2(g) \rightarrow 6CO_2(g) + 7H_2O(l)$ ✓
   $\Delta_c H^\circ = 6(-393) + 7(-285) - (-167) = -4186$ kJ/mol ✓

8. **EM** Students need to recall that sublimation is the conversion of a solid directly to form a gas. Hess's law can be used as reaction 1 is the sum of reactions 2 and 3.
   a $\Delta H_1 = \Delta H_2 + \Delta H_3 = (+6) + (+41) = +47$ kJ/mol ✓
   b $\Delta S^\circ = S^\circ(H_2O(g)) - S^\circ(H_2O(s)) = (189) - (41) = +148$ J/K/mol ✓

   The entropy of the system has increased as water vapour molecules are more disordered than water molecules that are highly ordered in ice crystals. ✓

9. **EM** Students are required to understand the difference between cellular respiration (an exothermic reaction) and photosynthesis (an endothermic reaction). Photosynthesis occurs in green plants and the energy required comes from sunlight. The glucose that is formed is in a much more ordered state than the gases or liquid water.
   a Sunlight (solar energy) ✓
   b $\Delta S^\circ = (+212) + 6(+205) - 6(+214) - 6(+70)$
   $= 1442 - 1704$
   $= -262$ J/K/mol ✓

   There is a decrease in entropy by the formation of glucose which is a highly ordered solid. ✓

10. **EM** Students need to use the reaction stoichiometry to calculate the standard entropy of methane given that the change in entropy is the sum of the entropies of the products minus the sum of the entropies of the reactants.
    a $CH_4(g) + 2O_2(g) \rightarrow CO_2(g) + 2H_2O(l)$ ✓
    b $\Delta S^\circ = -242$
    $= S^\circ(CO_2(g)) + 2S^\circ(H_2O(l)) - S^\circ(CH_4(g)) - 2S^\circ(O_2(g))$ ✓
    $-242 = (+214) + 2(+70) - S^\circ(CH_4(g)) - 2(+205)$
    $S^\circ(CH_4(g)) = (+214) + 2(+70) - 2(+205) + 242$
    $= +186$ J/K/mol ✓

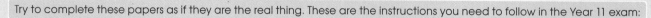

SAMPLE YEAR 11 EXAMINATION 1

Try to complete these papers as if they are the real thing. These are the instructions you need to follow in the Year 11 exam:

General instructions
- Reading time: 5 minutes
- Working time: 3 hours
- Write using black pen.
- Board-approved calculators may be used.
- Use the data sheet and periodic table in this book.

Total marks: 100

Section I: 20 marks
Section II: 80 marks
- Attempt all questions.

Section I: 20 Marks

Allow about 40 minutes for this section.

Objective-response questions   (1 mark each)

Choose the letter A, B, C or D that corresponds to the best answer.

1   The following half-equation shows one reaction that occurs in a battery:

$$2MnO_2(s) + 2NH_4^+(aq) + 2e^-$$
$$\rightarrow Mn_2O_3(s) + H_2O(l) + 2NH_3(aq)$$

Select the correct statement about this half-equation.

   A The oxidation state of manganese increases.

   B The oxidation state of manganese changes from +4 to +3.

   C The ammonium ions are reduced.

   D This half-reaction would occur at the anode.

2   Consider the information in the following table.

Element	Neutrons	Protons	Electrons
P	14	14	14
Q	14	11	11
R	6	6	6
S	7	6	6
T	10	9	9
U	14	11	11

Which of the groups contains three different elements?

   A P, R and S   B Q, R and T

   C R, S and T   D P, Q and U

3   The compound octanoic acid has the condensed structural formula $CH_3(CH_2)_6COOH$. Its empirical formula is:

   A $C_8H_{16}O_2$ B C_4H_8O

   C C_3H_7COOH D CHO

4   Consider the following chemical equation:

$$Cu(s) + 4HNO_3(aq)$$
$$\rightarrow Cu(NO_3)_2(aq) + 2H_2O(l) + 2NO_2(g)$$

Which of the following shows the maximum mass of copper (II) nitrate that can be produced from the given mass of copper?

	Mass of copper (g)	Mass of copper (II) nitrate (g)
A	0.6355	1.8757
B	0.3178	1.0767
C	0.2540	0.5020
D	0.1270	0.4690

5   A metal that dissolves in dilute hydrochloric acid and displaces iron from iron (II) nitrate solution is:

   A copper.   B silver.   C lead.   D zinc.

6   Which set of elements contains a semi-metal, a metal with a valency of +3 and a non-metal that is gaseous at room temperature?

   A silicon; zinc; bromine

   B aluminium; fluorine; germanium

   C phosphorus; arsenic; barium

   D copper; silicon; chlorine

7   22.2 g of calcium chloride is dissolved in 250 mL of water. The concentration of the solution is:

   A 1.18 mol/L   B 1.60 mol/L

   C 0.800 mol/L   D 3.20 mol/L

8   Ammonium sulfate solution and barium chloride solution are mixed and a white precipitate forms. Select the equation that shows a correctly balanced whole-formula equation.

   A $NH_4SO_4(aq) + BaCl(aq) \rightarrow BaSO_4(s) + NH_4Cl(aq)$

   B $Ba^{2+}(aq) + SO_4^{2-}(aq) \rightarrow BaSO_4(s)$

   C $(NH_4)_2SO_4(aq) + BaCl(aq) \rightarrow NH_4Cl(aq) + BaSO_4(s)$

   D $(NH_4)_2SO_4(aq) + BaCl_2(aq) \rightarrow 2NH_4Cl(aq) + BaSO_4(s)$

9 Which one of the following reactions would be classified as endothermic?

  A magnesium + nitric acid
  B potassium hydroxide solution + sulfuric acid
  C combustion of propane gas in air
  D decomposition of nickel (II) carbonate

10 A solid consists of blue crystals that melt at 740 °C. The solid does not conduct electricity but the molten liquid does. Which of the following substances could have the properties of this blue solid?

  A $C_{20}H_{42}$ B SiO_2 C $CoCl_2$ D PCl_5

11 The percentage by mass of carbon in lithium carbonate is:

  A 16.3%   B 17.4%   C 17.9%   D 36.7%

12 The number of oxygen atoms present in 8.00 g of ozone (O_3) is:

  A 3.011×10^{23} B 6.022×10^{23}
  C 1.807×10^{24} D 0.500

13 200 mL of 2.00 mol/L hydrochloric acid is added to water and the final volume adjusted by the addition of 1300 mL of water to a final volume of 1.50 L. Calculate the molarity of the diluted hydrochloric acid.

  A 0.143 mol/L   B 0.667 mol/L
  C 0.267 mol/L   D 0.308 mol/L

14 10.0 L of argon gas at 20 °C and 100 kPa is heated to a temperature of 35 °C at 100 kPa. Calculate the volume of the gas at 35 °C.

  A 17.5 L   B 9.5 L   C 5.7 L   D 10.5 L

15 Consider the following reaction:

  $Br_2(g) + 2I^-(aq) \rightarrow 2Br^-(aq) + I_2(s)$

  Which of the following statements is true?

  A Bromine is the reductant.
  B Iodide ions are the oxidants.
  C Bromine has been reduced.
  D Iodide ions have gained electrons.

16 Identify which change will result in a faster reaction rate.

  A powdering limestone chips before their reaction with hydrochloric acid
  B using a smaller beaker for the reaction between solid zinc oxide and dilute sulfuric acid
  C cooling a solid mixture of magnesium and iodine crystals
  D combustion of ethanol in air rather than in pure oxygen

17 1.50 g of a soluble salt was dissolved in 115 g of water in a polystyrene foam calorimeter. The temperature of the solution rose from 21.0 °C to 37.2 °C during the dissolution of the salt. Calculate the quantity of heat released in the dissolution process given that the heat capacity of the solution is 4.18×10^3 J/kg/K.

  A 6804 J   C 1021 J   B 7825 J   D 15 309 J

18 Select the process in which there is an increase in entropy.

  A $H_2O(s) \rightarrow H_2O(g)$
  B $Ca^{2+}(aq) + CO_3^{2-}(aq) \rightarrow CaCO_3(s)$
  C $H_2(g) + \frac{1}{2}O_2(g) \rightarrow H_2O(l)$
  D $BaO(s) + CO_2(g) \rightarrow BaCO_3(s)$

19 Calculate the enthalpy change for the following reaction:

  $2SO_2(g) + O_2(g) \rightarrow 2SO_3(g)$

  Data (standard enthalpies of formation):
  SO_2 (−297 kJ/mol); SO_3 (−396 kJ/mol)

  A +198 kJ   B −198 kJ   C +99 kJ   D −99 kJ

20 Use the supplied data to determine the enthalpy change for the following reaction (R).

  (R): $Li(s) + H^+(aq) \rightarrow Li^+(aq) + \frac{1}{2}H_2(g)$

  Data:

  (1) $LiCl(s) \rightarrow Li^+(aq) + Cl^-(aq); \Delta H_1 = -37$ kJ
  (2) $Li(s) + \frac{1}{2}Cl_2(g) \rightarrow LiCl(s); \Delta H_2 = -409$ kJ
  (3) $\frac{1}{2}H_2(g) + \frac{1}{2}Cl_2(g) \rightarrow H^+(aq) + Cl^-(aq);$
                                              $\Delta H_3 = -167$ kJ

  A +279 kJ   B −539 kJ   C −279 kJ   D −205 kJ

Section II: 80 Marks

Allow about 2 hours and 20 minutes for this section.

Extended-response questions

21 The following table shows the results of a series of experiments involving galvanic cells in which the $Hg \mid Hg^{2+}$ couple was used as a reference half-cell. This couple was connected to the negative terminal of a DC voltmeter with a central zero. The electrolytes were all 1 mol/L in concentration. A saturated potassium-nitrate salt bridge linked the two half-cells.

Cell	Cell notation	Cell voltage (V)
1	$Sr \mid Sr^{2+} \parallel Hg^{2+} \mid Hg$	3.75
2	$Co \mid Co^{2+} \parallel Hg^{2+} \mid Hg$	1.13
3	$Pd \mid Pd^{2+} \parallel Hg^{2+} \mid Hg$	−0.07
4	$Ni \mid Ni^{2+} \parallel Hg^{2+} \mid Hg$	1.04

  a Use the collected data to arrange the five metals in increasing order of strength as reductants. Justify your answer.   (3 marks)
  b Write a net cell equation for cell 3, and identify the cathode and anode in this cell.   (3 marks)

22 Ammonia, water and methane are small molecules with similar molar masses. Explain why methane has a melting point and boiling point so much lower than ammonia or water. (4 marks)

Molecule	m.p (°C)	b.p (°C)
ammonia	−78	−33
water	0	100
methane	−182	−161

23 a A student performed the following experiments:
  - Experiment 1: Silver nitrate solution is mixed with sodium chloride solution.
  - Experiment 2: Copper metal is added to dilute hydrochloric acid.
  - Experiment 3: Dilute nitric acid is added to solid zinc carbonate.

   A reaction was observed in two of the experiments. Describe what would be observed and write balanced equations for each reaction. (5 marks)

  b Explain why no reaction occurred in the remaining experiment. (1 mark)

24 Acids react with metallic sulfides and produce hydrogen sulfide gas. 10.0 g of solid potassium sulfide (K_2S) is reacted with excess nitric acid.

  a Write a balanced equation for this reaction. (1 mark)

  b Calculate the mass of hydrogen sulfide gas produced. (3 marks)

25 8.00 g of sodium chloride was weighed out and dissolved in 100.00 g of water in a calorimeter. The temperature of the mixture decreased from 21.0 °C to 19.9 °C during the dissolution process. Calculate the molar enthalpy of dissolution of sodium chloride. Assume the specific heat capacity for the mixture is 4.18 J/g/K. (3 marks)

26 Calculate the mass of carbon dioxide produced if on the complete combustion of hexan-1-ol, 100 kJ of heat is released. (Heat of combustion $C_6H_{11}OH(l)$ = 3984 kJ/mol) (3 marks)

27 Butane (C_4H_{10}) gas undergoes complete combustion in excess oxygen to form gaseous carbon dioxide and liquid water.

  a Write a balanced equation for the complete combustion of one mole of butane. (1 mark)

  b Use the supplied data to calculate the molar entropy change for the reaction in (a). (2 marks)

   Data:

$S°$ (J/K/mol)
$CO_2(g)$ = 214
$H_2O(l)$ = 70
$C_4H_{10}(g)$ = 310
$O_2(g)$ = 205

28 Natural gallium consists of 2 stable isotopes. Calculate the atomic weight of natural gallium from the following data. (2 marks)

   Ga-69: isotopic mass = 68.93 u
   percentage = 60.11%

   Ga-71: isotopic mass = 70.92 u
   percentage = 39.89%

29 Write balanced symbolic equations for the following reactions.

  a liquid undecane ($C_{11}H_{24}$) burns in oxygen gas to produce carbon dioxide and water (1 mark)

  b iron (II) oxide (solid) + carbon monoxide gas → iron (molten) + carbon dioxide gas (1 mark)

  c lithium (solid) + oxygen gas → lithium oxide (solid) (1 mark)

30 The gaseous hydride of element X has the formula XH_3. It can be produced by heating a mixture of X_2 gas and hydrogen gas under high pressure.

  a Write a balanced equation for this reaction. (1 mark)

  b A mixture of 100 mL of X_2 and 240 mL of hydrogen is allowed to completely react at a fixed temperature and pressure. After reaction is complete, the reaction mixture is returned to the same temperature and pressure conditions.

   Calculate the volume of each of the gases remaining after the reaction. (2 marks)

31 Classify the listed elements as solids, liquids or gases at 25 °C and 100 kPa using the melting point and boiling point data provided. (3 marks)

  a bromine: m.p = −7 °C; b.p = 59 °C

  b gallium: m.p = 30 °C; b.p = 2403 °C

  c fluorine: m.p = −220 °C; b.p = −188 °C

32 Sterling silver is an alloy of silver and copper. A 50.00 g sample of sterling silver contained 3.67 g of copper.

  a Calculate the percentage by weight of each metal in the sterling silver. (2 marks)

  b Explain whether or not this alloy would react with 0.10 mol/L hydrochloric acid. (2 marks)

  c Explain why sterling silver is used instead of pure silver to create knives, forks and spoons. (1 mark)

33 For each of the listed isotopes:

  a Calculate the number of neutrons in each nucleus. (1 mark)

  b Write the spdf notation for each element:

   i $^{11}_5B$

   ii $^{14}_7N$

   iii $^{39}_{19}K$ (3 marks)

34 a A student is supplied with a solid sample of hydrated barium chloride.

Describe the method of an experiment to determine the flame colour for barium ions and state the colour observed. (3 marks)

b The emission spectrum for barium is shown in Figure E1.1. Use the theory of electron energy levels to explain the existence of different wavelength lines in the emission spectrum. (3 marks)

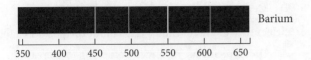

Figure E1.1 Barium emission spectrum

35 Nihonium (Nh) is a synthetic radioactive element with an atomic number of 113.

a Identify the periodic table group to which nihonium belongs. (1 mark)

b Classify nihonium as a metal, semi-metal or non-metal. Explain. (2 marks)

c Nihonium-278 was created originally by firing an accelerated zinc-70 ion into a bismuth-209 target. A neutron was also released. Write a nuclear equation for this synthesis. (1 mark)

36 The term *ionisation energy* refers to the removal of electrons from atoms. Successive ionisation energies refer to the energy required to remove successive electrons from an atom. Electrons in the outer electron shell are the first to be removed in the ionisation process. The following data was collected for successive ionisation energies (MJ/mol) for elements L, M and N. Use the data to identify and explain to which periodic group each element belongs. (3 marks)

L	0.43	3.06	4.42	5.88	7.98	9.66	11.35	14.95
M	1.01	2.26	3.37	4.57	7.02	8.50	27.11	31.68
N	1.02	1.91	2.92	4.96	6.28	21.28	25.40	29.86

37 A chemist collected a sample of waste water and determined the concentration of cadmium ions. Cadmium ions are toxic to living things. The experiment showed that the cadmium ion concentration was 200 ppm.

a Calculate the total mass of cadmium present in 2000 kg of waste water. (1 mark)

b The acceptable limit for cadmium ions in natural waters is 10 ppm. If the 2000 kg of waste water was diluted with fresh water to produce a total volume of 2 megalitres, determine whether the diluted solution is safe to discharge into the environment. (1 litre of water = 1 kilogram) (2 marks)

38 A student conducted an experiment to verify Charles' law. The apparatus used is shown in Figure E1.2. A fine capillary tube has a bead of mercury in it. This bead creates a column of trapped air. The other end of the capillary tube is open. The column of trapped air is heated in a water bath and the length of the air column (L) is measured as a function of temperature.

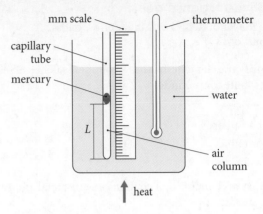

Figure E1.2 Charles' law experiment

a Explain why the capillary tube is open at one end. (1 mark)

b Explain why the length of the air column is a measure of the volume of the gas. (1 mark)

c The results of the experiment are tabulated below:

Temperature (°C)	10	20	30	40	50	60	70	80
Temperature (K)								
Length (L) (mm)	30.0	31.1	32.1	33.1	34.2	35.3	36.4	37.4

i Copy and complete the table by calculating the temperature in Kelvin units. (1 mark)

ii Plot a line graph of L versus the absolute temperature. Include absolute zero on the temperature axis. Draw a line of best fit that passes through absolute zero. (5 marks)

iii Has this experiment verified Charles' law? Explain. (2 marks)

39 A sample of water was electrolytically decomposed to produce hydrogen and oxygen. The hydrogen and oxygen that were formed were collected separately, dried and weighed.

water → hydrogen + oxygen

The mass of oxygen collected was 0.32 g.

a Write a balanced equation for the electrolytic decomposition. (1 mark)

b Calculate the number of moles of water decomposed. (2 marks)

c Calculate the mass of hydrogen formed. (2 marks)

SAMPLE YEAR 11 EXAMINATION 2

Section I: 20 Marks

Allow about 40 minutes for this section.

Objective-response questions

(1 mark each)

Choose the letter A, B, C or D that corresponds to the best answer.

1 Identify the element that has a common valency of −3 in its ionic compounds.

  A oxygen

  B phosphorus

  C bromine

  D tellurium

2 The set of elements that contains a semi-metal and two non-metals is:

  A sulfur, iodine, boron.

  B zinc, nitrogen, plutonium.

  C copper, iridium, bromine.

  D silicon, germanium, arsenic.

3 Identify the ionic compound.

  A selenium dioxide

  B nitrogen dioxide

  C sulfur dichloride

  D manganese (II) fluoride

4 Identify the reaction in which heat and light energy are released.

  A combustion of magnesium powder in oxygen

  B neutralisation of barium hydroxide with nitric acid

  C electrolysis of molten sodium chloride

  D rusting of cast iron

5 Identify the transition element.

  A osmium

  B lead

  C radium

  D thallium

6 When nickel in placed in dilute sulfuric acid, a slow effervescence is observed. Select the correct statement about this process.

  A Each nickel atom loses 2 electrons as it oxidises.

  B Gaseous sulfur dioxide is evolved.

  C This reaction is faster than the reaction between magnesium and dilute acid.

  D The sulfate ions in the acid lose electrons to the metal.

7 Select the correct statement concerning the trends from left to right across a period for elements in the second period (Li to Ne) of the periodic table.

  A First ionisation energy decreases.

  B Electrical conductivity increases.

  C Electronegativity increases.

  D Melting point increases.

8 Select the statement that is true about the periodic table.

  A The elements are arranged according to increasing proton number.

  B The elements across a period have similar physical properties.

  C The atomic weights increase sequentially in Period 5.

  D All lanthanoid elements are radioactive.

9 Identify a molecule that has hydrogen bonding between its molecules.

  A CH_4 B HI   C H_2 D NH_3

10 Ten moles of nitrogen dioxide gas are placed in a closed vessel at 0 °C and 100 kPa. Nitrogen gas is placed in an equal-sized vessel at the same temperature and pressure. Select the correct statement.

  A The mass of nitrogen present in the second container will be 28.0 g.

  B The mass of nitrogen dioxide gas present is 460.1 g.

  C There are ten times as many molecules of nitrogen dioxide as nitrogen.

  D 3.01×10^{23} molecules of nitrogen dioxide are present in the first vessel.

11 Select the statement that is true concerning an ideal gas.

  A Dispersion forces exist between gaseous molecules.

  B The volume of gas molecules is negligible compared with the total volume occupied by the gas.

  C Ideal gases only obey Boyle's law over moderate temperature ranges.

  D Sulfur dioxide behaves as an ideal gas.

12 Some solutes were tested for their solubility in water. Identify the solute that has the greatest solubility at room temperature.

  A copper (II) nitrate

  B iron (II) oxide

  C silicon dioxide

  D nitrogen gas

13 The number of moles of nitrate ions present in 400 mL of a 0.20 mol/L solution of barium nitrate is:

A 0.080 mol

B 0.16 mol

C 0.060 mol

D 0.32 mol

14 The molar mass of iron (III) sulfate is:

A 399.91 g/mol

B 215.62 g/mol

C 263.62 g/mol

D 344.06 g/mol

15 0.500 kg of water at 15 °C is heated until its temperature is 80 °C. Calculate the quantity of heat that is required (specific heat capacity of water = 4.18×10^3 J/kg/K).

A 135.85 J

B 67 925 J

C 156.75 J

D 135 850 J

16 At 20 °C, a fixed mass of methane gas occupies a volume of 550 mL at 100 kPa. Calculate the volume of the gas at 100 kPa if the temperature is raised to 110 °C.

A 3025 mL

B 421 mL

C 719 mL

D 110 mL

17 Select the correct statement concerning the allotropes of carbon.

A Graphite is a covalent network crystal.

B Diamond is a covalent molecular crystal.

C Graphite is harder than diamond.

D Graphite and diamond have the same crystalline structure.

18 Select the correct electron spdf notation for neon.

A $1s^2\, 2s^2\, 2p^3$

B $1s^2\, 2s^2\, 2p^6$

C $1s^2\, 2s^2\, 2p^6\, 3s^1$

D $1s^2\, 2s^2\, 2p^6\, 3s^2\, 3p^6$

19 The oxidation state of nitrogen in nitric acid is:

A +3   B +4   C +5   D +6

20 The rate of the oxidation reaction between red-hot iron sheets and air could be increased by:

A injecting nitrogen into the vessel.

B rolling the iron sheets into a tight ball.

C cooling the iron.

D increasing the oxygen concentration in the air.

Section II: 80 Marks

Allow about 2 hours and 20 minutes for this section.

Extended-response questions

21 Azurite ($Cu_3(CO_3)_2(OH)_2$) is a deep-blue mineral and malachite ($Cu_2CO_3(OH)_2$) is a green mineral. Both crystals consist of copper (II) ions, carbonate ions and hydroxide ions.

a A chip of malachite is added to a beaker containing sufficient dilute hydrochloric acid so the solid just dissolves. Malachite reacts with dilute hydrochloric acid to produce a green-blue solution. Write a balanced equation for this reaction. (1 mark)

b Explain whether any differences in the reaction of malachite and azurite with hydrochloric acid would be observed by a student in a school laboratory. (1 mark)

c An excess of magnesium powder is added to the green solution and the mixture stirred. The green-blue colour gradually fades until the liquid is colourless and a red-brown solid settles on the base of the beaker.

   i Write a balanced ionic equation for this reaction. (1 mark)

   ii Account for the observations. (2 marks)

22 Chemists investigate methods to increase the rate of a reaction. Three common methods that can be used to increase the reaction rate are:

A increasing the temperature.

B increasing the surface area of any solids.

C adding a catalyst.

For each method above, identify a reaction that illustrates that procedure. In each case write a balanced equation for the reaction. (3 marks)

23 The concentration of lead ions in water was determined via a gravimetric analysis in which the lead ions were precipitated as an insoluble sulfate. A sodium sulfate solution was added in excess to 200 mL of the lead ion solution. The precipitate was filtered, washed, dried and weighed. The mass of the dried precipitate was 1.900 g.

a Write an ionic equation for the precipitation reaction. (1 mark)

b Calculate the concentration of lead ions in the original solution in the units of:

   i mol/L

   ii ppm (2 marks)

c Explain why the collected precipitate must be thoroughly washed and dried before weighing. (2 marks)

24 Powdered silver oxide was heated with methane gas until all the silver oxide had been reduced to metallic silver. Carbon dioxide and water vapour also form.

   a Write a balanced equation for the reaction of silver oxide with methane. (1 mark)

   b Explain why the reactants had to be heated for a reaction to occur. (1 mark)

   c Calculate the mass of silver which formed from the reduction of 15.0 g of silver oxide. (2 marks)

25 Aluminium powder when heated in oxygen burns brilliantly, emitting heat and light.

$$4Al(s) + 3O_2(g) \rightarrow 2Al_2O_3(s); \Delta H = -3352 \text{ kJ}$$

   a Calculate the mass of aluminium that is required to produce 300 kJ of energy on combustion. (3 marks)

   b Explain why firework manufacturers use powdered aluminium rather than using larger pieces in their fireworks. (1 mark)

   c Identify the species that is reduced in the reaction. (1 mark)

26 At 27 °C a fixed mass of oxygen gas occupies a volume of 900 mL at 100 kPa. Calculate the volume of the gas at 100 kPa if the temperature is raised to 227 °C. (2 marks)

27 Figure E2.1 shows a Hess's law pathway at 298 K for the formation of NO and NO_2.

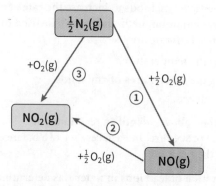

Figure E2.1 Hess's law diagram

The following data for paths 1 and 3 are provided:
Path 1: $\Delta_f H°(NO) = +90$ kJ/mol
Path 3: $\Delta_f H°(NO_2) = 133$ kJ/mol
Calculate the standard enthalpy change for path 2.
(2 marks)

28 A student conducted a Boyle's law experiment using the apparatus shown in Figure E2.2. A small sample of air is trapped by mercury in a J-shaped tube. When the height of the mercury columns in both arms of the tube are equal, the pressure gauge (P) shows that the pressure of the trapped air is equal to the atmospheric pressure. The student then adds additional mercury to the right-hand arm of the J-tube and observes that the

pressure of the trapped air increases as it undergoes compression.

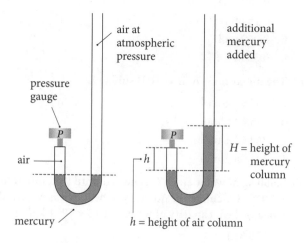

Figure E2.2 Boyle's law experiment using mercury

The student collected data on the height (h) of the trapped air column versus the height (H) of the mercury column. In each experiment the pressure gauge reading was recorded.

H (mm)	50	100	150	200	250	300
h (mm)	32.0	30.1	28.5	27.0	25.7	24.5
P (kPa)	106.6	113.2	119.7	126.3	132.9	139.5

   a Explain why the volume of trapped air decreases as more mercury is added to the right arm of the J-tube. (1 mark)

   b How is the height of the air column (h) related to the volume of the air? (1 mark)

   c Calculate $\frac{1}{h}$ for each pressure reading and plot a line graph of P versus $\frac{1}{h}$. Explain how this graph demonstrates Boyle's law. (6 marks)

29 Many brands of liquid-fuel lighters use butane as a fuel. Both liquid and gaseous butane are present in the storage tank of such lighters. Butane has a boiling point of −0.5 °C.

   a Butane (C_4H_{10}) boils below room temperature. Explain the existence of liquid butane in the fuel reservoir. (1 mark)

   b Each time the lighter is used, approximately 1000 J of energy is released and 0.0300 g of fuel is consumed. The flame that is produced is yellow in colour.

     i Calculate the heat released from the combustion of the butane (in kJ/mol). (1 mark)

     ii Explain why the answer in (i) differs from the published heat of combustion (2877 kJ/mol) for butane. (1 mark)

30 a Two vessels of equal volume and the same temperature and pressure contain two different gases. One vessel contains hydrogen (H_2) gas and the other vessel contains an unknown hydrocarbon gas. The mass of hydrogen gas is 4.000 g and the mass of the unknown hydrocarbon is 115.3 g. Determine the molar mass of the hydrocarbon.

(2 marks)

b The general formula of this group of hydrocarbons is C_nH_{2n+2}, where n is an integer. Determine the molecular formula of the unknown hydrocarbon.

(1 mark)

c Draw two possible structural formulas for the hydrocarbon. (2 marks)

31 300 mL of 0.12 mol/L magnesium bromide and 200 mL of 0.20 mol/L potassium bromide are mixed.

a Calculate the molarity of bromide ions in the final solution.

(3 marks)

b Water is then added to the mixture until the total volume is 3.00 litres. Calculate the molarity of bromide ions in the diluted solution. (2 marks)

32 When iodine solid is heated it sublimes into a gas without passing through the liquid state. Given the standard entropies of the initial and final states, calculate the standard entropy change. (2 marks)

Data: $S°(I_2)(s) = +116$ J/K/mol; $S°(I_2)(g) = +261$ J/K/mol

33 Silver carbonate solid thermally decomposes to form silver metal, oxygen gas and carbon dioxide gas.

a Write a balanced equation for the decomposition of 1 mole of silver carbonate. (1 mark)

b Calculate the change in Gibbs free energy and determine whether the reaction is spontaneous under standard conditions.

(3 marks)

Data:

	$Ag_2CO_3(s)$	$Ag(s)$	$O_2(g)$	$CO_2(g)$
$\Delta_fH°$ (kJ/mol)	−506	0	0	−394
$S°$ (J/K/mol)	+167	+43	+205	+214

34 Calculate the bond energy of the C−H bond in methane (CH_4) using Figure E2.3 and the following data. (4 marks)

Data: $\frac{1}{2}H_2(g) \rightarrow H(g)$; $\Delta H° = +218$ kJ/mol

$C(s)_{(graphite)} \rightarrow C(g)$; $\Delta H° = +718$ kJ/mol

$\Delta_fH(CH_4) = -75$ kJ/mol

Tetrahedral structure of methane

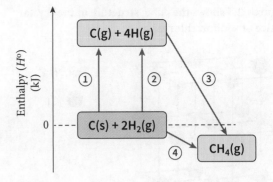

Figure E2.3 C−H bond energy calculation

35 The following table shows the result of the reaction of four metals (W, X, Y and Z) with water.

Metal	W	X	Y	Z
Reactivity with water	no reaction with water	reacts with hot water releasing hydrogen gas; a solution containing hydroxide ions forms	reacts with steam when metal is heated to red heat; surface oxides form and hydrogen forms	rapidly reacts with cold water to form a solution containing hydroxide ions; hydrogen gas is released

a The metals used are (in random order): Zn, Cu, K, Mg
Identify metals W, X, Y and Z. (2 marks)

b Write balanced equations for the reaction of metals X, Y and Z with water. (3 marks)

36 16.0 g of sucrose ($C_{12}H_{22}O_{11}$) is dissolved in sufficient water to make 250 mL of solution.

a Calculate the number of moles of sucrose that has been dissolved. (1 mark)

b Calculate the molarity of the sucrose solution. (1 mark)

c Figure E2.4 shows the structure of sucrose. Use this structure to explain why sucrose is soluble in water.

(2 marks)

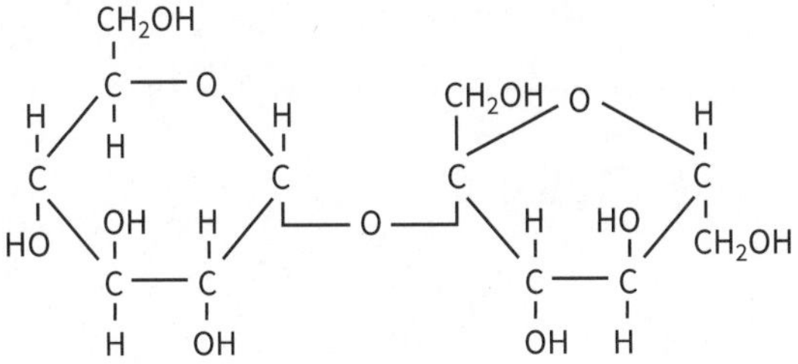

Sucrose

Figure E2.4 Sucrose structure

37 Draw Lewis electron dot diagrams for:

a Cl_2O (1 mark)

b CaI_2 (1 mark)

38 Figure E2.5 shows the cubic structure of the crystal lattice of sodium chloride.

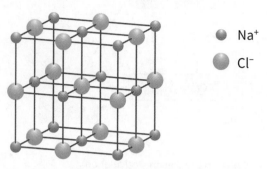

Figure E2.5 Sodium chloride lattice

a Explain why crystalline sodium chloride does not conduct electricity but molten sodium chloride does conduct. (2 marks)

b Write a balanced equation for the dissolution of sodium chloride crystals in water. (1 mark)

c Figure E2.6 shows the arrangement of a sodium ion and water molecules in a sodium chloride solution. Explain the attraction and orientation of the water molecules around the sodium ion. (2 marks)

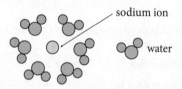

Figure E2.6 Sodium ion interacts with water molecules

39 A metal (M) is divalent. Common divalent metals include iron, zinc, calcium, cobalt and copper. The sulfate of M is an ionic salt with a percentage composition by weight of:

38.02% M; 20.69% S; 41.29% O

a Use this data to calculate the atomic weight of M. (3 marks)

b Use the periodic table to identify M. (1 mark)

c Identify the periodic group to which M belongs. (1 mark)

40 Write a whole formula equation and a net ionic equation for each of the following reactions:

a Barium chloride solution + silver nitrate solution forms white silver chloride precipitate + barium nitrate solution. (1 mark)

b Nickel (II) sulfate solution + potassium sulfide solution forms black nickel (II) sulfide precipitate + potassium sulfate solution. (1 mark)

SAMPLE YEAR 11 EXAMINATION 1

Objective-response questions

1 **B.** MnO_2: $x + 2(-2) = 0$, $x = +4$; Mn_2O_3: $2x + 3(-2) = 0$, $x = +3$. **A** is incorrect as the oxidation state of manganese decreases from +4 to +3. **C** is incorrect as N in ammonium ions and ammonia does not change its oxidation state. **D** is incorrect as the reaction would occur at the cathode as electrons are gained.

2 **B.** Q, R and T have different proton numbers. **A** and **C** are incorrect as R and S are the same element. **D** is incorrect as Q and U are the same element.

3 **B.** $MF = C_8H_{16}O_2$; $EF = \frac{1}{2}MF = C_4H_8O$. **A** is incorrect as this is the molecular formula. **C** is incorrect as the simplest ratio of elements is not shown. **D** is incorrect as the 1 : 1 : 1 ratio is not correct.

4 **A.** $M(Cu(NO_3)_2) = 63.55 + 2(14.01) + 6(16.00) = 187.57$ g/mol
1 mol Cu forms 1 mol $Cu(NO_3)_2$
63.55 g Cu forms 187.57 g $Cu(NO_3)_2$
0.6635 g Cu forms 1.8757 g $Cu(NO_3)_2$
Thus **B**, **C** and **D** are mathematically incorrect.

5 **D.** Zinc is the strongest reductant listed. **A**, **B** and **C** are incorrect as copper, silver and lead are too weak as reductants.

6 **B.** Aluminium is a metal with a +3 valency, fluorine is a gas and germanium is a semi-metal. **A** is incorrect as bromine is a liquid non-metal. **C** is incorrect as phosphorus is a solid non-metal. **D** is incorrect as copper has a +2 valency.

7 **C.** $M(CaCl_2) = 40.08 + 2(35.45) = 110.98$ g/mol
$n = m/M = \dfrac{22.2}{110.98} = 0.200$ mol
$c = n/V = \dfrac{0.200}{0.250} = 0.800$ mol/L
A, **B** and **D** are mathematically incorrect.

8 **D.** Formulas are correct and atoms balance. **A** is wrong as the incorrect formulas of barium chloride and ammonium sulfate are shown. **B** is incorrect as this is a net ionic equation. **C** is incorrect as the barium chloride formula is incorrect.

9 **D.** Decomposition reactions require an energy input. **A**, **B** and **C** are incorrect as they are all exothermic.

10 **C.** Cobalt chloride is ionic; molten ionic salts conduct electricity. **A** and **D** are incorrect as they are covalent molecular compounds. **B** is incorrect as silicon dioxide is a covalent network solid.

11 **A.** $M(Li_2CO_3) = 2(6.941) + 12.01 + 3(16.00) = 73.892$ g/mol
$\%C = \dfrac{12.01}{73.892} \times 100 = 16.3\%$
Thus **B**, **C** and **D** are wrong as they are mathematically incorrect. The correct formula for lithium carbonate must be used.

12 **A.** $M(O_3) = 3(16.00)$
$\quad = 48.00$ g/mol
$n(O_3) = m/M = \dfrac{8.00}{48.00}$
$\quad = 0.167$ mol
$n(O) = 3n(O_3) = 0.500$ mol

$N = nN_A = (0.500)(6.022 \times 10^{23})$
$\quad = 3.011 \times 10^{23}$ atoms of O
Thus **B**, **C** and **D** are incorrect. **D** only shows the number of moles.

13 **C.** $c_1V_1 = c_2V_2$
$(2.00)(0.200) = c_2(1.50)$
$\quad c_2 = 0.267$ mol/L
Thus **A**, **B** and **D** are incorrect. The units must be the same for volume; the total final volume is 1.5 L and not 1.3 L.

14 **D.** $V_1/T_1 = V_2/T_2$
$\dfrac{10.00}{293} = \dfrac{V_2}{308}$
$V_2 = 10.5$ L
Thus **A**, **B** and **C** are incorrect. Temperatures must be converted to Kelvin temperatures.

15 **C.** Bromine's oxidation state has reduced from 0 to −1. **A** is incorrect as bromine is the oxidant. **B** is incorrect as iodide ions are reductants. **D** is incorrect as iodide ions have lost electrons.

16 **A.** Powdering increases the surface area. **B** is incorrect as the size of the beaker has no effect. **C** is incorrect as cooling will lower the rate. **D** is incorrect as the rate increases when combustion occurs in oxygen.

17 **B.** $q = mc\Delta T = (0.115)(4.18 \times 10^3)(37.2 - 21.0) = 7825$ J. Thus **A**, **C** and **D** are incorrect. The mass of solution is not 100 g as the 15 g of solute must be added.

18 **A.** Gases are more disordered than solids. **B** is incorrect as the formation of the solid leads to a more ordered state. **C** is incorrect as liquid water is a more ordered state. **D** is incorrect as the carbon dioxide is in a more disordered state than the product.

19 **B.** $\Delta H = 2(-396) - 2(-297) = -198$ kJ. **A** is incorrect as the enthalpy change is calculated by subtracting the enthalpy of reactants from the enthalpy of formation of the product. **C** and **D** are incorrect as molar stoichiometry must be included.

20 **C.** Reaction (R) = reaction (1) + reaction (2) − reaction (3)
$R = Li(s) + \frac{1}{2}Cl_2(g) + H^+(aq) + Cl^-(aq) + LiCl(s)$
$\quad \rightarrow LiCl(s) + \frac{1}{2}H_2(g) + \frac{1}{2}Cl_2(g) + Li^+(aq) + Cl^-(aq)$
$R = Li(s) + H^+(aq) \rightarrow Li^+(aq) + \frac{1}{2}H_2(g)$
$\Delta H_R = \Delta H_1 + \Delta H_2 - \Delta H_3$
$\quad = (-37) + (-409) - (-167) = -279$ kJ
Thus **A**, **B** and **D** are wrong as the equations have been incorrectly added or subtracted.

Extended-response questions

21 **EM** The weakest reductant is listed first and this will be palladium as it has the lowest cell potential. The remaining metals can then be ordered according to increasing potential difference. As the voltage of cell 3 was negative then the palladium must be the cathode and mercury the anode.

a Pd < Hg < Ni < Co < Sr ✓
Strontium is the strongest reductant listed; its cell produced the highest voltage. ✓
Palladium is the weakest reductant listed; its cell produced the lowest voltage. ✓

b $Hg(l) + Pd^{2+}(aq) \rightarrow Hg^{2+}(aq) + Pd(s)$ ✓

Mercury is the anode and mercury is oxidised. ✓ Palladium is the cathode and palladium ions are reduced. ✓

22 **EM** Students need to revise intermolecular forces and molecule polarity to ensure maximum marks are attained. Although C–H bonds are polar the methane molecule is non-polar as it has a tetrahedral shape. Ammonia, however, has polar N–H bonds but due to its pyramidal shape it is polar.

Methane is a non-polar molecule and weak dispersion forces are the only attractive intermolecular forces. ✓ Thus its melting and boiling points are lowest. ✓ Ammonia and water are polar molecules. Hydrogen bonding exists between their molecules. ✓ The hydrogen bonding is stronger between water molecules than ammonia molecules. Thus water has the highest m.p and b.p. ✓

23 **EM** Experiment 1 is a precipitation reaction and a knowledge of solubility rules is essential in predicting the compound that precipitates. Experiment 2 can be answered using a knowledge of the activity series of metals. Experiment 3 involves the evolution of carbon dioxide gas when an acid reacts with a carbonate.

a Exp. (1)—a white precipitate forms: ✓

$AgNO_3(aq) + NaCl(aq) \rightarrow AgCl(s) + NaNO_3(aq)$ ✓

Exp. (2): no reaction ✓

Exp. (3): effervescence occurs as the zinc carbonate dissolves ✓

$ZnCO_3(s) + 2HNO_3(aq) \rightarrow Zn(NO_3)_2(aq) + H_2O(l) + CO_2(g)$ ✓

b Copper is too weak a reductant to reduce the hydrogen ions in the dilute HCl. ✓

24 **EM** Valency rules must be remembered to write the correct formulae and then a correct balanced equation. The correct stoichiometry in the equation is essential for the subsequent mole calculation.

a $K_2S(s) + 2HNO_3(aq) \rightarrow 2KNO_3(aq) + H_2S(g)$ ✓

b $M(K_2S) = 2(39.10) + 32.07 = 110.27$ g/mol ✓

$n(K_2S) = \dfrac{10.00}{110.27} = 0.0907$ mol ✓

$n(H_2S) = n(K_2S) = 0.0907$ mol

$M(H_2S) = 2(1.008) + 32.07 = 34.086$ g/mol

$m(H_2S) = nM = (0.0907)(34.086) = 3.09$ g ✓

25 **EM** The temperature decreases and so the dissolution is endothermic. Therefore a positive sign is required for the enthalpy change. Three significant figures are required in this answer.

$q = mc\Delta T = (100.0)(4.18)(1.1)$

$= 459.8$ J

$= 0.4598$ kJ ✓

$n(NaCl) = m/M = \dfrac{8.00}{22.99 + 35.45} = 0.137$ mol ✓

$\Delta H = +q/n = \dfrac{0.4598}{0.137} = +3.36$ kJ/mol ✓

26 **EM** To balance the combustion equation start by balancing carbon atoms and then hydrogen atoms. Use a fraction to balance the oxygen atoms. The ratio of heat released to the heat of combustion determines the number of moles of hexan-1-ol. Three significant figures are required in this answer.

$C_6H_{11}OH(l) + \frac{17}{2}O_2(g) \rightarrow 6CO_2(g) + 6H_2O(l)$ ✓

$n(C_6H_{11}OH) = \dfrac{100}{3984} = 0.0251$ mol ✓

$n(CO_2) = 6n(C_6H_{11}OH) = 6(0.0251) = 0.1506$ mol

$m(CO_2) = n.M = (0.1506)(12.01 + 2(16.00)) = 6.63$ g ✓

27 **EM** To balance the combustion equation start by balancing carbon atoms and then hydrogen atoms. Use a fraction to balance the oxygen atoms. Use the stoichiometry to calculate the entropy change.

a $C_4H_{10}(g) + \frac{13}{2}O_2(g) \rightarrow 4CO_2(g) + 5H_2O(l)$ ✓

b $\Delta S^o = 4(214) + 5(70) - (310) - \frac{13}{2}(205)$

$= (1206) - (1642.5)$ ✓

$= -436.5$ J/K/mol ✓

28 **EM** The atomic weight of natural gallium is the weighted average of the isotopic masses. Four significant figures are required in this case.

Atomic weight $(Ga) = \dfrac{60.11}{100} \times 68.93 + \dfrac{39.89}{100} \times 70.92$

$= 41.43 + 28.29$ ✓

$= 69.72$ u ✓

29 **EM** Ensure the states of matter are shown in each equation.

a $C_{11}H_{24}(l) + 17O_2(g) \rightarrow 11CO_2(g) + 12H_2O(l)$ ✓

b $FeO(s) + CO(g) \rightarrow Fe(l) + CO_2(g)$ ✓

c $4Li(s) + O_2(g) \rightarrow 2Li_2O(s)$ ✓

30 **EM** This question is answered using Gay-Lussac's law of combining gas volumes as well as Avogadro's law that equal volumes of gases contain equal number of molecules. Thus the volume ratio equals the molecule ratio and provides the coefficients in the balanced equation.

a $X_2(g) + 3H_2(g) \rightarrow 2XH_3(g)$ ✓

b X_2 and H_2 react to form XH_3 in the volume ratio 1 : 3 : 2. Thus 80 mL of X_2 reacts with 240 mL of H_2 to form 160 mL of XH_3. ✓

Gases remaining = 100 − 80 = 20 mL of X_2 and 160 mL of XH_3. ✓

31 **EM** Substances are solids if their melting points are above 25 °C; substances are liquids if their melting points are below 25 °C but their boiling points are above 25 °C; substances are gases if their boiling points are below 25 °C.

a liquid ✓   **b** solid ✓   **c** gas ✓

32 **EM** The mass of silver can be found by subtraction of the two masses; a knowledge of the firsthand investigation of the reactivity of metals is required to answer (b); alloys have different physical properties to their constituent metals.

a $m(Cu) = 3.67$ g; $m(Ag) = 50.00 - 3.67 = 46.33$ g

$\%Cu = \dfrac{3.67}{50.00} \times \dfrac{100}{1} = 7.34\%$ ✓

$\%Ag = \dfrac{46.33}{50.00} \times \dfrac{100}{1} = 92.66\%$ ✓

b There would be no reaction ✓ as copper and silver are very low on the activity series (they are very weak reductants). ✓

c The alloy is much harder than pure silver, which is relatively soft and malleable. Cutlery should not bend when used. ✓

33 **EM** The number of neutrons = A − Z; the number of electrons in a neutral atom is the same as the atomic number; the orbital notations show how many electrons are present in each atomic orbital.

a **i** $n = 11 - 5 = 6$ **ii** $n = 14 - 7 = 7$

iii $n = 39 - 19 = 20$ ✓

b **i** $1s^2\, 2s^2\, 2p^1$ ✓   **ii** $1s^2\, 2s^2\, 2p^3$ ✓

iii $1s^2\, 2s^2\, 2p^6\, 3s^2\, 3p^6\, 4s^1$ ✓

34 **EM** The electrons in the barium ions in the flame become excited and then emit energy of specific wavelengths that are characteristic of the metal; in atomic emission spectra these wavelengths can be detected and displayed on a screen; each spectrum is characteristic of the element.

a 1 Dissolve the solid sample in water. ✓

2 Dip a clean platinum wire loop in the solution.

3 Hold the drop of solution on the platinum in a blue Bunsen flame and observe the colour of the flame. ✓

Flame colour = pale yellow-green ✓

b When atoms are heated their electrons can absorb energy and can be excited into higher energy levels. ✓ When these electrons de-excite they can fall back to lower energy states in the atom. Photons of light of various wavelengths are emitted. ✓ Red spectral lines indicate smaller energy transitions than blue or violet lines. ✓

35 **EM** Element 113 is at the bottom of the boron group, which is Group 13; all these elements have 3 valence electrons. Boron is a semi-metal whereas all other elements in this group are metals. When writing nuclear equations students need to check that atomic numbers and nucleon numbers are conserved.

a Group 13 ✓

b metal ✓

The trend down Group 13 is from non-metal to metal and so nihonium would be metallic. ✓

c $^{70}_{30}\text{Zn} + ^{209}_{83}\text{Bi} \rightarrow ^{278}_{113}\text{Nh} + ^{1}_{0}\text{n}$ ✓

36 **EM** Successive ionisation energies refer to the energy required to remove electrons one at a time starting in the outer valence shell. Only the first 8 ionisation energies are listed for each element. Students should examine the trends and look for a magnitude increase. Count the number of electrons prior to this large increase.

- L: Group 1. The first ionisation energy is very much smaller than subsequent ionisation energies and so only 1 valence electron is present. ✓
- M: Group 16. The first 6 ionisation energies are much lower than the remaining 2 ionisation energies; consequently there are 6 valence electrons, which is characteristic of Group 16. ✓
- N: Group 15. The first 5 ionisation energies are much lower than the remaining 3 ionisation energies; consequently there are 5 valence electrons, which is characteristic of Group 15. ✓

37 **EM** The ppm unit is related to other units as follows:
1 ppm = 1 mg/kg or 1 mg/L. The prefix *mega* means 'million', thus 2 megalitres = 2 ML = 2×10^6 L.

a $c(\text{Cd}^{2+}) = 200$ ppm = 200 mg/kg

Therefore in 2000 kg of water, the mass of cadmium
= $200 \times 2000 = 400\,000$ mg = 4×10^5 mg ✓

b 2 megalitres = 2×10^6 L = 2×10^6 kg ✓

Concentration of cadmium = 4×10^5 mg/2×10^6 kg
= 0.2 mg/kg
= 0.2 ppm < 10 ppm

Thus the diluted solution is safe to discharge into the environment. ✓

38 **EM** For Charles' law to be verified, the pressure of the gas must not change. This is achieved in this experiment by having the capillary tube open at the top end. When plotting a graph ensure the temperature scale starts at zero Kelvin. This is essential to show that volume is directly proportional to temperature. Ensure the graph has a title. Use a ruler to extrapolate the straight line of best fit.

a The open end allows the air pressure of the column of air to always equal the external atmospheric pressure as the gas expands on heating. Thus the pressure remains constant. ✓

b As the capillary tube is of uniform cross-section, the length of the air column is proportional to its volume. ✓

c **i**

Temperature (°C)	10	20	30	40	50	60	70	80
Temperature (K)	283	293	303	313	323	333	343	353
Length (L) (mm)	30.0	31.1	32.1	33.1	34.2	35.3	36.4	37.4	✓

ii Figure AE1.1 shows the application of Charles' law.

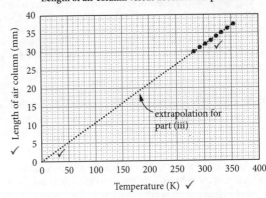

Length of air column versus absolute temperature ✓

extrapolation for part (iii)

Figure AE1.1 Length of air column versus absolute temperature

iii The linear graph, which passes through the origin, shows that the length of the air column is directly proportional to the absolute Kelvin temperature. ✓

As the volume of the air (V) is proportional to the length (L), then the volume of the gas is directly proportional to its absolute temperature. Thus Charles' law is confirmed. ✓

39 **EM** Ensure states of matter are shown in the balanced equation. Oxygen and hydrogen are diatomic gases; use the stoichiometry in the equation to calculate the number of moles of water that have decomposed.

a $2\text{H}_2\text{O(l)} \rightarrow 2\text{H}_2\text{(g)} + \text{O}_2\text{(g)}$ ✓

b $m(\text{O}_2) = 0.32$ g

$n(\text{O}_2) = m/M = \dfrac{0.32}{2 \times 16.00} = 0.010$ mol ✓

2 moles of water produce 1 mole of oxygen on decomposition

Thus $n(\text{H}_2\text{O}) = 2 \times 0.010 = 0.020$ mol ✓

c $n(\text{H}_2) = 2n(\text{O}_2) = 0.020$ mol ✓

$m(\text{H}_2) = nM = (0.020)(2 \times 1.008) = 0.040$ g ✓

Objective-response questions

1 **B.** Phosphorus is in Group 15 and can gain 3 electrons to form a stable ion. **A** is incorrect as oxygen has a typical −2 valency. **C** is incorrect as bromine has a valency of −1. **D** is incorrect as tellurium has a −2 valency.

2 **A.** Boron is a semi-metal and sulfur and iodine are non-metals. **B** is incorrect as zinc is a metal. **C** is incorrect as copper and iridium are metals. **D** is incorrect as all these elements are semi-metals.

3 **D.** Manganese is a metal and fluorine is a non-metal. Ionic compounds are formed when metals react with non-metals. Thus **A**, **B** and **C** are incorrect as no metals are present.

4 **A.** Magnesium is a reactive metal that burns with a bright, white flame. **B** and **D** are incorrect as no light energy is produced. **C** is incorrect as this process is endothermic.

5 **A.** Osmium is located in Period 6, Group 8. **B** and **D** are incorrect as they are p-block elements. **C** is incorrect as radium is an s-block element.

6 **A.** Nickel forms a stable 2+ ion when it is oxidised by hydrogen ions. **B** is incorrect as hydrogen gas is evolved. **C** is incorrect as magnesium is a more active metal and the reaction is faster. **D** is incorrect as the sulfate ions are spectator ions.

7 **C.** Non-metals have greater electronegativity than metals. **A** is incorrect as first ionisation energy increases. **B** is incorrect as non-metals have very low electrical conductivity. **D** is incorrect as non-metals have very low melting points.

8 **A.** The atomic number is the number of protons in the nucleus. **B** is incorrect as the physical properties change significantly across a period. **C** is incorrect as tellurium has a higher atomic weight than iodine. **D** is incorrect as lanthanoids are not radioactive.

9 **D.** N is a very electronegative atom and H is very electropositive. The H-bonding is quite strong between ammonia molecules. **A** is incorrect as methane is non-polar. **B** is incorrect as iodine is not sufficiently electronegative to create hydrogen bonding in HI. **C** is incorrect as hydrogen has only dispersion forces as it is non-polar.

10 **B.** $n = 10$ mol; $m(NO_2) = nM = 10(14.01 + 2(16.00)) = 460.1$ g. **A** is incorrect as 28 g is the mass of 1 mole and there will be 10 moles present. **C** is incorrect as Avogadro's law states that equal numbers of molecules are present. **D** is incorrect as there would be 10 times' Avogadro's constant molecules present.

11 **B.** Ideal gases are assumed to consist of point particles that do not attract one another. **A** is incorrect as ideal gases have no dispersion forces. **C** is incorrect as real gases only obey Boyle's law over moderate ranges of pressure and temperature. **D** is incorrect as sulfur dioxide is polar and cannot be classified as ideal.

12 **A.** All nitrates are water soluble. **B** and **C** are incorrect as iron (II) oxide and silicon dioxide are insoluble solids. **D** is incorrect as nitrogen gas is non-polar and has a very low solubility.

13 **B.** $n(NO_3^-) = 2n(Ba(NO_3)_2)$; $n(NO_3^-) = cV = 2(0.20(0.400)) = 0.16$ mol/L. Thus **A**, **C** and **D** are mathematically incorrect.

14 **A.** $Fe_2(SO_4)_3$: $M = 2(55.85) + 3(32.07) + 12(16.00) = 399.91$ g/mol. **B**, **C** and **D** are wrong as the incorrect formula has been used to calculate the molar mass.

15 **D.** $q = mc\Delta T = (0.500)(4.18 \times 10^3)(80-15) = 135\,850$ J. **A** is incorrect as the mass has not been converted to grams. **B** and **C** are mathematically incorrect.

16 **C.** $V_2 = V_1 \times T_2/T_1 = 550 \times \dfrac{383}{293} = 719$ mL. **A**, **B** and **D** are wrong as incorrect numbers have been substituted into the Charles' law formula, which requires kelvin units.

17 **A.** **B** is incorrect as diamond is also a covalent network solid. **C** is incorrect as diamond is harder than graphite. **D** is incorrect as diamond's structure is based on interlocking tetrahedra whereas graphite's carbon atoms form sheets of hexagonal rings.

18 **B.** Neon is a noble gas with a stable octet in the L shell ($n = 2$). Its atomic number is 10. **A**, **C** and **D** are incorrect as these configurations do not show 10 electrons.

19 **C.** HNO_3: N = +5 as H = +1 and *each* O is −2; $1 + 5 + 3(−2) = 0$. Thus **A**, **B** and **D** are incorrect as the oxidation states do not sum to zero.

20 **D.** More oxygen will increase the number of collisions with the iron atoms. **A** is incorrect as nitrogen will inhibit the oxidation. **B** is incorrect as the surface area decrease will slow the reaction. **C** is incorrect as removal of heat slows the rate of the reaction.

Extended-response questions

21 **EM** Carbonate ions react with acid to release carbon dioxide gas. Hydroxide ions are neutralised by acids to form water. Azurite and malachite will therefore produce the same products on reaction with hydrochloric acid. To write an ionic equation, ensure spectator ions (in this case chloride ions) are not shown.

  a $Cu_2CO_3(OH)_2(s) + 4HCl(aq) \rightarrow 2CuCl_2(aq) + 3H_2O(l) + CO_2(g)$ ✓

  b No differences as the final solution contains copper (II) chloride. Both minerals release bubbles of gas and both solids dissolve in excess acid to form green-blue copper (II) chloride. Heat is also released in both reactions. ✓

  c i $Cu^{2+}(aq) + Mg(s) \rightarrow Cu(s) + Mg^{2+}(aq)$ ✓

     ii The green-blue colour fades as the copper ions are reduced to copper metal. ✓ The red-brown solid is copper that has been displaced from solution. ✓

22 **EM** To demonstrate an increase in rate with a change in variables students should select an example where a macroscopic change can be observed. Gas evolution, colour changes and rates of dissolution are readily observed.

  A Add a strip of magnesium to dilute sulfuric acid. Increase the temperature of the system by placing the tube in a hot water bath. The rate of gas effervescence will increase as the acid gets hotter.

    $Mg(s) + H_2SO_4(aq) \rightarrow ZnSO_4(aq) + H_2(g)$ ✓

  B Powder calcium carbonate (rather than using chips) in its reaction with dilute hydrochloric acid. The rate of gas evolution will increase.

    $CaCO_3(s) + 2HCl(aq) \rightarrow CaCl_2(aq) + H_2O(l) + CO_2(g)$ ✓

  C Place a piece of zinc in dilute hydrochloric acid. Allow a piece of copper wire to touch the zinc. The reaction speeds up as the copper acts as a catalyst. Hydrogen gas is produced at a greater rate.

    $Zn(s) + 2HCl(aq) \rightarrow ZnCl_2(aq) + H_2(g)$ ✓

23 **EM** The sodium ions are spectators and they will not appear in the ionic equation. There is a 1 : 1 stoichiometry for Pb : $PbSO_4$ in the equation. To convert a mol/L concentration to parts per million (ppm) the mass of lead (in milligrams) must be calculated.

In gravimetric analysis the precipitate must be pure. Thus it needs to be washed to remove any adsorbed soluble ions. Drying to constant weight ensures no water is present.

a $Pb^{2+}(aq) + SO_4^{2-}(aq) \rightarrow PbSO_4(s)$ ✓

b i $M(PbSO_4) = 303.27$ g/mol

$n(PbSO_4) = m/M = \dfrac{1.900}{303.27} = 6.265 \times 10^{-3}$ mol $= n(Pb^{2+})$

$c(Pb^{2+}) = n/V = \dfrac{6.265 \times 10^{-3}}{0.200} = 0.0313$ mol/L ✓

ii $m(Pb^{2+}) = nM = (6.265 \times 10^{-3})(207.2) = 1.298$ g $= 1298$ mg

$c(Pb^{2+}) = \dfrac{1298}{0.200} = 6490$ mg/L $= 6490$ ppm ✓

c If water or adhering salts ✓ are present then the precipitate will weigh too high. The calculation will lead to a value for the lead concentration that is too high. ✓

---

24 **EM** Chemical reactions have an activation energy barrier and reacting substances must have sufficient kinetic energy on collision to overcome this energy barrier. Heating increases the kinetic energies of reactants and also the proportion of reactants with higher kinetic energies. The reaction stoichiometry shows a 1 : 2 mole ratio for Ag_2O : Ag.

a $4Ag_2O(s) + CH_4(g) \rightarrow 8Ag(s) + CO_2(g) + 2H_2O(g)$ ✓

b The particles must have sufficient kinetic energy on collision to overcome the activation energy barrier for the reaction. ✓

c $M(Ag_2O) = 231.8$ g/mol

$n(Ag_2O) = m/M = \dfrac{15.0}{231.8} = 0.064\,71$ mol ✓

Each mole of silver oxide produces 2 moles of silver.

$n(Ag) = 2 \times 0.064\,71 = 0.1294$ mol

$m(Ag) = nM = (0.1294)(107.9) = 14.0$ g ✓

---

25 **EM** The enthalpy change represents the heat liberated for the reaction of 4 moles of aluminium and 3 moles of oxygen. In fireworks a fast chemical reaction must occur. Powdering the aluminium increases its surface area and therefore reaction rate. Reduction is the decrease in oxidation state and oxygen's oxidation state decreases from 0 to −2.

a 4 mol of Al on combustions produces 3352 kJ of energy.

x mol of Al on combustion produces 300 kJ of energy. ✓

Thus $\dfrac{4}{3352} = \dfrac{x}{300}$

Solve for x.

$x = 4 \times \dfrac{300}{3352} = 0.3580$ mol Al ✓

$m(Al) = nM = (0.3580)(26.98) = 9.66$ g ✓

b The higher surface area increases the reaction rate. ✓

c oxygen ✓

---

26 **EM** Students should recall the equation relating to Charles' law and convert temperatures to Kelvin units.

Initially $V_1 = 900$ mL; $T_1 = 27 + 273 = 300$ K

Finally $T_2 = 227 + 273 = 500$ K ✓

$V_1/T_1 = V_2/T_2$

$\dfrac{900}{300} = \dfrac{V_2}{500}$

$V_2 = 1.500$ mL $= 1.50$ L ✓

---

27 **EM** Hess's law states that the change in enthalpy for a reaction is independent of the path taken. Thus nitrogen can be directly converted to nitrogen dioxide or via a path in which NO forms, which is then oxidised to NO_2.

$\Delta H_1 + \Delta H_2 = \Delta H_3$ ✓

$(+90) + \Delta H_2 = (+33)$

$\Delta H_2 = (+33) - (+90)$

$= -57$ kJ/mol ✓

---

28 **EM** Mercury is very dense and adding extra mercury causes compression of the gas in the J-tube. Thus the volume of the gas decreases as pressure increases. Boyle's law can be expressed mathematically as $PV = k$, or $P = k(1/V)$. The graph of P versus $1/V$ should therefore be linear.

a The increasing weight of the mercury column exerts an extra pressure on the gas in the left-hand tube. The gas becomes compressed as a result. ✓

b As the tube has a uniform cross-sectional area, the volume (V) of the gas is directly proportional to h. ✓

c The following table is used to plot the graph in Figure AE2.1.

$1/h$ (mm^{-1})	0.03125	0.0332	0.03509	0.0370	0.03891	0.04082
P (kPa)	106.6	113.2	119.7	126.3	132.9	139.5

✓

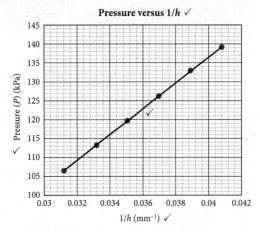

Pressure versus $1/h$ ✓

Figure AE2.1 Boyle's law demonstrating P versus $1/h$

The graph is linear and therefore $P = k(1/h)$ ✓

Or, $P.h = k = $ constant

As $V \propto h$, then $P.V = k$ (i.e. Boyle's law) ✓

---

29 **EM** The normal boiling point of butane is measured at 100 kPa. Raising the pressure changes the boiling point. The yellow colour of the butane flame demonstrates the presence of carbon particles in the flame. Therefore insufficient oxygen is present to allow complete combustion.

a The pressure is higher than 100 kPa and so the gas can liquefy. ✓

b i $M(C_4H_{10}) = 4 \times 12.01 + 10 \times 1.008 = 58.12$ g/mol

$n(\text{butane}) = m/M = \dfrac{0.0300}{58.12} = 5.162 \times 10^{-4}$ mol

Heat $= q = \dfrac{1000}{5.162 \times 10^{-4}}$

$= 1.937 \times 10^6$ J/mol

$= 1.94 \times 10^3$ kJ/mol (3 significant figures) ✓

ii The combustion is incomplete and so less heat is evolved. The literature value refers to complete combustion. ✓

30 **EM** Avogadro's law states that equal gas volumes at the same temperature and pressure contain equal numbers of molecules. Thus the number of moles will be equal. To determine the molecular formula, various integers should be tried in the general formula until a result agrees with the calculated molar mass. The two structural formulas show different arrangement of the same number of C and H atoms. These molecules have the same molecular formulae but different structures and are called isomers.

a $N(H_2) = N(\text{hydrocarbon})$

$n(H_2) = n(\text{hydrocarbon})$

$(m/M)_{\text{hydrogen}} = (m/M)_{\text{hydrocarbon}}$ ✓

$$\frac{4.000}{2(1.008)} = \frac{115.3}{M}$$

$M = 115.3 \times \dfrac{2.016}{4.000} = 58.11 \text{ g/mol}$ ✓

b $n = 4$; MF = C_4H_{10}; $M = 4(12.01) + 10(1.008) = 58.12$ g/mol ✓

c Figure AE2.2 shows the structures of the two isomers for C_4H_{10}.

Figure AE2.2 Isomer structures for C_4H_{10}

31 **EM** The two salts dissolve and the bromide ion concentration is the total number of moles of bromide ions divided by the total volume in litres. Use the dilution formula for (b).

a $MgBr_2(aq) \rightarrow Mg^{2+}(aq) + 2Br^-(aq)$

$n(MgBr_2) = cV = (0.12)(0.300) = 0.036$ mol

$n(Br^-) = 2(0.036) = 0.072$ mol ✓

$KBr(aq) \rightarrow K^+(aq) + Br^-(aq)$

$n(KBr) = cV = (0.20)(0.200) = 0.040$ mol

$n(Br^-) = 0.040$ mol ✓

Final volume = 300 + 200 = 500 mL = 0.500 L

Total $n(Br^-)$ = 0.072 + 0.040 = 0.112 mol/L

$c(Br^-) = n/V = \dfrac{0.112}{0.500}$

$= 0.224$ mol/L

$= 0.22$ mol/L (2 significant figures) ✓

b $c_1V_1 = c_2V_2$ ✓

$c_2 = c_1V_1/V_2 = \dfrac{(0.224)(0.500)}{(3.00)}$

$= 0.0373$

$= 0.037$ mol/L (2 significant figures) ✓

32 **EM** Some solids, such as iodine and dry ice (solid carbon dioxide), do not melt on heating under standard pressure but form a vapour directly.

$I_2(s) \rightarrow I_2(g)$ ✓

$\Delta S^o = S^o(I_2(g)) - S^o(I_2(s)) = (+261) - (+116) = +145$ J/K/mol ✓

There has been an increase in the entropy of the system as heat has been absorbed and the iodine molecules have become less ordered in the gaseous state.

33 **EM** Use a fraction to balance the number of moles of oxygen. Use the Gibbs free energy equation and substitutes the enthalpy and entropy changes into the formula. The standard temperature is 298 K.

a $Ag_2CO_3(s) \rightarrow 2Ag(s) + \frac{1}{2}O_2(g) + CO_2(g)$ ✓

b The standard enthalpy change can be calculated:

$\Delta H^o = \Sigma \Delta_f H^o(\text{products}) - \Sigma \Delta_f H^o(\text{reactants})$

$= 0 + 0 + (-394) - (-506)$

$= +112$ kJ/mol ✓

The standard entropy change can be calculated:

$\Delta S^o = \Sigma \Delta S^o(\text{products}) - \Sigma \Delta S^o(\text{reactants})$

$= 2(+43) + \frac{1}{2}(+205) + (+214) - (+167)$

$= +154.5$ J/K/mol

$= +0.1545$ kJ/K/mol ✓

The standard Gibbs free energy change can be calculated:

$\Delta G^o = \Delta H^o - T\Delta S^o$

$= (+112) - (298)(+0.1545)$

$= +66$ kJ/mol > 0

Thus the reaction is not spontaneous at 298 K as the Gibbs free energy change is positive (> 0). ✓

34 **EM** Relate each step in the Hess's law diagram to the supplied data. Use the structure of the methane molecule to determine the number of C–H bonds.

$\frac{1}{2}H_2(g) \rightarrow H(g)$; $\Delta H^o = +218$ kJ/mol

$C(s)(\text{graphite}) \rightarrow C(g)$; $\Delta H^o = +718$ kJ/mol

Hess's law:

path 1 + path 2 + path 3 = path 4 ✓

$\Delta H_1^o + \Delta H_2^o + \Delta H_3^o = \Delta H_4^o$

$\Delta H_1^o = +718$ kJ;

$\Delta H_2^o = +4(218) = +872$ kJ;

$\Delta H_4^o = \Delta_f H(CH_4) = -75$ kJ ✓

$(+718) + (+872) + \Delta H_3^o = (-75)$

$\Delta H_3^o = (-75) - (718) - (872) = -1665$ kJ

Methane has four C–H bonds. ✓

$BE(\text{C–H}) = \dfrac{1665}{4} = 416$ kJ/mol ✓

35 **EM** Revise the practical investigations conducted in class and relate the observations to the activity series of metals. Use the tabulated information to identify the reaction products.

a W = Cu, X = Mg ✓; Y = Zn, Z = K ✓

b $Mg(s) + 2H_2O(l) \rightarrow Mg(OH)_2(aq) + H_2(g)$ ✓

$Zn(s) + H_2O(g) \rightarrow ZnO(s) + H_2(g)$ ✓

$2K(s) + 2H_2O(l) \rightarrow 2KOH(aq) + H_2(g)$ ✓

36 **EM** Sucrose (table sugar) is quite soluble in water. Students should examine the structure to determine the large number of polar –OH groups.

a $M(C_{12}H_{22}O_{11}) = 12 \times 12.01 + 22 \times 1.008 + 11 \times 16.00$

$= 342.296$ g/mol

$n(\text{sucrose}) = m/M = \dfrac{16.0}{342.296} = 0.0467$ mol ✓

b $c = n/V = \dfrac{0.0467}{0.250} = 0.187$ mol/L ✓

c Sucrose is a polar molecule with numerous polar hydroxyl (OH) groups. ✓ These groups interact with polar water molecules by hydrogen bonding. This interaction assists the dissolution process. ✓

---

37 **EM** For OCl_2 ensure an octet of electrons are present in each element's valence shell. In CaI_2 the calcium ion has lost its valence electrons to the 2 iodide ions.

Figure AE2.3 shows the electron dot structures for OCl_2 and CaI_2.

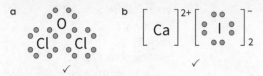

Figure AE2.3 Lewis electron dot diagrams

---

38 **EM** Ionic crystals have ions in fixed positions. Conductivity relies on moving charge carriers. Water is an excellent solvent for many ionic salts as the solvation process lowers the potential energies of the ions and helps to drive the dissolution process, as does the increase in entropy.

a The sodium ions and chloride ions cannot move out of their lattice positions in the solid state and so no mobile charge carriers are present to carry the current. ✓ However, when melted, the ions become free to move and can carry the current. ✓

b $NaCl(s) \rightarrow Na^+(aq) + Cl^-(aq)$ ✓

c The positive sodium ion attracts the slightly negative oxygen atom in the water molecule. ✓ This is called ion−dipole attraction and this assists the dissolution of NaCl in water as the ions become stabilised. ✓

---

39 **EM** Sulfate ions have a −2 valency so the formula is MSO_4. Thus the mole ratio of $M : S : O = 1 : 1 : 4$. By calculating the number of moles of sulfur, the number of moles of M can be determined. The metal is cobalt, which is the first metal in Group 9 in the d block.

a The metal is divalent so the formula of the sulfate salt is MSO_4. The mole ratio of $M : S = 1 : 1$.

Calculate the number of moles of M and S in 100 g of the compound.

Let x = atomic weight of M

$m(M) = 38.02 \text{ g}; n(M) = \dfrac{38.02}{x}$

$m(S) = 20.69 \text{ g}; n(S) = \dfrac{20.69}{32.07} = 0.6452 \text{ mol}$ ✓

Thus $\dfrac{38.02}{x} = 0.6452$ ✓

Solve for x.

$x = 58.93 \text{ g/mol}$

Atomic weight of M = 58.93 g/mol ✓

b cobalt (58.93 is the published atomic weight of cobalt) ✓

c Group 9 ✓

---

40 **EM** To obtain the net ionic equation, cancel out spectator ions. These are the barium and nitrate ions in (a) and the potassium and sulfate ions in (b).

a $BaCl_2(aq) + 2AgNO_3(aq) \rightarrow 2AgCl(s) + Ba(NO_3)_2(aq)$
$Ag^+(aq) + Cl^-(aq) \rightarrow AgCl(s)$ ✓

b $NiSO_4(aq) + K_2S(aq) \rightarrow NiS(s) + K_2SO_4(aq)$
$Ni^{2+}(aq) + S^{2-}(aq) \rightarrow NiS(s)$ ✓

INDEX

© 2018 Geoffrey Thickett and Pascal Press
Reprinted 2019

ISBN 978 1 74125 675 8

Pascal Press
PO Box 250
Glebe NSW 2037
(02) 8585 4044
www.pascalpress.com.au

Publisher: Vivienne Joannou
Project editor: Mark Dixon
Edited by Karen Enkelaar
Reviewed by Jim Stamell
Answers checked by Janette Ellis
Indexed by Puddingburn Publishing Services
Cover, page design and typesetting by Sonia Woo
Printed by Vivar Printing/Green Giant Press

Students
All care has been taken in the preparation of this study guide, but please check with your teacher
or the NSW Education Standards Authority about the exact requirements of the course you are
studying as these can change from year to year.

The validity and appropriateness of the internet addresses (URLs) in this book were checked at
the time of publication. Due to the dynamic nature of the internet, the publisher cannot accept
responsibility for the continued validity or content of these web addresses.

NOTES